ISABEL BUCHANAN

Isabel Buchanan was born in Dundee in 1987. She studied at the Universities of Glasgow and Harvard. She is a barrister at Blackstone Chambers in London.

Praise for *Trials*:

'[A] superbly assured debut that lifts the lid on an important but neglected subject in a way that is both intellectually and emotionally compelling'
Judges of the Saltire Society Literary Awards

'I'll be surprised if I come across a braver, more necessary debut this year' *The National*

'In *Trials*, her utterly brilli
about human rights activi
stan, Isabel Buchanan of
law that is deeply persona
her subtle renderings of th
and the choices they and their advocates have made.

But the book is equally a fine exploration of universal human themes, not least the power and limits of the law itself to make the world a bit less bad. There is no better introduction to the paradoxes of human rights on the ground today.' Samuel Moyn, Professor of Law and History, Yale University

'An important, must-read work' *The Skinny*

'As events unfolded this year, it was reassuring to read superb non-fiction that celebrated expertise ... *Trials: On Death Row in Pakistan* tells how Isabel Buchanan, fresh from a law degree, applied her feeling and intelligence to apprentice in a jurisdiction which, by 2014, saw a person executed every day' Kate Womersley *Spectator*

'This is much more than a well-written coming-of-age memoir: it is a thoughtful reflection on the legal system of an important country in the modern geopolitical world' Roger Smith, *Law Society Gazette*

'Altruism, empathy and a sense of justice cannot be eradicated by anyone—this book testifies to that' Kapil Summan, *Scottish Legal News*

ISABEL BUCHANAN

Trials

On Death Row in Pakistan

VINTAGE

1 3 5 7 9 10 8 6 4 2

Vintage
20 Vauxhall Bridge Road,
London SW1V 2SA

Vintage is part of the Penguin Random House group of companies
whose addresses can be found at global.penguinrandomhouse.com

First published in Vintage in 2017
First published in hardback by Jonathan Cape in 2016

penguin.co.uk/vintage

A CIP catalogue record for this book is
available from the British Library

ISBN 9781784700195

Printed and bound by Clays Ltd, St Ives Plc

Penguin Random House is committed to a sustainable future
for our business, our readers and our planet. This book is made
from Forest Stewardship Council® certified paper.

For Sohail

Prologue

Mr Hussein made the best chips and curry sauce in East Lothian. Every morning, I caught the train to school in Edinburgh from the station a few streets from his shop. Every evening, be it *sinny* or *bleerie*, queues of children wound their way to the Salter Fry. The shop is now under new management. Mr Hussein is on death row in Pakistan. Accused of blasphemy, he awaits his execution. By strange coincidence, I ended up working on his defence team.

Salmon-like, Naveed Hussein had long planned to retire to the place of his birth. Scotland, he said, was too cold a country to grow old in. And so, in 2010, aged sixty-seven and suffering from chronic illnesses that had hastened his early retirement, he travelled to northern Pakistan, to the town where he had grown up. He wanted to confirm that his properties and pension were in order.

They weren't: his bank account was empty, a decade's worth of rent payments missing. Several families were living illegally in his home. An argument ensued between Naveed Hussein and a tenant. When Naveed filed a civil claim, the tenant reported him to the police: *'Naveed Hussein insulted the Prophet; I have five witnesses.'* In Pakistan, blasphemy is a capital offence. That afternoon, whilst running errands in the bazaar, Naveed Hussein was arrested. For four years he remained in a small prison cell in a provincial jail – in solitary confinement, owing to the prison authority's fear that another prisoner would assassinate him. In early 2014, he was sentenced to death.

Rawalpindi's jail is south-west of the city, close to the point where South Asia's ancient Grand Trunk Road, which joins Kabul to Calcutta, intersects Pakistan. It is about thirty miles from the house where Naveed Hussein was born. In the north of Pakistan, close to Kashmir's mountain ranges, Naveed's eight-foot-square cell knows a cruel climate: bitter in winter and brutal in summer. And from his wing of the jail – several shed-like cells, enclosing a square of concrete – he can glimpse the gallows.

So great is the risk of an attack on Naveed Hussein's life – blasphemy, in Pakistan, is a deeply sensitive, controversial issue and civilians have been known to kill alleged apostates – the court considers it too dangerous to move him to and from the jail for his hearings. Instead, his trial is conducted in the jail's makeshift courtroom. The court has ordered that lawyers and judges travel with guards and in protected vehicles. Excepting a spell in hospital, Naveed Hussein hasn't left the confines of the jail complex since his arrest. Angry mobs led by mullahs gather outside clamouring for the execution of this seventy-year-old man, and of anyone trying to help him.

I was, and remain, a child of the post-9/11 world. Whilst I sat my Highers and A levels in Edinburgh, Guantanamo Bay was opened; wars began in Iraq and Afghanistan; new, urgent anti-terrorism legislation was passed in both Britain and America. In July 2005, two months before I began my undergraduate law degree, an attack on the London transport system brought those threats first articulated on New York's skyline closer to home. Headlines in the *Guardian* declared it Britain's first suicide attack; the country's 'Orphans of Islam', they warned, had turned to terror. 7/7 now stood with 9/11 as numerical shorthand for our worst fears. What the world should do in response to these acts and to quell these fears became a pressing political question; how it would do it a pressing legal one.

Questions of legality – the legality of military prisons and tribunals, of war, of invasion and occupation, of indefinite detention, of rendition, of Sharia in the UK – were front-page news. The law, or so it seemed to my seventeen-year-old self, determined everything. My first jurisprudence seminars buzzed with immediate relevance. We discussed grand abstract nouns – Liberty, Security, Justice, Freedom – in relation to tabloid headlines and the ten o'clock news. We were taught to read the legal justifications for those recent interventions, detentions and renditions in the light of Viscount Stair's *Memorial Encyclopaedia*, John Locke's *Two Treatises of Government*, Jean-Jacques Rousseau's *Social Contract*. To embark on our first academic encounter with sovereignty and constitutionalism as American law professors were drafting the Iraqi constitution gave these weighty concepts a glitz and a thrill. Enlightenment Edinburgh of the eighteenth century might, I imagined, have felt similar. World events reverberated through the university.

Pakistan was not in these headlines, but it lingered close behind them. In 2009, President Obama announced that American strategy for defeating the Taliban in Afghanistan was to treat both sides of the Afghanistan–Pakistan border as a 'single theatre'. Richard Holbrooke, then US Special Envoy to Afghanistan and Pakistan, declared Pakistan the source of many of Afghanistan's problems: *'We must recognise that the heart of the threat to [the West] comes from the people in western Pakistan . . . You*

3

can't succeed in Afghanistan if you don't solve the problems in western Pakistan.' A busy man, Holbrooke coined 'Af-Pak' as shorthand for two countries with a long and tangled history. Regional experts and foreign correspondents suspected Pakistan's Inter-Services Intelligence (the ISI; Pakistan's military intelligence agency) of supporting various militant organisations, including the Afghan Taliban. These commentators held Pakistan at least vicariously responsible for many of the major terrorist attacks of the past decade. The British government, as well as the American, expressed concern over both Pakistan's accommodation of militant groups and its vulnerability to them; 'duplicitous' was an adjective frequently levelled at the government in Islamabad. Nonetheless, foreign ministers and special envoys on both sides of the Atlantic stressed the impossibility of disengagement with Pakistan and the importance of maintaining a friendship. But even from my student flat in Glasgow, it was clear that the relationship between Pakistan, America and Britain was characterised by mistrust.

As a student, I saw several Pakistans. One was a dystopia of terrorist training camps and political machination, founded on an ideal of Muslim purity and intolerant of anything else. *Pakistan: Terrorism Ground Zero, The Most Dangerous Place, The Scorpion's Tail* and *Deep Inside the World's Most Frightening State* were just a handful of the titles published the year I graduated from law school. Every dust jacket showed firearms or militants. Another Pakistan was local to me. Glasgow has a large British Pakistani population. Many of our city councillors, neighbours, newsagents and restaurateurs were of Pakistani heritage. And greed was my way into this world. For four undergraduate years, my favourite puddings were the *gulab jamun* – sweet russet-coloured balls of milk curds, deep-fried and served saturated in rose-water cardamom

4

syrup – sold by Mr Ali, my local newsagent. Rawalpindi was to me, until I visited the city in 2011, a tandoori restaurant on Sauchiehall Street. On filthy wet *dreich* Glasgow days we bought warm, sweet peshwari nan to take away and scoff on the rain-stained baroque steps of Kelvingrove Museum.

This scant introduction to incongruous extremes – sweets, *sag aloo*, Sharia – sparked my interest in Pakistan. A little research into its legal system alarmed me. 13,223 people had been sentenced to death in the decade before I began university. And when I began writing this book, in 2013, there were estimated to be at least 8,000 people detained on death row, making Pakistan's death-row population one of the world's largest. It was also one of the most unjust: Pakistan's former Minister for Human Rights estimated that roughly two-thirds of those 8,000 people were innocent.

But at the same time I found myself intrigued by Pakistan's legal system. Drafted by British barristers during the Raj, Pakistan's laws (since the country's creation in 1947) had gradually been amended by its courts and governments, creating an odd medley of British statute with Sharia-compliant alterations and Indian and Pakistani case law. Moreover, close as the country looked to a failed state, and despite widespread corruption and injustice, Pakistan seemed to have a remarkably independent legal system, in which courts could order government action and Bar Association protests could halt the impeachment of the Chief Justice. As a young student with relatively straightforward ideals and ideas, I wanted to understand these contradictions – and perhaps to help where I could. Soon after I graduated, I volunteered with a legal charity in London, where I worked solely on the cases of British citizens on death row in Pakistan. Naveed Hussein's was the first I opened.

Through these first post-university months, I developed my understanding of Pakistan and South Asia from the culinary to the social, historical and legal. Between scanning, photocopying, navigating the Pakistan Penal Code and sorting vast medical files into trial evidence, I regularly accompanied the lawyer I worked for on visits to the families of our condemned clients, several of whom lived in suburbs of Birmingham. It was during the course of these trips to the Midlands that I decided to learn Urdu, move to Pakistan and work in Lahore.

Like Glasgow, Birmingham has a large British Pakistani population. Many of these people either are, or are descended from, those citizens of the British Commonwealth who, like Naveed Hussein, moved to the UK in the 1950s. The British Nationality Act, passed by Clement Attlee's Labour government, allowed citizens of the Commonwealth to take up residence and, ultimately, to acquire nationality. Most of the men took jobs in the foundries and set up family homes in east Birmingham; today almost a quarter of Birmingham's population is of Asian ethnicity (with over half of Birmingham's Asian population of Pakistani ethnicity). My first day in Birmingham was spent in Alum Rock, one of those predominantly Pakistani-populated suburbs. By lunchtime we had visited several families, each in a situation of comparable tragedy yet each almost completely unaware of the others.

First was the family of a Bangladeshi girl who had recently eloped to Pakistan with her Pakistani fiancé. They lived in a relatively new housing development, the buildings semi-detached and constructed of red brick, sporadically faced with tiles. We spoke mostly with the father, who – vehemently opposed to the match – had severed communications with his daughter. Upon arrival in Pakistan she (then second-trimester pregnant) and her husband had been accused of murder, and soon afterwards found themselves on death row. Our visit was to inform her family of this. They received us and the news with hostile indifference.

From there we drove a few streets to the family of the girl's Pakistani husband. The girl's father had had no contact with his daughter's in-laws; during our brief meeting, he had spoken ominously of what he thought of the boy and his kin. The boy's family, however, received us with friendly gratitude and spoke fondly of their daughter-in-law. We were plied with milky sweet spiced chai, tangerine coils of *jalebi* and digestive biscuits whilst we chatted about the couple's misfortune. I was surprised and touched by the conviviality of these legal meetings.

A few more streets away – past corner shops with the proprietor's name and wares written in Urdu's slanting *nastaliq* script, international calling rates and Pakistani SIM cards advertised in the windows – to the home of an extended family composed of the brothers, uncles, nephews and nieces of two young men charged with murder in Kashmir. Theirs too was a simple brick house in a modern development. Here, neater front gardens and newer cars displayed the residents' relative affluence. In the front room we talked with the boys' father. He had moved to Birmingham in the 1950s and all his children had been born there. Aged nineteen and twenty, the boys had returned to Pakistan to visit their relatives, staying with aunts and cousins in the Kashmiri town where their father had grown up and where he still owned some land. One summer evening, there had been a shooting on the other side of town. Someone had been killed. The boys had strong alibis, no motive and no forensic evidence against them. They were charged with the murder and imprisoned. The family suspected the complainant, a neighbour who was envious of the boys' father's land, of falsely accusing them. With more local influence than the sons of an absentee landlord, the neighbour easily found eyewitnesses to the crime. At the time of our visit, the boys were having their bail application argued. The legal proceedings had cost the family thousands of pounds, reducing them to near penury. Our visit was pastoral and friendly – the lawyer had known this family for some time. We drank yet more cardamom-y chai and ate stacks of samosa and pakora (freshly made and hot from the pan, stuffed with richly seasoned diced potato, peas and onion). When interviewing families, we volunteers had been told on our induction day, you must never decline food.

Between these visits, during a lunchtime hour where we had neither need nor desire to eat, we struck west to Birmingham's jewellery quarter. Once a hive of workshops, a gem of the Industrial Revolution, it is now a conservation area of handsome brick houses with pilastered front doors; home to vegan restaurants, cocktail bars and the loft-conversion offices of a law firm famous for bringing cases that challenge the government. Given their expertise, we spoke to these lawyers about concerns we had over delays in Foreign Office action for British citizens charged with crimes in Pakistan. Listening to the ensuing discussion, I realised that the cases I had first understood as isolated, dreadful events were in fact part of a larger narrative of injustice, connected to Pakistan's diaspora and legal system.

These death-penalty cases often share a fact pattern. The men and women we represented were the children or grandchildren of immigrants from Pakistan who had moved to the UK in the 1950s and 60s. At that time, the daily wage in the UK was up to thirty times that of

Pakistan. As a result, many Pakistani immigrants used money earned in the UK to support dependants they had left behind. Today, over £1.2 billion is still sent in remittances annually from the UK to Pakistan, over three times the amount Pakistan receives each year in aid payments from the UK government. (This movement of money is part of a larger global flow: expatriate Pakistanis around the world send over $13 billion to Pakistan annually.) A large number of these Pakistani-born British citizens also own land in Pakistan. When their children reach a suitable age, many of them make long trips to Pakistan to visit relatives and learn about their parents' country and heritage. It is on these trips that expat Pakistanis and their children encounter problems: false charges of murder and blasphemy are levelled by envious neighbours or business rivals pursuing old vendettas. Absentee landlords and their anglicised children are easily framed as guilty parties.

I have continued work on these and other death-penalty cases for several years, living in Pakistan for significant spells of time. In 2011, I arrived at a fledgling legal office in Lahore, where I began work as an intern. Since then, that office has expanded in staff numbers, desks and caseload. What was once a solely capital-defence practice grew to represent casualties of America and Britain's War on Terror: the Pakistani men (and boys) detained without trial at Bagram airbase in Afghanistan, and their families and neighbours in the northern areas of Pakistan where women, children, the elderly and the infirm have been killed in US drone strikes. When I worked there, the office remained one of the very few chambers in Pakistan willing to take on blasphemy cases (as for defendants in blasphemy cases, the risk of assassination for defence lawyers is high) and to confront the police about the torture so many suffer by their hand.

As the office and the scope of its work grew, I was able to learn more about Pakistan and its legal system. Through apprenticing myself to our clerk, I understood something of how to navigate the filing rooms of the Lahore High Court and the filing systems of the local police. Through days spent in the courtroom, I learnt how lawyers argued a defence, challenged a confession and exposed police malpractice. Conversation with my Urdu teacher taught me a certain amount of grammar, but more importantly, I learnt about the everyday lives of lower-middle-class working Lahoris. Hours spent meeting with and talking to judges and other lawyers helped me to understand the personalities of court and prison.

I was confused, however, as to how this detailed local knowledge should relate to the grander themes of law, justice and human rights. After my first period of living in Pakistan, I undertook postgraduate study at Harvard. In classes on human rights, constitutional law and moral philosophy, I didn't pass an hour without reflecting on what our readings and the theories behind them said about my work in Pakistan. What did Susan Sontag in *Regarding the Pain of Others* tell me about watching a policeman beat up a client? How could I use Ronald Dworkin's *Taking Rights Seriously* to criticise judicial reasoning in a blasphemy case? How did Adam Smith's *The Theory of Moral Sentiments* help me to understand why execution was so popular in Pakistan? What of empathy and our natural social sympathy? What could Montaigne's scepticism about the fundamental nature of human rights teach international experts expounding the virtues of the UN charter? I met some of these experts – usually kind, clever, idealistic people – in classrooms, international workshops and conferences; many were ambitious and optimistic about the law's power to do good. And yet my time in Pakistan made me wonder about the limits of what the law could do. I was struck by the ability of Pakistan's Supreme Court to stand up to the government and protect fundamental rights. I was impressed by the lobbying power of High Court advocates on strike. But I was sceptical of the power of the law. Could legal change alone stop a policeman behaving in the same way he had for the last forty years of his career? Could it make a poor and illiterate Christian labourer – tortured and terrified into confessing to a crime he didn't commit – confident that his family would be safe if he reported police corruption and malpractice to the local authorities? Could the ratification of international conventions offer a panacea to a people's ills? When a country's poor are so used to seeing the law routinely bent to disadvantage and maim them, and a country's rich are so used to seeing it bent to accommodate them, who will take seriously the suggestion that legal change means social change?

I wrote this book to explore these questions, and to tell the stories of some of the people – little known and often overlooked – who taught me what answers I have been able to find. It is a story of Pakistan, and an enquiry into what the law can and cannot do.

I

Four death warrants had been issued in Zulfikar Ali Khan's name before he wrote to his local newspaper in Lahore in the spring of 2009. Ten years earlier, Zulfikar Ali Khan had fired three fatal shots. He was arrested and charged with murder. Unable to afford a lawyer, his case was argued piecemeal and badly. He was sentenced to death twice over: once by hanging, once by firing squad. *'The date of my execution is drawing near and has now been fixed for 7 April,'* his letter to the newspaper said, written on 1 April. *'I seek sympathy from civil society, NGOs and welfare organisations. I appeal to the President to commute my capital punishment.'*

Sitting at her breakfast table late on a Wednesday morning – smoking a fourth cigarette and still in her pyjamas – Sarah Belal flicked through the week's papers. Skimming headlines, she turned to the back pages. Zulfikar Ali Khan's plea caught her eye. Something about it piqued her interest. Perhaps it was the sense of a clear injustice. Perhaps it was curiosity about the strange circumstances of the murder, the double death sentence. Perhaps it was the fact that Sarah had no other work, and little hope of getting any.

Sarah was one of Pakistan's least successful lawyers. The daughter of a wealthy textile merchant, she had been brought up between Boston, Geneva and Lahore. Taught by nuns, she spent six years at a private convent in Lahore before leaving Pakistan – for good, she had hoped – to finish her education at an elite east-coast US boarding school and its neighbouring liberal-arts college. When she returned to Pakistan in 2001, Sarah had few links to the tightly knit world of Lahore's legal profession and little interest in forging any. By the time she read that letter to the newspaper, she had been through a succession of legal jobs, from which, when she wasn't ignored, she had been fired: for being too Western, too attractive, too lazy, too argumentative, too female.

Law had never been what Sarah's family had wanted for her, nor what she had wanted for herself. Having spent a small fortune on her education, her parents had planned for her to work in the family textile business in Lahore. But Sarah cared little for such a career. She wanted to stay in America – Miami, preferably. Maybe she would be a writer, or an historian, perhaps a political activist, or an immigration case-worker. Her first act of defiance was to switch her major from economics to modern history (her parents only found out in 2001, at her graduation ceremony). But she never did find her dream job, and her parents gave her an ultimatum: become financially independent or return to Pakistan. She soon found herself back in Lahore.

Unemployed, depressed, dependent, Sarah was apprenticed to the manager of two of her father's factories, which were then the biggest textile manufacturers in Lahore. Every day she drove along Lahore's rust-coloured canal to buildings crammed with over 5,000 workers. A slogan hung above the entrance: *If you can dream it, you can do it*. But the Pakistan she saw belied the phrase: many of her father's workers earned a pittance, with no job security and scant hope of a pension. Corruption cloaked every encounter with the government and silenced the poor. Returning from work each evening, staring from her chauffeur-driven car's air-conditioned cool, Sarah got used to seeing the rows of dirt-stained homeless bodies sleeping on the road's central reservation. By the time she arrived at the guarded gates of her father's large house in the affluent Gulberg district, she'd forgotten them.

All around, the gulf between rich and poor was as clear as the window glass between her and the homeless. The life of Lahore's moneyed elite was a never-ending round of partying at huge, homogeneous houses. The same people. The same families. Some had second, entirely separate houses just for parties. At one, a Porsche – costing hundreds of thousands of pounds to import, and undrivable on Lahore's potholed roads – stood as a stationary showpiece in the driveway. Whole rooms were built as bars, stacked with Johnnie Walker Black Label, Grey Goose, Bombay Sapphire. At weekends, US hip hop – Akon, Jay Z, Lil Wayne – shook the walls. Outside, in large green gardens, on balconies and roof terraces, bodies lounged, engulfed in clouds of *'Asia's finest dope, yaar.'*

Most of the partygoers, Sarah's set of friends in Lahore, worked for their parents. They were apprenticed to inherit the corporations that ran Pakistan's industry, those corporations certain to inherit the government contracts that, with the stroke of a pen, made millionaires of their CEOs. This world, Sarah said, underpinned a structure that she disliked and which put her off Pakistan. If she was going to stay, advised her therapist, she would need a change of career.

Scanning back issues of *Time* at her father's house one evening in 2003, Sarah noticed that all the jobs that interested her – at the UN, with large charities, with well-known

NGOs, government postings – preferred candidates with a law degree. The next day she wrote her applications for law school; a close friend in Geneva recommended Oxford, and she applied there. The following month she handed in her notice. The next year, aged twenty-six, she moved to England.

But Sarah was as ill-suited a law student as she was a factory manager. High school and college in America had imbued in her an American style of education. The American law degree is three years of postgraduate study, taught in large groups, intensively, with regular assignments and close contact with professors. At most of the US Ivy League schools, human rights clinics give students the opportunity to work on real, and important, cases alongside their seminars and lectures. But at Oxford, with very few lectures and a lot of solitary reading, Sarah felt like she was teaching herself. And there was no sign of the human-rights courses she had imagined law school to be made of. Within the law department she was lonely, and bored: she wasn't brilliant. Once again she entertained escapist fantasies about not returning to Pakistan. But this time she knew they were futile: she was in love and engaged to be married, that summer, in Lahore. Foot-dragging and fed up, she ploughed through her Oxford law degree and London bar exams, passing both and returning to Lahore in 2007.

Legal training in Lahore bears a colonial imprint. In moving to London to train as a barrister, Sarah was following in a long line of South Asian lawyers who had begun their profession in Britain's imperial metropolis. The mid-nineteenth century onwards saw the British drafting large swathes of India's laws: men like Jeremy Bentham and Thomas Babington Macaulay had codified India's justice system. Given the origins of India's laws and its

British imperial government, it made sense for the country's lawyers – including Mahatma Gandhi, Jawaharlal Nehru, the first prime minister of India, and Muhammad Ali Jinnah, founder of Pakistan – to learn their trade in London.

Having completed a law degree, these lawyers joined one of London's four Inns of Court. The Inns – professional associations of barristers – are medieval societies, dating back to at least the fourteenth century. They spread lawyers' chambers, dining halls, chapels, libraries and gardens across several acres of land, centred on the Royal Courts of Justice on Fleet Street. Today their cobbled streets are thick with purposefully striding silks, and clerks ferrying stacks of grey ring binders to and from court. Gandhi and Nehru joined Inner Temple; Jinnah joined Lincoln's Inn, because, he said, it was the only one of the four Inns that included the Prophet Muhammad in the history of the world's great lawmakers (a large fresco in the Great Hall of Lincoln's Inn, titled *Justice, A Hemicycle of Lawgivers*, depicts Muhammad beside Justinian, Moses and Solon). I, in a bid to impress Lahore's High Court judges, also joined Lincoln's Inn. Sarah joined Gray's Inn, the least South Asian, the least predictable, of the four.

Today, Lahore's locally trained lawyers must complete five years of undergraduate study at one of Pakistan's universities – the final three years devoted to specialised study of Pakistan's laws. At Oxford, Sarah studied only English law, and for only two years, not five. Upon graduation, the locally trained Pakistani student must apply for and undertake an apprenticeship with a lawyer licensed to the Lahore High Court who has been practising for at least a decade. The apprenticeship will last for six months to a year, and the student will work on a minimum of twenty cases. After these six months, the student can enrol for the bar exams, success in which grants them a practising licence. But this licence is limited in scope: the student must then spend two years practising in the lower courts before being eligible to apply for a High Court licence, which will be granted after a successful interview before a panel of sitting High Court judges. All in, the process from A level to High Court licence takes a minimum of seven years for the locally trained lawyer.

To learn law in London is to take a dramatic short cut. Sarah, like all graduates of London's bar courses, benefited from a waiver of both the six-month apprenticeship requirement and the obligation to spend two years practising in the lower courts. On return to Pakistan, graduates like Sarah simply fill out a form, pay an application fee, have a brief interview with a panel of High Court judges and are instantly – without a moment's experience of practice in Pakistan nor an hour's study of Pakistan's legal system – granted a High Court licence.

If Sarah's legal training in England allowed her to fast-track her licence, it was otherwise of extremely limited use in Pakistan. In the summer of 1947, India had become independent from the British Empire. Hurried negotiations between India's main political parties and the British government resulted in an agreement that the subcontinent would be partitioned along broadly religious lines: Pakistan was created as a homeland for India's Muslims. (The name 'Pakistan' was chosen for both its literal meaning – land of the pure – and as a neat acronym of the British names for the new country's five provinces: Punjab, Afghan (border areas), Kashmir, Sindh, Baluchistan.) With Independence and Partition, the relevance of a British legal training began to wane. When India and Pakistan's nascent leaders – Jinnah, Nehru and Gandhi – studied law in England, India was under colonial rule and the legal systems of England and India were broadly comparable: training in one was transferable to the other. Jinnah returned to Bombay, Nehru to Allahabad, both well equipped to practise. Gandhi used his knowledge of India's laws more strategically, travelling from London to South Africa, where he spent twenty years working as a civil-rights lawyer before returning to India to set in motion India's independence movement. But when Sarah studied law in England, Pakistan was fifty-seven years old and had a legal system quite different from England's. The country does still use nineteenth-century British statutes – like the 1898 Code of Criminal Procedure and Thomas Babington Macaulay's 1860 Indian Penal Code (such statutes make up the bulk of the country's laws, and most court hearings are still conducted in English as a result) – but Sarah's training in England taught her nothing of nineteenth-century statutes and made no mention of Pakistan's own case law and precedent. In Pakistan in 2007, the granular knowledge she had of English civil and criminal procedure was next to useless. She returned to Pakistan a High Court lawyer without the faintest idea how the law in Pakistan worked.

For the next couple of years, Sarah went through a succession of low-level legal jobs. Marriage had brought her one connection to Lahore's lawyers: her husband's great-grandfather had been a Chief Justice of the Lahore High Court. This was enough to get her through the doors of Lahore's most famous firms. But no job lasted more than two months. Leaving aside her defining character traits – argumentative, idealistic, hot-headed, stubborn – being a woman hindered employment. In Pakistan's criminal courts, women (both as lawyers and defendants) are unexpected and often unwelcome. The rough and tumble of adversarial argument and the gritty facts of criminal cases are deemed unsuitable for female sensitivities. In many of these firms, Sarah was the first female employee. At one job, there were no ladies' bathrooms, and as most male employees were unhappy to work in the same room as her, Sarah had no desk. Those women who were working as lawyers in these firms were generally hostile towards the young upstart – with her sharp wit, closely cropped, boyish hair, fine features and large dark eyes. They resented her family connections. Throughout Lahore, many clients categorically refused to have a woman argue their case.

In late 2007, only six months after beginning her abortive career, Sarah, along with many other lawyers in Pakistan, stopped work. Following a challenge to his authority by some of the country's most senior judges, the then military dictator General Pervez Musharraf had twice impeached the Chief Justice, Iftikhar Chaudhry, and scores of other judges. Lawyers revolted. Musharraf imposed martial law. Hundreds of thousands of people marched in solidarity with the judiciary – a doubly remarkable event in a country where judges are often accused of elitism. The police tear-gassed protesters and made arrests by the hundred. Suicide bombers stormed the Lahore High Court. Most of Pakistan's senior judiciary and lawyers were placed under house arrest; the rest boycotted the courts. Sarah lost her job again. Musharraf maintained martial law for several months.

The 'Lawyers' Movement', as it has come to be known, received global news coverage. Even I, as a nineteen-year-old second-year Scottish law student, heard about what was happening in Pakistan. For the international press, it was a perfect example of the separation of powers, a surprising vindication of elegant legal theory in a country usually lambasted for its human-rights abuses, corruption and fostering of terrorism. It was a picture of mass political participation and democracy. It gave people hope for Pakistan's future. But for Sarah, it was just another vector of unemployment. For the next two years, she continued to ricochet from firm to firm.

By this point, early in 2009, Zulfikar Ali Khan – the author of the letter to the newspaper – was about to be executed. He had been on death row in Lahore Central Jail for over ten years, and the jail authorities swore that this week would be his last. His death sentence had been confirmed, his execution date set. His only chance for reprieve was a presidential pardon, which, given the state of the government, was unlikely. Frantic, he told his brother of his idea to write to the editor of a national newspaper. A week before his scheduled execution, they drafted the letter, a last-ditch plea for help. The newspaper printed it. That afternoon, the brother's phone rang: it was a young, upper-class-sounding woman with an American twang to her Urdu. Within an hour, he had delivered the case files to her doorstep.

Starting your own law firm is common practice in Pakistan. Graduating from university in Lahore, or returning from study in England or America, young lawyers train with a well-established firm, spend several years working as an associate and then, having gained experience, connections and clients, set up on their own. Unlike law firms in London or New York, which often have hundreds of partners, the majority of Pakistan's civil and criminal firms have one or two. Their relatively small offices collect in clusters. Criminal firms huddle in the streets surrounding the Lahore High Court. Once referred to, during the Raj, as 'Sharks' Lane' (an allusion to the notoriety of criminal barristers), the streets south of the court are lined with unattractive tall glass office buildings faced with shiny brown and green foil that reflects the sun's heat and gives a certain sleazy gaudiness to the area. Inside are floors of lawyers' firms, the names of Lahore's most famous criminal lawyers lined up by the buttons of battered steel lifts: *Khwaja Sultan, Azam Tarrar, Salman Safdar*. Civil firms lie further from the court, away from the old city and towards the British-built army cantonment, in the modern residential area of town.

Although office practices vary, almost all legal firms are characterised by their dependence on – and consequent privileging of – *munshis*, legal clerks. The firm's most important hire, a *munshi* with the right experience and connections is instrumental in moving cases quickly and resolving them favourably. Without one, a lawyer will struggle to get a case through the courts. They flank law-firm partners like familiars: a clerk is a constant confidant, a true *consigliere*. In Lahore's larger firms, where positions are organised on a strict hierarchy, the partners' *munshis* are senior in status to all junior lawyers.

Sarah's firm did not correspond to this model. For a woman to start up a law firm is uncommon. And for that firm to focus on only one area of law, death sentences, of which the founder had no prior experience and knew next to nothing, was unprecedented. As people on death row are almost invariably poor – the wealthy can pay bribes and use influence to avoid charges, let alone punishments – the work is not well remunerated. Sarah's intention to found a firm with no money, and to work for free, struck even the uninitiated as a bizarre business model. Unsurprisingly, she couldn't begin to afford a clerk. In her naivety, she thought she could do it herself. Ignorance and inexperience were a blessing. Anyone better informed would have assumed that the whole enterprise was impossible.

One of the few things Sarah did know was that she needed some help. Since taking on Zulfikar Ali Khan's case, she had been working with an experienced investigator and the support of Clive Stafford Smith, founder of Reprieve, an international organisation that supported the cases of people facing execution around the world. Sarah and the investigator had drafted a mercy petition (a plea to the President of Pakistan asking that he pardon the accused) for Zulfikar Ali Khan, which surprisingly, as in Pakistan these petitions rarely have any practical effect, had gained him a stay of execution of ten days. During that respite, they persuaded the prison authorities to stay his execution for another fourteen days. Then eighteen. In this piecemeal way, Sarah achieved her first small successes. But she had no local legal help, and the ragged ring binders on her kitchen table and the constant phone calls from Zulfikar Ali Khan's desperate family members made too much work for one person. Racking her brains, she remembered Maryam, a sympathetic young lawyer at a commercial law firm with whom she'd shared cigarette breaks and complaints about corporate law.

From a studious, quiet and understated upper-class family, Maryam had grown up in a Lahore some distance from the Porsches and Johnnie Walker of Sarah's social circle. Not yet married, she lived with her parents and sisters in a modest, handsome home built by her grandfather in the early 1960s. The second of four headstrong daughters, she had been to a good girls' school – Lahore Grammar, or LGS – and had read law at University College Lahore, which is affiliated with the University of London. Upon graduating in 2006, aged twenty-two, she had started at one of Lahore's best law firms, Ramday Law Associates. Maryam specialised in domestic and international corporate law. She was hard-working but bored, so when Sarah briefly worked for the same law firm in 2008, the two young women quickly became friends. By 2009 – when Zulfikar Ali Khan wrote to the newspaper and Sarah decided to start her firm – Maryam had spent seven years familiarising herself with legal Lahore, deep in the arduous qualification process that Sarah had side-stepped. Seeing in her a friend, an ally and a vital source of local knowledge and relative experience, Sarah offered her an unpaid job. The pair of them – a twenty-five-year-old commercial lawyer and a thirty-two-year-old unemployed lawyer – made an unlikely set of founding partners.

For the first two months, they worked long hours at the same kitchen table where Sarah had first read Zulfikar Ali Khan's plea. Amongst Sarah's empty iced-coffee cartons, scattered newspapers and magazines with half-filled-out crosswords were now piles of documents, legal textbooks and copies of Pakistan's statutes. As Maryam was still working out her notice period, they began work at 8 p.m. and continued late into the night. More frequently than he liked, Sarah's husband's driver was hauled awake to drive Maryam home in the wee hours. Zulfikar Ali Khan's case became Sarah and Maryam's crash course in capital-defence law.

Again, money caused Sarah a problem: she didn't have enough. It was January 2010. Sarah and Maryam could no longer fit their law books on Sarah's kitchen table. The weighty tomes – Criminal Procedure Code, Pakistan Penal Code, textbooks on writs and laws of evidence – were causing family arguments. But rent prices for criminal offices beside the court were prohibitively high. And so the young lawyers camped in one of the spare rooms at Sarah's father's factory headquarters, and paid a nominal rent. Their office was little more than a walk-in cupboard, with one desk, one chair, one computer and a stained, sagging sofa. They couldn't afford to install an air-conditioning unit or buy a printer (they would sneak into Sarah's father's office to print out important court documents). Electricity shortages punctuated their days, with power cuts of increasing length as spring progressed towards summer. With no independent power source, they had to second-guess the national grid, making sure to save everything on the computer ahead of unannounced blackouts. In this hot, dark room, Sarah and Maryam tried to teach themselves the law whilst running a practice where each of them was lawyer, clerk, investigator and administrator.

Where their unorthodox business model did correspond to other Pakistani law firms was in relying on the counsel of senior lawyers. The first lesson they learnt was that in Pakistan – as in many other countries, including Britain – legal knowledge is best garnered through apprenticeship. Pakistan's law, especially the criminal variety, owes as much to the accrued habits of lawyers, judges and police officers as to statutes. Many points of procedure, techniques for examining a police file, systems for spotting fake documents are unknown to the Criminal Code of Procedure and are only learnt through experience. Success depends to a great degree on the pedigree of a person's training. Assistance from the most highly esteemed lawyers is not only the most valuable form of teaching but will of itself advance cases. Eminent names lend gravity in court. 'Who are your seniors?' is often barked across a courtroom by judge or opposing counsel.

In their search for a mentor, Sarah and Maryam's aborted careers were crucial. The first months of a young lawyer's life in Pakistan involve nothing much more than following seasoned professionals through court. From 8 a.m., juniors shadow their seniors. In Lahore, in the summer, this means ten-hour days entombed in hot red sandstone, with no air-conditioning. Through this shadowing, the young practitioner learns how to read police files, police handwriting and Urdu legal jargon. The long days allow juniors to gradually grasp the Lahore High Court's tetris-like constellation of courtrooms, to study styles of argument and advocacy, and to come to know the characters of the Bar and Bench – the favourite counsel, the sharpest clerk, the spiciest fried egg sandwich. Given the number of jobs she had started and left, Sarah had absorbed those lessons many times over.

What she saw of the Lahore High Court during these apprenticeships served as Sarah's lodestar through the instability of her early career. She had sat in the courtrooms of many High Court judges, under the auspices of many High Court lawyers. She had been appalled. She had seen corrupt court readers fixing hearing dates for a fee. She had witnessed a gang of lawyers physically abuse a man who had questioned the integrity of his patently corrupt advocate. She had watched judges snooze through bail applications. She had seen ancient cases postponed yet further by the death – simply from old age – of lawyer, judge or one of the parties. But she had also been inspired. From amidst the murk, glimpses of goodness and equity had shone.

From her disastrous early legal career, Sarah also managed to salvage some mentors. 'Waseem Sahib' had once sat at the next-door desk to her. An earnest middle-aged man, he invariably dressed in an immaculate suit and was always clean-shaven. Every day, when she arrived at work, he would be there, bent over some documents with a light furrow in his brow, his dark eyes attentive, his high forehead creased in concentration. He knew Pakistan's legal system – both practically and procedurally – as a mother knows a child: every contour of its temperament and predilections. To a new lawyer, documents in a criminal file are incomprehensible. The Urdu is different from anything spoken on the streets of Lahore. Police handwriting is scrawled and illegible. The significance of minor differences in the dating, filing and stamping of a document is lost. Waseem Sahib could read legal Urdu and police reports. Beside and behind his desk, like a corner of an English country-house library, were vast bookshelves of leather-bound High and Supreme Court law reports. Faded gold embossed numbers on the spine told the year, court and status of the cases inside. Within moments, he would have one of these on his lap, open at the relevant case, instructing Sarah how to use it. Computers were alien to him, and superfluous. To enliven long hours of drafting witness statements and skeleton arguments, Sarah and Waseem Sahib would race to find the best case-law precedent: she used the search function of Pakistan Law Site, an almost complete online database; he pulled books from shelves. He nearly always won.

When Sarah had first worked through the documents of Zulfikar Ali Khan's case – police statements, court judgments, witness statements, lists of evidence, forensic reports – she had been confused. The criminal process didn't match that of the textbooks, the facts were unintelligible, it looked like clear legal provisions had been ignored. As she and Maryam puzzled over the file, Waseem Sahib began to visit their one-roomed office, dropping by for the odd hour or two during a lunch break or after work. A veritable textbook of legal statutes and criminal procedure in practice, he talked them through routine criminal law petitions, the dynamics of the clerks' room, the workings of a police station, the susceptibilities of the judiciary. Putting up with what many would have deemed inappropriate – by the late summer of 2010, Sarah was heavily pregnant and insisted on wearing short summer dresses and eating bright neon ices throughout meetings – Waseem Sahib began to make criminal lawyers of the two women.

*   *   *

In Pakistan, the death penalty is popular. But governments have nonetheless equivocated over executions. In 2008, the year before Sarah and Maryam took on Zulfikar Ali Khan's case, the government had begun to pause executions. 'The Moratorium', as it came to be known, gave opponents of the death penalty some hope: moratoriums often lead to abolition. From 2008 to 2009, the Moratorium remained unofficial and not fully enforced; some death-row inmates, including Zulfikar Ali Khan, continued to be given execution dates. In 2010, however, the Moratorium was formalised by the President, Asif Ali Zardari, leader of the Pakistan People's Party (PPP) and widower of Benazir Bhutto, who upheld his party's traditional opposition to execution. But Pakistan's other main political party, the Muslim League, was known to be in favour of the death penalty. During the League's recent terms in office (1990–3 and 1997–9), Pakistan had one of the highest execution rates in the world, close behind China, Iraq, Iran, Saudi Arabia and the United States. The Moratorium could easily be repealed if the League came back to power. It was unlikely to survive an election. Meanwhile, even with the Moratorium in force, people still continued to receive death sentences – at a rate of almost one a day – swelling ever further the population of Pakistan's death row.

Pakistan's hesitations about the death penalty, combined with several cases of British citizens on Pakistan's death row, prompted the British legal charity Reprieve (who had until that point been supporting Sarah remotely) to travel to Lahore and meet with Sarah and other local lawyers willing to work on these cases. They arrived in March 2010, and soon afterwards gave Sarah and Maryam enough money to rent an office and employ essential staff. Maryam was paid £400 a month, Sarah £525. The remaining funds covered rent, utility bills and the salaries of a cleaning lady and a part-time trainee clerk.

This financial injection was transformative. Sarah and Maryam left the factory floor and rented a windowless flat consisting of two bedrooms, a bathroom and a kitchen – a simple apartment sandwiched between the homes of two families on a narrow cul-de-sac behind one of Lahore's main roads. An erratic assortment of tables, chairs, bookshelves and the odd AC unit donated by family members furnished the offices. They made board members of erstwhile bosses and registered with the government as a new NGO, calling themselves 'Justice Project Pakistan' (JPP).

The workload increased. One other lawyer was taken on part time, then another – both very young. Following the lawyers came a generator, protection against power cuts. Following the generator, an investigator. And in May 2011, a foreign volunteer: me.

During my first weeks in Lahore, I lived in what had been Sarah's childhood home. Set in a square of smooth green lawn in an upmarket residential district of Lahore, the house was of simple lines and open spaces, in the style of the 1960s. I stayed in Sarah's younger brother's room; now a well-known fashion designer, he had decorated it in dark red, with bright red leather sofas to match. Wall-eyed and restless from jet lag, I spent those first evenings sitting on the floor, with paper and files spread all around me, trying to get up to speed with the cases Sarah had shown me that day. Zulfikar Ali Khan's case was the first I read. Although mediated through paper and filtered through cigarette breaks and cold coffee, my first encounter with Pakistan's legal system remains one of the most memorable.

This much I learnt from the trial court judgment:

On the afternoon of 13 April 1998, Zulfikar Ali Khan's brother, Khurshid, took a bus from Shakargarh to Islamabad. The family home, where Khurshid lived with six of his siblings and their decrepit father, was in a small village ten kilometres north of the bus station, on the banks of the River Ravi, wedged between Pakistan's borders with India and Kashmir. Zulfikar Ali Khan himself had recently been posted to Islamabad, working as a gym instructor in Pakistan's navy. But given his father's frailty, he acted as the head of the family. As often as he could afford, he paid for his siblings to travel north and visit him.

The following day, 14 April, was a Tuesday. Zulfikar Ali Khan's household was busy at breakfast time: he had cadets to exercise, his daughter had to go to school and his heavily pregnant wife had to make sure they were both well fed. According to Zulfikar Ali Khan and Khurshid's version of events, Khurshid woke with them and set off for a day of walking in the mountain air on the banks of Simly Dam.

Simly Dam, built in the early 1980s, forms a reservoir from a mountain river. Its two million cubic metres of water are cupped in a valley some twenty miles north-east of Islamabad, in the foothills of the mountain range joining Central and South Asia, where the northernmost point of the Punjab meets Kashmir and the Khyber Pakhtunkhwa. For the past thirty years, the lake has provided drinking water and a day-trip destination for the people of Rawalpindi and Islamabad. On weekends and holidays it is a popular spot – particularly during the summer migration from the punishing heat of the Punjab's plains.

The tree-covered hills surrounding the lake are a welcome counterbalance to Islamabad's utopian grid-block design. Where the administrative capital of Pakistan is audaciously artificial – houses grouped into numbered and lettered cubes, imposed on flattened land – the settlements in the hills follow watercourses and natural contours. Where Islamabad's trees are regimented, metro-nomic markers flanking roads and framing parks, the nature reserves to the north and east are thick with tangled fronds. At Simly, these unkempt hills come right to the water's edge, and there isn't a house to be seen on its northern bank. With some craggy tree-covered islands and interlocking spurs of blurred green hills receding right to the horizon, the scene is reminiscent of a Scottish loch. The shoreline, casually cared for by Islamabad local government's Capital Development Agency, is littered with remnants of barbecues, evening parties and children's games. On that Tuesday morning in April, Khurshid said in his defence, it was almost deserted.

It was at this point, Khurshid later said when questioned by the court, that he met with some men whom he identified as 'two persons from the village of Pehont' – a place eight kilometres from Simly Dam. A fight broke out. The court was not told why. It was by then about 9.30 a.m., said Khurshid. He said that he was badly wounded in the fight, and so walked to the nearest police station to report that he had been assaulted.

All criminal complaints in Pakistan must be lodged with the police: an injured person arrives at the *thana* (small police station) and reports an incident to the officer in charge (known, locally and legally, as the 'incharge'). What happens next depends on the mood of the police, the evidence of the victim and the willingness of witnesses. Faced with an injured person or an alleged crime, it is effectively the incharge's choice whether or not to formally register the complaint. If registered, the complainant's account becomes the dominant narrative of any subsequent trial. As most of Pakistan's police stations have no forensic training, rarely gather DNA evidence and often have to wait several months for results from laboratories (results that are often inconclusive in any event: blood samples, for example, are only tested to determine whether the blood is animal or human, and until 2009 there was no national fingerprint database), the police are rarely able to compellingly prove or disprove complaints. If the complaint isn't registered, nothing further happens at all. More often than not, the incharge will exercise his discretion according to the relative influence of the person making the complaint and the persons named in it. All else being equal, a stranger will usually be unsuccessful in registering a case against a local, and witnesses – on whose evidence the bulk of police investigation is based – tend to be closer to their neighbours than they are to the truth, and easily intimidated in any event. As a consequence, Khurshid claimed in his defence, the police refused to file his complaint against the two men, though the incharge did send him, accompanied by two officers, to the local hospital. Khurshid presented in evidence an outpatient receipt from a hospital in Islamabad: it was time-stamped 10.47 a.m. At about 11 a.m., he said, he phoned his brother, Zulfikar Ali Khan, and told him what had happened.

At about 1 p.m., Zulfikar Ali Khan told the court, he went to Pehont to 'enquire about the argument'. Zulfikar Ali Khan did not explain to the court how he travelled to Pehont, nor what he intended to do once he got there. The court was not told what Khurshid was doing at that time. Zulfikar Ali Khan was carrying a loaded pistol on 14 April, which was licensed to him. (The court did not comment on the fact that he was carrying a loaded gun, and it was not considered evidence of his guilt. This may seem strange to an Anglo-European reader, since the mere fact of carrying a weapon in England and other European countries may point toward an intention to cause injury. However, in Pakistan it is more common for a person to be armed when travelling in a rural area they do not know well, and as Zulfikar Ali Khan had a gun licence, he was not breaking the law in doing so.) He told the court that he met with four men, including the two whom Khurshid had encountered that morning. He said that 'hard words' were exchanged, and a fight broke out. The police reports say that the incident took place roughly half a kilometre from Pehont, on a road with crops to one side and uncultivated *jangal* – an old Sanskrit word for wasteland, from which we get our 'jungle' – to the other. There were neither homes nor people nearby.

One of the men, Zulfikar Ali Khan said, took a revolver out of the folds of his *shalwar kameez* – it would later be presented as evidence, bloodstained and in a sealed bag – and told Zulfikar Ali Khan to leave. Zulfikar Ali Khan didn't move. The man holding the gun, Zulfikar Ali Khan told the court, fired a shot at him. Zulfikar Ali Khan returned fire with three shots.

Zulfikar Ali Khan was unscathed. He admitted that two of his three shots, however, gravely wounded two of the four men. He referred to this as an 'accidental murder'. According to the police report, these shots were fired at 3.45 p.m. Zulfikar Ali Khan told the court that after the shooting he waited with the wounded men before they were taken to hospital. Police were called from a town six kilometres away, and whilst the two healthy men tended to the two wounded, Zulfikar Ali Khan went to meet the investigating officer in order to direct him to the scene of the incident. Zulfikar Ali Khan said that he was then arrested and taken to the police station. His gun and three bullet casings were bound in a sealed parcel. The wounded men were taken to hospital, where they were declared dead.

Some time before 5 p.m., Zulfikar Ali Khan told the court, he arrived at the *thana*, where he met his brother Khurshid. Both Zulfikar Ali Khan and Khurshid were adamant that they were not together when the shooting took place. But both were in police custody by 5.30 p.m. that day.

It turned out that the four men at Pehont had been closely related to one another. The survivors, the father and brother of one of the deceased, left the hospital and went to the police station to register a complaint at 5.35 p.m. They and the investigating officers remained at the police station until 11 p.m. During that time, the officers took down the complainant's full account. On the basis of this report, the police decided that they had evidence enough to justify the further detention of both Zulfikar Ali Khan and Khurshid. At this point, neither side disputed that the two men had died from shots fired by Zulfikar Ali Khan. But whereas Zulfikar Ali Khan claimed that the shots were fired in self-defence, the victims' family portrayed Zulfikar Ali Khan as an assassin and armed robber. The narrative officially recorded was that given by the father of the deceased:

> I was walking to my village, Pehont, along with my sons . . . and my wife's brother in law . . . in the morning on a track. When we reached half a kilometre from Pehont, a boy, whose legs and hands were tied, shouted for help from behind some bushes. He pointed to a taxi parked by the side of the road and told us that two men had hired his taxi from Faizabad and had grabbed his taxi with its documents by threatening him with a weapon, and had left him tied in the bushes. We saw two men – one taller, wearing pants and shirt, the other shorter in height, wearing shalwar kameez – approaching the taxi. [My son] and [brother-in-law] rushed toward the taxi while I untied the boy . . . Then we rushed, yelling for help, towards the taxi parked some 200 yards away. The young man wearing pants and shirt was in the driver's seat and was trying to start the taxi. When [my son] and [brother-in-law] got closer to the taxi, the man sitting in driver's seat . . . shot straight at my son . . . which he received in the right part of his abdomen, and he fell on the ground.

*The other man sitting alongside the driver in front
seat . . . then fired from his 30-bore pistol, two consec-
utive shots at [my brother-in-law] which injured him in
the right side of his chest and the left portion of his
abdomen. The same shooter fired two/three shots at me
when I stepped forward, but they missed me. On hearing
our cries, the people in the area gathered and both
accused men escaped to the nearby woods while [the
police] arrived. They searched the woods and arrested
the culprits. I got both my wounded dear ones into a
Suzuki, to carry them to Polytech Hospital for medical
aid but they died on the way to the hospital. Their
dead bodies have been placed in the hospital while I
have come here to request you take action against the
cruel deed.*

In other words, the father claimed that he and his
sons and brother-in-law had apprehended two men
(Khurshid and Zulfikar Ali Khan) who were in the process of committing highway robbery. This became the
prosecution case: that Khurshid and Zulfikar Ali Khan
had hired a taxi to Pehont, and then stolen that taxi at
gunpoint and bound and gagged the driver. On finding
the driver by the road, the men from Pehont had acted
in his defence and been shot at. Khurshid and Zulfikar
Ali Khan, the prosecution told the court, had then run
from the scene into the *jangal*, where they had ultimately both been apprehended by people from the
village, arrested by the police and taken to the police
station (though the prosecution presented no witness
statements from those villagers who were said to have
apprehended the brothers).

At the police station, Khurshid and Zulfikar Ali Khan
had no access to a lawyer. They had also not been told
the full extent of the prosecution case. Khurshid claimed

that he had no idea what he had been charged with, what he had been arrested for. Zulfikar Ali Khan was adamant that he had fired in self-defence. The brothers were then detained for eleven days, during which time they were interrogated by the police. In Britain, an independent custody officer records each stage of an accused's arrest and continued custody is reviewed at roughly nine-hourly intervals. But in this rural Pakistani police station, no note of Khurshid and Zulfikar Ali Khan's arrest was entered into the police diary, and no independent officer oversaw their treatment.

From what Sarah had told me, and the little study I'd done of Pakistan's criminal law, I knew that it was illegal for the police to keep an accused for more than twenty-four hours unless approved by a magistrate. And it was unlawful for a magistrate to approve further detention if, during those twenty-four hours, either no investigation had been done, or the investigation had been completed, or the person had been tortured, or the police had made no proper record of the initial detention. I had also learnt that where a magistrate wrongly grants further detention, an accused can appeal that decision to a higher court. And, guaranteed by the constitution, a detainee has the right to a lawyer. On the statute books, therefore, there are significant protections available for an accused.

But in practice, it seems, magistrates give the police what they ask for, and their decisions are rarely questioned. The lack of a comprehensive system of legal aid means that few accused can employ a lawyer (an average murder case will cost about Rs. 60,000, or £400 – as much as six times a labourer's monthly salary) and have to rely instead, where eligible, on counsel provided by the government. And, particularly in murder cases, the extensions granted by the magistrate – during which the accused has no access to a lawyer and rarely learns of the case against him – are characterised by torture. The police are relatively open about this. When interviewed by a local human rights group, one superintendent said: *'In effect, the police have complete and unchecked powers. And the lack of modern investigative techniques means that we are forced to torture to secure confessions.'* Common techniques include sleep deprivation, heat exposure, rolling heavy objects over a person's limbs, beatings with a leather racket, attaching electrodes to a person's genitals and running a current through them. Other practices are *kursi* – forcing the detainee to crouch as though sitting in a chair for hours on end; *manji* – tying the right arm and leg to a wooden bed, the left arm and leg to a parallel wooden bed, leaving the body hanging in the middle, then pulling the beds further apart, forcing the joints to sustain the entire body's weight; and *strappado* – hanging from the wrists, with arms twisted behind the back, for long periods of time.

Such torture – illegal in Pakistan under both domestic and international law – often serves police officers well: it speeds up a confession, which eliminates the need for further investigation. Moreover, the worse a beating, the more someone will pay for it to stop. Even if they do not know their rights in detail, Pakistan's poor generally know these police station economies. After days drifting in and out of consciousness, delirious with pain, heat, thirst and hunger, few can remember what they've confessed to, or how exactly their confessions were induced.

In the case file, I read that on 15 April 1998, the day after their arrest, the magistrate granted the police further detention of Khurshid and Zulfikar Ali Khan. On the brothers' version of events, this was unlawful. There were no police diary entries of their detention, and beyond speaking to the deceased men's families and packaging a gun and some bullet casings as evidence, no investigation had been carried out. But neither Khurshid nor Zulfikar Ali Khan had a lawyer at that stage, so no one had appealed against the detention.

Police torture is pervasive in Pakistan. And so, without attempting to abolish the practice, but in order to mitigate against one of its greatest harms – false confessions from innocent men – the country's legislature declared, in 1984, that confessions, or indeed any witness statements, obtained in police custody were inadmissible in court. Most countries presume confessions to the police to be admissible unless it appears to the court that the police used oppressive tactics. But in Pakistan, the risk of torture-induced confessions is so high that the legislature sees all confessions as unreliable – a sorry indictment of their national law enforcement officers. In one circumstance, however, police officers in Pakistan can rely on a confession made in their custody: if physical evidence is found as a result of the confession (that is, if the confession is corroborated in some way), then the part of that confession that relates to the evidence found will be admissible in court, regardless of the fact that the confession was made to the police. In order to legitimise confessions, therefore, police have been known to plant corroborating physical evidence. Khurshid and Zulfikar Ali Khan, like many, confessed to knowing the whereabouts of further physical evidence related to the offence.

From the incident outside Pehont, only one weapon was taken: Zulfikar Ali Khan's gun. (Zulfikar Ali Khan says that he handed this over to the police when he voluntarily surrendered himself to custody; the prosecution and the police say that it was discovered in the *jangal* near where the incident occured when Zulfikar Ali Khan was forcibly arrested.) For the evidence to match the prosecution's case, however, two 30-bore revolvers were needed: one fired by Zulfikar Ali Khan, the other by Khurshid. On the tenth day of his detention, Khurshid told the police that he had left a pistol lying in the *jangal* outside Pehont, hidden under some stones. Under interrogation, Zulfikar Ali Khan told the police that his ID card might be found lying in the dirt by the side of the road, half a kilometre outside Pehont. The second gun and the ID card, pieces of physical evidence – discovered by the police eleven days after the offence, from a crime scene that had not been secured in the interim – served to corroborate the prosecution's case.

It took over a year for the case to be tried. Zulfikar Ali Khan and Khurshid were in custody for the duration. Curiously, they were both charged with committing a 'terrorist act', at the time defined in statute expansively and almost incomprehensibly in the following terms:

> *Whoever, to strike in the people, or any section of the people, or to alienate any section of the people or adversely affect harmony among different sections of the people, does any act or thing by using bombs, dynamite or other explosive or inflammable substances, or firearms, or other lethal weapons or poisons or noxious gasses or chemicals or other substances of a hazardous nature in such manner as to cause, or be likely to cause the death of, or injury to, any person or persons, or damage to or destruction of property or disruption of any supplies of services essential to the life of the community or displays firearms, or threatens with the use of force public servants in order to prevent them from discharging their duties commits a terrorist act.*

By this definition, a person who spills kerosene (a substance of a hazardous nature) on his neighbour's (thereby adversely affecting harmony among different sections of the people) garden chair cushion (thereby causing damage to property) commits a terrorist act. And all people charged with a terrorist act were tried in special anti-terrorism courts that allowed for rushed, expedited trials, limited evidence and – where the police had any material evidence (such as Zulfikar Ali Khan's gun) – an inverted burden of proof requiring the accused to prove they didn't commit the act. Only a year after it was drafted, much of the Anti-Terrorism Act was held to be unconstitutional.

At the close of the brothers' trial in an anti-terrorism court in September 1999, the case was disposed of relatively quickly. A poorly paid government lawyer had been appointed to defend the two men. All of the police officers acted as witnesses for the prosecution, with the exception of the investigating officer, the first to the scene, who was out of the country for the duration of the trial and gave no evidence at all – something that concerned the trial judge as a *serious defect* in the case. The police and court questioned Khurshid and Zulfikar Ali Khan, but the brothers didn't give evidence on oath in court, nor were there any other defence witnesses. The defence evidence was scant: Khurshid gave no account of where he was on the afternoon of 14 April; Zulfikar Ali Khan did not explain how he travelled to Pehont; there were no ballistics reports matching a gun either to the deceased or the other two men (necessary to corroborate the defence case of self-defence). The court held that the key piece of evidence corroborating the defence case (the doctor's note from the hospital, stamped at 10.47 a.m.) was a forgery. The government defence counsel didn't look into how the hospital recorded outpatient receipts (which may have been done on a twenty-four-hour clock and would thereby have been immune from this sort of error), nor did he check with the hospital for records of Khurshid's visit. The prosecution case was equally thin, failing to explain why it took almost two weeks to gather both weapons and other material evidence from the scene of the shooting; why – given the allegation that the taxi driver had been forced to hand over his vehicle documents and keys to Zulfikar Ali Khan and Khurshid – no registration documents or keys were ever found; why the complainant's account of events said that the shooting took place in the morning, whereas the police recorded it as taking place at 3.45 p.m.; why the site plan of the incident – hand-drawn by the police, who rarely take photographs of a scene – indicated only one accused, making no mention of Khurshid anywhere near Pehont on the afternoon of 14 April.

In September 1999 – a year and five months after the brothers' arrest – Islamabad's Special Court for Anti-Terrorism handed down its judgment. Khurshid was sentenced to life and a fine of Rs. 100,000 (£1200) for the murder of one of the men; to life and a fine of Rs. 100,000 for the murder of the other; to fourteen years' imprisonment for robbery committed on a highway; to ten years' imprisonment and a fine of Rs. 10,000 (£120) for the attempted murder of the father. He was not sentenced to death, because the court had been baffled by the evidence against him: the judge held that his case was 'shrouded in mystery'. Zulfikar Ali Khan was sentenced to death by hanging for the murder of one of the men; to death by firing squad for the murder of the other; to fourteen years' imprisonment for robbery on a highway. The anti-terrorism court prized itself on its speed, in sharp contrast to the regular court system, where cases have formed a backlog since long before the partition of India, but its cost was the loss of strict laws of evidence and a thorough system of appeals. The court ultimately found the brothers not guilty of committing terrorist acts, but it was still deemed efficient to try the remaining charges – of murder, attempted murder and robbery – in the anti-terrorism court, with its special rules of evidence.

To make up for relaxed evidentiary rules and the speed of the trials, the Anti-Terrorism Act put in place heightened procedural protections. Under the Act, for example, any police officer who conducts a defective investigation is liable to two years' imprisonment. But Khurshid and Zulfikar Ali Khan's government-appointed defence lawyer did not press charges against the police. The anti-terrorism court concluded that '*The report of the Forensic Science Laboratory as regards the comparison of weapons recovered from both the accused and with empties recovered from the spot is positive and this evidence alone is sufficient to convict the accused.*' As the forensic report in itself could not exclude the reasonable possibility of the shots being fired in self-defence, a conviction on that basis alone was unsafe, and left itself open to challenge.

In due course, both prosecution and defence appealed this decision. The appeal was heard two years later. The defence argued that the prosecution hadn't proved their case and appealed against both conviction and sentence. The prosecution, by contrast, argued that Khurshid, as well as Zulfikar Ali Khan, should be sentenced to death. Both appeals were dismissed. The High Court (to whom the trial court judgment was appealed) did concede, however, that both Khurshid's presence at the scene of the crime and the allegation that he had fired any shot '*could not be proved beyond a reasonable doubt*'. The High Court was also not satisfied that either Zulfikar Ali Khan or Khurshid had had any intention to steal the taxi and doubted the discovery of a second gun, eleven days after the offence. It nonetheless held that '*putting the defence version in juxtaposition to the prosecution case it was safely held that [the defence] has no plausible appeal available [. . .] For the forgoing reasons, we [. . .] dismiss their appeals.'*

The government lawyer acting for the accused then requested a review by the Supreme Court, but the application was submitted 204 days late and was refused. Khurshid and Zulfikar Ali Khan's sentences were confirmed: *'Prosecution succeeded in proving its case against the petitioners. The impugned judgment does not suffer from any legal or factual inaccuracy. Therefore the High Court decision is upheld and the petition is dismissed.'*

By the time Sarah had those documents dropped on her doorstep, Khurshid had been released from prison but Zulfikar Ali Khan had spent over a third of his life in the same square cell; his execution date had been scheduled and cancelled more than fifteen times. In 1999, he was twenty-nine years old. When Sarah met him in 2010, he was forty. His second daughter had been born, and following the death of his wife (she was unable to afford medical treatment for her cancer), both the baby and her sister were effectively orphaned.

But eleven years on death row is a long time, and Zulfikar Ali Khan had not been idle. Whilst in prison, he began to study, then to teach. He obtained two masters degrees, more than thirty diplomas and the sobriquet 'Dr Zulfikar, The Educator'. More than 400 prisoners owe their literacy to him, and are grateful: *'Brother Zulfikar made me understand how precious our time is and how important education is. He offered to be my teacher and took full responsibility for my education'; 'When I was on death row I was completely uneducated. Thanks to [Dr Zulfikar's] hard work, I am now preparing for my bachelor's degree.'* During his time in prison, Zulfikar Ali Khan became well known, and was used globally as one of the best arguments against the death penalty, with human rights organisations often citing his case.

But the odds were stacked against him. His execution could occur at any time, something of which the prison's design – still built on the nineteenth-century model, with gallows prominent in the complex – kept him keenly aware. The Punjab's death rows are among the few prisons in the world that the International Committee of the Red Cross aren't allowed to access. Even Somalia, Colombia and the Democratic Republic of the Congo are more open to humanitarian visits.

Zulfikar Ali Khan's case offers many readings. To most of us, it's confusing. To his students, it's inspiring. To other prisoners, it's depressing. To lawyers, it's a cause for concern. To the senior judiciary of Pakistan, it's regrettable. To the police, it's all lies.

For me, as I closed the file at 4 a.m. and pushed it to one side of my bedroom floor, it was disconcerting. From what I had read, it seemed that the court – both at trial and on appeal – could not possibly have been in a position to make any findings on guilt or innocence in this case. The evidence – of both prosecution and defence – was weak. Oral accounts were confused, conflicting and unconvincing. Key witnesses were missing. The court itself had stated that certain elements were not proved beyond reasonable doubt. And yet one man had been sentenced to spend a life sentence in prison, and another had been sentenced to death.

As my first experience of a case outside the classroom, Zulfikar Ali Khan's file made me think hard about the relationship between laws and those they aim to punish, protect and regulate. Pakistan has laws prohibiting torture and is a signatory to the United Nations Convention

Against Torture, which it ratified in 2010. But between 2006 and 2012, in one district of the country, doctors found that 76 per cent of those alleging abuse by the police had certainly been tortured, while the remaining 24 per cent showed *'signs indicating injury'*. No police officer was prosecuted. Pakistan's Qanoon-e-Shahadat (Law of Evidence) was drafted in full knowledge of this police malpractice and with the specific intent of mitigating its harms, and yet the police can use it to rely on confessions extracted by torture. Pakistan's constitution cites the fundamental and inviolable right to a fair trial, and yet statutes create 'special courts' with the power to sentence to death on little evidence. Before Zulfikar Ali Khan's case even reached trial, it seemed, a lack of proper investigation and profound flaws in the legal system had already sentenced him to death.

There was only one man who could save Zulfikar Ali Khan's life, Sarah told me with a touch of melodrama, and that man's name was Arthur Wilson. It was my first week in Lahore, and Sarah had arranged a meeting at our offices with Mr Wilson; he would be here shortly. Who was this Arthur Wilson? I wondered. An international lawyer? A British judge somehow overseeing the case? A diplomat? The director of an international charity? I was somewhat surprised, therefore, when a tall, round-faced and definitely Pakistani man, with swept-back greying hair and long white sideburns, bounced into the office.

Arthur Wilson, it transpired, was a mediator. Deploying the charm that so often got people to do what she wanted, Sarah explained that he 'worked *tirelessly* for Pakistan's prisoners' and 'had done *more than any other* for the rights of those on death row'. He ran Pakistan's Prison Fellowship International, a Christian charity that provided food and basic healthcare to prisoners, and supported their families. But during his career, he had also taught himself to mediate disputes – a rare and useful skill, for which Sarah relied on him heavily. Arthur could resolve disagreements between hostile adversaries. His techniques were both ancient and novel, the coincidental outcome of his holding strong Christian values in a country with increasingly Islamic laws.

Arthur Wilson's working day was sustained by innumerable cups of tea, into which he dissolved more sugar than anyone I'd ever known. His time in our office, therefore, was largely spent in the kitchen. Unhurried, languid and immune from anxiety, Arthur was many things Sarah was not. But unlike Sarah's other staff, he was never chased to work harder, never scolded for spending an hour in conversation. For Sarah was well aware that conversation and a tendency never to rush were what made him so good at his job.

From Monday to Friday, Arthur would work on active cases: travelling to jails to meet prisoners, to villages to talk with complainants, to marketplaces, shops and businesses in an attempt to network his way into communities. Saturdays were a day off. Sundays were saved for pastoral visits. After church – which, all over Lahore, ended in tea and conversation on the lawn – he would ride his motorbike around town, visiting the households of men still on or recently released from death row. Initially, these meetings were merely to update mothers, wives and daughters about the mental and physical health of their menfolk in jail. But Arthur had soon become a friend to many. He helped the children with their exam revision, encouraged college applications and would often arrive with baskets of home-cooked food, to ease the strain on newly single mothers. The decades people spent in prison allowed him to establish close relationships, and he had been seeing some families every Sunday for many years.

Vocation and empire had brought Arthur Wilson's family to Lahore. Baghdin, Arthur's paternal grandfather, spent his life living and working in the Punjab, on both sides of the border that would separate Muslim and Hindu when the British left India. Raised between Delhi and Amritsar, he moved to Gurdaspur when he was eighteen and spent three years training to be a Presbyterian minister at the city's American-founded seminary. His first posting was to Narowal – then in India, now narrowly in Pakistan – where he served as minister for a decade. By then he had a wife, also from Amritsar, and they came to have four sons, all raised in Narowal. The town was remote, and Baghdin, a fit young man, visited parishioners on foot or horseback – a fact that his grandchildren, raised many years later in Lahore, where only the very poor walk from place to place, found astonishing.

With the creation of Pakistan in 1947, Baghdin found himself in a new country. Gurdaspur was no longer an hour's drive from Narowal, Delhi no longer a simple day trip. He now held a different nationality from his brother, the principal of Gujranwala's seminary, where Baghdin had once hoped to retire. It was a time of great trauma: the partition of India resulted in the largest and most rapid movement of people in the world's history. By 1951, Pakistan was home to seven million refugees, and as Indian Muslims fled to the newly created country and Hindus fled from it, they slaughtered one another in hundreds of thousands. Because he was from a Christian family, and perhaps also because he and his brothers held senior positions in the Church, Baghdin did not suffer the persecution and bloodshed faced by many during Partition. Instead of cursing his new-found isolation, he thanked God that his family had been spared from slaughter. He learnt to rely on Pakistan for his family's future.

In 1952, when the Zenana Bible and Medical Mission first accepted male staff and offered him a job, Baghdin moved his family to Lahore, further from Kashmir – a territory that would be fought over by Pakistan and India from Partition until today – and its related insecurity. At this point, his eldest son had already left home to work as a clerk to the deputy commissioner of Mianwali, a city further into Pakistan, six hours west of Narowal. His second son had recently completed his own training as a minister – and was to remain in Narowal and take over his father's post. Baghdin's youngest son was still a child and could easily be taken with them to Lahore. But the third, unmarried son posed a problem: the women's mission, where the family were to live, did not allow single men. So Baghdin found a local wife for his son, and Arthur's parents, Nazira and Wilson ('Willie' to his friends), were hurriedly married the week before the family moved to Lahore.

The Zenana Bible and Medical Mission (the 'Bible Women', as they were nicknamed) was founded in 1852 by a group of evangelical British Christian women concerned about Indian women's access to education and medical care. They were part of a larger movement of British missionaries in India who, throughout the nineteenth century, converted considerable numbers of the Hindu and Muslim lower castes and largely created present-day Pakistan's small Christian population. Besides eternal salvation, Christianity promised many of its converts escape from an entrenched social position that determined everything from career and marriage prospects to the area of town they could live in (the lowest castes often lived outside villages and were restricted to jobs higher castes considered unclean, such as skinning animals, carrying out executions and disposing of animal carcasses). But being Christian soon became associated with being from a low caste. Today, Christians in Pakistan, who make up roughly 1.6 per cent of the country's population, lead difficult lives. They are disproportionately at risk of being charged with blasphemy (21 per cent of blasphemy cases registered are against Christians), Christian residential areas are vulnerable to sporadic attacks by lynch mobs, and on several occasions whole church congregations have been the target of suicide bombs.

But in the 1950s, the political context in which the Bible Women worked was not yet so fraught. They lived in a compound of twenty-eight *kanals* (about three and a half acres) between Empress Road and Allama Iqbal Road, just south of Lahore's railway station and next door to St Andrew's Church. In the centre of the compound was a large bungalow, where some Bible-study classes were held and the mission's principal lived. Surrounding the bungalow stretched grass playing fields, bright green and immaculately kept, tropical tendrils overflowing carefully curated flower beds. On the Empress Road side of these, at the compound's perimeter, was a large dormitory, home to the mission's students – women of sixteen or older who hoped to be teachers. On the Allama Iqbal Road side were the staff quarters, shared between Baghdin's family, the gardener's family and the gatekeeper's family.

The Bible Women gave jobs to all of Baghdin's family. Nazira cooked for the school's staff and students. Willie managed the administration of the compound – at the time, the women relied on the compound's men, who were in short supply, to negotiate all contracts, manage public relations and sit on the mission's board. Alongside their jobs, Nazira and Willie raised five children, each born two years apart between 1960 and 1968 – Rubina, Selina, Arthur, Almaas and Shahla. As is common in Pakistan, the children all took their father's first name as their surname.

With five children, Baghdin's three-roomed living quarters were fit to burst, but on the edge of those expansive playing fields, the three families never felt cramped. Outside teaching hours, the campus belonged to Arthur and his siblings who, every day after their 5 p.m. rest, would spill across the grass, playing tag and elaborate games of hide and seek. When they could find willing partners amongst the female students, the children held badminton and basketball competitions on the compound's courts. And as their parents became closer to the principal, the Wilson siblings moved freely in and out of her bungalow, playing with brilliantly colourful toys and watching their two favourite TV programmes – *The Saint* and *The Six Million Dollar Man* – on a little black-and-white set. Aged seven, Arthur's hero was Roger Moore.

Arthur's time at high school – a nearby boys' school recently founded by the Catholic Archdiocese of Lahore and managed by the Church to this day – was untroubled. He spent most of his time playing sport: idolising Bruce Lee as he practised karate, participating in volleyball championships with his classmates. Every morning at assembly, he played the flute in the school band as it blasted through the national anthem.

But the 1970s was a volatile period in Pakistan. In 1971, East and West Pakistan fought a bloody civil war and the country's eastern wing declared itself independent as Bangladesh. Zulfikar Ali Bhutto, president of what remained of Pakistan, drafted a new constitution – still in force today – which was prefaced with confirmation of Islam's position at the heart of the country and, for the first time since Pakistan's creation, declared Islam the state religion. In 1977, as Arthur entered the seventh grade and joined the judo team, General Zia-ul-Haq, Chief of Army Staff and a man with a mission to Islamise, seized power from Zulfikar Ali Bhutto.

General Zia-ul-Haq came to power in 1977 by way of a military coup. In keeping with a wave of similar projects across the Islamic world – Islamic legislation was introduced in Libya in 1971, in Iran in 1982, and in Sudan in 1983 – Zia intended to Islamise his country's legal system, which included drafting an Islamic criminal law. This was contrary to the vision of Pakistan's founder, Muhammad Ali Jinnah, who had imagined Pakistan as a secular state. *'Religion'*, Jinnah famously said, *'has nothing to do with the business of the state.'* And yet, soon after Jinnah's early death from tuberculosis in 1948, his vision for the country was swiftly subverted. In 1949, Prime Minister Liaquat Ali Khan declared Pakistan to be a state founded on Islamic principles. The 'Objectives Resolution', as his declaration was titled, described Pakistan as a state *'wherein the principles of democracy, freedom, equality, tolerance and social justice as enunciated by Islam shall be fully observed; wherein the Muslims of Pakistan shall be enabled individually and collectively to order their lives in accordance with the teachings and requirements of Islam as set out in the Holy Quran and Sunnah.'* In 1956, the drafters of Pakistan's short-lived second constitution – it was suspended following the country's first military coup in 1958 – inserted the Objectives Resolution as its preamble. Since Jinnah's death, Pakistan's rulers have used Islam to their advantage, relying on Islamic idiom to co-opt conservative religious groups and contain a disparate electorate. Sharia-compliant law reforms had been on, or close to, government agendas from the late 1940s. But it was ultimately General Zia, who began to formalise Pakistan as a strictly Islamic nation: as part of his programme of legal reform, he incorporated the Objectives Resolution into the text of the constitution in 1985. With Zia, Pakistan became an exclusively Islamic republic.

General Zia's Islamism aimed to make more robust and religious the country's collective morals. In 1980, alongside unsuccessful attempts to impose dress codes on women, make the growing of beards compulsory and ban pigeon flying, he established a Federal Shariat Court. According to Zia's blueprint, the court would be supported by *ulema* – scholars and Islamic legal experts – and would have the power to change any of Pakistan's laws that it deemed un-Islamic, or *'repugnant to the injunctions of Islam'*. Confounding General Zia's conservative impulses, however, Pakistan's Federal Shariat Court proved itself a site of relative liberalism and a guardian of fundamental rights. During Zia's rule, the court declared repugnant a law that prescribed death by stoning as punishment for adultery. In 1991, it would announce its mandate to *'ensure and guarantee all fundamental human rights and [to emphasise] social, economic, and political justice for all'*. And in fulfilment of this mandate, the court would rule handcuffs and extended prison sentences un-Islamic, and repeatedly emphasise the Islamic values of liberty, equality and freedom of expression. General Zia made many attempts to rein in the court's liberal tendencies.

In Pakistan, the power to declare laws 'repugnant' itself was not new. In an attempt to secularise the subcontinent's laws, the British had granted Indian courts a power to find local religious laws (such as Muslim and Hindu personal law) invalid where *'repugnant'* to (British concepts of) *'natural justice'*. Inverting the British legislation, Pakistan's own repugnancy clause was first drafted in 1956; it allowed courts to invalidate British-drafted laws where repugnant to the injunctions of Islam, and thereby re-Islamise the legal system. Established seventeen years before Islam was even declared Pakistan's state religion (with Bhutto's Constitution of 1973), and twenty-four years before Zia established the Federal Shariat Court in 1980, Pakistan's repugnancy clause was therefore one of the country's first moves toward institutionalising Islam.

But General Zia's legislative amendments were far more thoroughgoing, and his re-emphasis of the repugnancy clause, together with the creation of a specialist Islamic court with relative autonomy and wide-ranging powers for Islamic legal reform, marked him as the most ambitious of Pakistan's Islamic reformers.

Zia's Islamisation programme threatened Lahore's Bible Mission with closure. In the newly pressurised environment, the small compound was riven with argument. To Arthur, then thirteen years old, the disagreement was simple: some people in the government wanted all foreign missionaries to leave; others wanted them to stay. The head of the mission resigned. The project was handed over to local management, and an elderly Englishwoman, Miss Edith Williams, who had just travelled to Lahore from India, was appointed principal. For the next two years, the government, which had previously provided some funding to the mission, stopped doing so.

Edith Williams, a tiny, white-haired and pale-skinned woman who had spent most of her life in India, became very close to Arthur's family. For his parents she was a combination of spiritual guide, teacher, babysitter and patient. Arthur himself saw her as a grandmother, a friend and one of the most important influences on his early life, and he was deeply impressed by the changes she brought about. She founded the mission's first nursery for local children, both Christian and Muslim, and she instilled in everyone a work ethic and renewed faith. Despite her frailty – a few years after joining, she fell and broke her leg and had to live, bedridden, with Arthur's family – she remained a strong presence in the compound. Even from her sickbed she gave lessons every day. Each morning a gaggle of girls would flood into Baghdin's household clamouring, 'Auntie, where is the milk, can we have some tea?' at Arthur's beleaguered mother. In the small house, the girls filled the floor, gathered around Miss Williams' bed.

Decades later, whilst reflecting on his career, Arthur would look back on this period as formative. He valued his parents' and Edith Williams' sense of service, faith in God and respect for one another. But he saw that these qualities were not enough to hold the mission together. Fissures from the arguments of the late seventies split the small community. Arthur's father, Willie, became increasingly embroiled in a dispute with the other trustees about ownership of the mission compound, which a number of them wanted to sell. In central Lahore, those twenty-eight *kanals* were a valuable asset. This disagreement became a court case that would worry Willie late into his nineties. As one of his first experiences of justice and its vulnerabilities to power, Arthur still talks about the case at length. By 1979, these domestic pressures had taken their toll on Arthur's mother, her diabetes ultimately resulting in kidney failure. And so Arthur, the eldest son of a father trapped in a long and complicated legal dispute, and an invalid mother, was forced to leave school and get a job.

Just out of school and reluctantly contemplating a career, the sixteen-year-old Arthur spent much of the summer of 1980 bored. Most of the time it was too hot to go out, and instead he and his friends spent their days sitting inside, listening to music – ABBA, Boney M., Kenny Rogers. Dizzy with images of wide-legged flares and shoulder-length hair, the boys plotted their way to pop stardom.

First, he needed to learn an instrument. Arthur had always fancied the guitar. Unfortunately, there were few guitar teachers in Lahore in 1980, and even fewer willing to teach a penniless schoolboy for free. After several weeks, the boys found a guitarist living in a nearby Christian community. One Saturday afternoon they knocked on his front door and asked if he would help. He advised them to join the local church choir – it was the best in town and had won seventeen Christmas choral competitions in a row – where they would get free musical tuition.

Built by the British in 1860, St Andrew's Church was at the midpoint between Arthur's family home and the guitarist's. With large gates and walls shielding it from the busy Empress Road, to walk into its grounds was to enter a sanctuary. Every evening and all day on a Sunday, the lawns were alive with children, the community hall packed with tea-drinkers conversing around huge metal urns, several hundred cups and trestle tables draped in cloth. While older children played basketball, younger ones crouched on the floor in a sea of crayons, women cooked large meals in the makeshift kitchen, men sat in cliques on creaking white plastic chairs.

Originally planning to use the church merely as a means to musical fame, Arthur and his friends ended up joining the choir and spending more and more time there. Arthur liked the fact that there were lots of other kids his age. Throughout the 1980s, as he bounced from job to job – banking clerk, travel agent, insurance broker, factory manager – he brought in just enough rupees for his family to get by. But as his jobs ended with predictable regularity, while the mission unravelled in legal disputes and his mother died, St Andrew's Church became the only constant in his life.

Climbing through the hierarchy of youth leadership roles, Arthur was first assistant, then joint, then general secretary of the youth fellowship. He never learnt to play the guitar. Instead, working under the wing of a church elder – a prosperous local businessman who earned so much that he was able to donate large sums to the church every year – he learnt how to manage a business. Within a few years, Arthur had founded his own company. He called it Excellent Services, which he had proudly emblazoned in coloured italics across letter paper and business cards. The firm provided cleaners, drivers and cooks to large corporations working in Lahore. With his first contract, Arthur bought himself a light blue Italian scooter, which soon became something of a trademark as he whizzed across Lahore meeting clients and church elders. Still in his early twenties, he was making money and showing it off: dark sunglasses, coiffed hair, self-iron shirts, shiny suits and pointed shoes. By thirty, he was rich, with a large office, a brand-new car, tens of employees and several *lakh* (hundred thousand) rupees (about £2,500) of disposable income. He soon married Violet, his first cousin, to whom he'd been betrothed since birth. After a year of family arguments caused by living in a three-bedroom apartment with Arthur's four siblings and his elderly father, the couple moved into their own house and in time had three children.

But with his success, Arthur's conscience began to nag. Looking to appease it, he turned to the Church and discovered their prison fellowship, a charitable mission, managed in Lahore by a Mr Baptist, that preached to Christian prisoners and gave alms to their families. Arthur was upset by the state of the Christian prisoners in Lahore Central Jail. Having grown up in a mission, he was appalled to see that these inmates had no books, bibles or prayer room. The poverty of the surroundings, the overcrowding and the dirt hit him viscerally. Reflecting on that first visit today, he unfailingly cites it as transformative: 'Since that day, I have never truly left Pakistan's prisons.' He employed managers to run his business and became obsessed with the prison fellowship. Within four years, he had sold his home services company and was spending all his time with prisoners.

Through the prison fellowship, Arthur began to cultivate 'leadership skills', as he proudly refers to them now. Leaving Pakistan for the first time, he took courses in Singapore, Canada and Africa, where he fostered an interest in basic human psychology. Back home, he found that he had a knack for appeasing arguments within the congregation and mediating between the parties to his father's land dispute. Had his father been more open, Arthur thought, he might not have had to spend his whole life bound up in a decades-long legal case (which always seemed to me, when Arthur described it, to be straight from the pages of *Bleak House*). It helped that Arthur's was a gentle, reassuring presence. Then, as now, his calm, reasonable way of speaking encouraged others to be cooperative and open. And although he saw communal prayer as the best way to reach agreement, his piety was mixed with a surprising pragmatism, which enabled him to craft subtle compromises between antagonists. The leadership courses had given his predisposition a professional focus, with the result that his occasional tendency to be judgemental and his capacity to hold grudges in his personal life evaporated when he was helping others. At some point in the 1990s, it struck him that his reconciliation skills could possibly help the prisoners he worked with.

As part of General Zia's programme of Islamisation, the Federal Shariat Court had the power to undertake penal reform. In the 1980s, the validity of a death sentence for murder was challenged. The court held that where the victim's family had forgiven the accused, a sentence of death was un-Islamic (or repugnant to Islam).

As a result of this judgment, the *Qisas* and *Diyat* Ordinance ultimately became law in 1990. *Qisas* is a principle of Islamic law that, like the biblical 'eye for an eye', allows for retaliation. Either the victim or their next of kin can punish the accused by inflicting an equal injury on them. Crucially, it is also in the power of the victim, rather than the state, to forgive the accused. *Diyat* is a principle that, like many old European legal traditions, allows a murdered person's heirs to accept financial compensation in lieu of criminal charges. It has become notorious as 'blood money'. Negotiations over *Qisas* and *Diyat* often run parallel to the criminal case being tried in the courts, and have sometimes led to last-minute reprieves at the foot of the gallows. The prisoners Arthur worked with were all at varying stages of the criminal process – some were pre-trial, others had exhausted their final appeal – but for all, forgiveness by the victim or their heirs would end the criminal case and have the accused released from jail.

These provisions evidence a conception of crime profoundly different from modern European traditions. According to European legal theory, a crime is committed against the state. The state prosecutes and punishes that crime, and it is only the state that can drop charges. Broadly speaking, it is only in civil law that the parties can settle cases financially. Other than giving evidence, the victim and their family generally have no role in the criminal proceedings. But under *Qisas* and *Diyat*, crimes are understood as committed against a person and their family, or *wali* (legal heirs). And unless a person reports a crime, it will generally go unpunished – where there is no victim, there is no offence. Where European Enlightenment legal theorists expounded elegant theories for why crimes were communal rather than personal, the Islamic provisions mark a practical approach to legal punishment. In Pakistan – a country devoid of a welfare state – the widow of a murdered man, left to raise their children, has lost her livelihood as well as a loved one. The *Qisas* and *Diyat* provisions are often condemned, rightly, for allowing the rich to buy their way out of a case, and for privatising the justice system. But compensation, or 'blood money', means something very different when you can no longer afford to feed your children. Hobbes, Locke and Rousseau have little to offer a penniless Pakistani widow.

In the early 1990s, when Arthur first shared meals and prayer with families of those accused, he was often shown case documents and told in detail about the circumstances of the crime. He was frustrated by the unfairness, injustice and confusion common to most of these tales. And so, tentatively, he began to contact the complainants. He wanted to understand the full story, to work out what had actually happened. Some of the disputes, he soon discovered, were based on simple misunderstandings – unpaid rents and other straightforward arguments over money – which he found he could easily and persuasively explain away. With facts set straight, victims and their families often forgave the accused, resulting in instant exoneration.

It was through Islamic laws, therefore – the result of General Zia's programme of Islamisation – that Arthur was able to use his mediating skills to try to get men like Zulfikar Ali Khan off death row. This irony was not lost on him. Arthur's negotiation techniques, although not explicitly religious, were firmly founded on his experience as a Christian in Pakistan. It was the Church that afforded him access to Lahore's prisons and prisoners. He owed his highly respected social position to his status as head of the prison fellowship, a Christian organisation. And yet, in the concept of 'forgiveness', both Muslim and Christian found a common resource before the law.

But even Arthur was struggling to resolve Zulfikar Ali Khan's case. He had managed to get the complainants to consider compromise, but they would accept nothing less than £35,000. Zulfikar Ali Khan had no money.

4

September 1992
First information report
Statement of husband and father of the three deceased
(prosecution witness 3)
Inquest reports of the three deceased
Hand-drawn plan of the place of occurrence
Recovery memo 1: sealed parcels of blood
Photographs of bloodstained fingerprints on wall,
cupboard, doorway
Statement of eyewitness (prosecution witness 4)
Recovery memo 2: clothing of deceased (bloodstained
shalwar kameez, dupatta, brassiere, cotton shirt)
Senior police officer annotations on plan of place of
occurrence
Post-mortem report of three deceased: deep incised wounds
to front neck of both boys – death by haemorrhage; ligature
mark around the woman's neck – death by strangulation
Parcels sent to chemical examiner: sealed jar of liver,
spleen and kidney; sealed jar of stomach contents
Arrest warrant for Ghulam Mustafa
Medical examination of Ghulam Mustafa, broken hand
Zimnis [police diary recorded every day of accused's
detention]
Statement of Ghulam Mustafa (accused 1)
Recovery memo 3: bloodstained knife

Recovery memo 4: VCR, suitcase, watch, two gentlemen's suits
Plan of the place of recovery
Application to magistrate to take fingerprints of accused 1
Sample of fingerprints
Certificate of proficient fingerprints
Arrest warrant for Aftab Masih (accused 2)
Transfer of investigation to Nawan Kot, Lahore

October 1992
Proceedings issued against Aftab Masih
Magistrate's proclamation
Arrest of Aftab Masih

November 1992
Transcript of interrogation of Aftab Masih
Statement of Aftab Masih
Zimnis
Recovery memo 5: strangulation wire
Plan of place of recovery
Recovery memo 6: golden ring and two gold necklaces
Plan of place of recovery
Application to magistrate to take fingerprints of accused 2
Samples of fingerprints
Certificate of proficient fingerprints
Reports of fingerprints bureau matching photographs to samples
Chemical examiner's report

April 1993
Challan [the charge]: Ghulam Mustafa and Aftab Masih charged with house trespass, robbery, attempted murder of a one-year-old child, murder of an eight-year-old boy, murder of a three-year-old boy, murder of their thirty-six-year-old mother

Statement of Ghulam Mustafa, pleads not guilty
Statement of Aftab Masih, pleads not guilty
Fourteen prosecution witnesses (no defence witnesses)
Speedy trials court judgment: '*I convict Ghulam Mustafa and Aftab Masih accused under Section 302(b) for the murders of three persons and sentence each of them to death on each of the three counts. They shall be hanged by the neck until dead.*'

March 1994
Supreme Court Appeal, Lahore Bench: '*We are convinced that the appellants committed the gruesome murders of three innocent persons and were rightly convicted. In view of the enormity of the crime they do not deserve any clemency in the matter of sentence. Their death sentences are confirmed.*'

Sarah delivered Aftab Masih's case file to my desk: 'Work through these and write up a case record sheet. Nasar will help you.' I had no idea what a case record sheet was. Who was Nasar?

The case file appeared fragile, obscure and ancient, more precious archival material than an active piece of litigation. Handwritten police records, ceaselessly photocopied, are as delicate as ancient parchment, as incomprehensible as cuneiform. With diary entries, investigation records, site inspection reports and witness statements, these notes take up a large proportion of the case file. Drafted in the heat of the moment – literally and metaphorically – the documents are filled with minor mistakes, translucent where the paper has been smudged with sweat. They present page after page of pallid palimpsest; annotated, amended, stamped and dated like a glossed monastic text. I wondered at the specialist training it would take to decipher them.

Nasar, it turned out, was our clerk: our *munshi*. In exasperation with the untrained schoolboys she had initially hired to save money, Sarah had finally employed a professional clerk. When he had first arrived, in late 2011, we hadn't been introduced, but I had noticed him around the office – with his distinctive starched white shalwar kameez and pointy black leather shoes, reflective aviator sunglasses and natty Samsung smartphone. He was tall and dark-skinned, with a head of thick, near-black hair. His brow jutted out over his eyes and was usually furrowed: in disdain, thought, or an attempt to shield his eyes from Lahore's bright sun. He came and went, and was never in the office more than an hour or two. And he enjoyed a privileged position as the only member of staff to have a 'company car' – through wrangling with Sarah (who guarded her tiny budget ferociously), he'd negotiated a red Honda scooter as part of his employment contract.

My desk was too small for both Nasar and me to sit at. We took the scrappy bundle of documents instead to the 'conference room' – what had once been the dining room in the secluded abandoned bungalow that was now our office. Here, as in the other front rooms, the windows stretched the room's full height. It was sparsely furnished: a long table, some office chairs, a whiteboard along one wall. Wicker and wooden bookshelves housed an amateur attempt at a legal library. Some UN manuals on the Convention Against Torture and the report of a Special Rapporteur on human rights were sandwiched between the several-inch-wide spines of the tomes of British liberalism: the Criminal Procedure Code and Pakistan's Penal Code. A fan turned lazily at the centre of the ceiling. The air-conditioning unit, on the opposite wall, wasn't working. From the table we looked out on to the garden: short, wide blades of grass, unruly vines with flashes of colour. The gardener's fighting cock was outside, its clatters and screeches shooting through the room as it attacked its reflection in the window.

Nasar and I were mutually suspicious, and curious. *'Case record sheet kia heh?'* 'What's a case record sheet?' I enquired. His face showed surprise that I spoke some Urdu. And annoyance that I was asking stupid questions. He shrugged. I pulled the case file towards me and attempted to read out loud. The enraged cockerel was hurling itself against the window. Irritatedly smoking a cigarette, Nasar watched the lank figure of the gardener scuff one of his hens away from the flower bed. I continued in my attempt to read the file, bludgeoning pronunciation, making no sense. Nasar put out his cigarette, uncrossed his legs and took the file from me. He began by working through the layers of annotation scrawled down the margins before returning to the top to read from right to left. Here was a true scholar. As he read, Aftab Masih's case started to unfold. And as we took breaks for tea, sunlight and cigarettes on the veranda, I learnt more of Nasar's life as a *munshi*.

Nasar was born in Pindi Bhattian, a village some 130 kilometres north-west of Lahore, near the Chenab river, on the way to Islamabad. The village sits on fertile river plains and, with sun-soaked days and riverside irrigation, is part of a busy farming community. Nasar's spartan family home, comprising just a bedroom and a kitchen, was built from mud and straw by his great-grandfather. Born in that house when Pindi Bhattian was still part of British India, Nasar's grandfather, Nadi Bukhsh, was a thirteen-year-old boy when the partition of India created Pakistan. He raised Nasar on stories of the village and his own childhood. As he talked about the break-up of the village during Partition – the departure of his Hindu friends and the arrival of strangers, the Muslim relatives of their neighbours – Nasar wondered about life beyond Pindi Bhattian, something few members of his family knew anything about.

Nasar's family have worked the same trade for generations: they are the shoemakers of Pindi Bhattian. Nasar's father, grandfather and great-grandfather made *khussa*, a light, leather-soled Punjabi slipper often embroidered with metallic threads, sparkling with sequins or curled up dramatically at the toe. Traditionally worn by both prince and peasant throughout much of northern India and Pakistan, *khussa* have also travelled abroad. Factory-made imitations sell in the summer collections of high-street stores – Topshop, Office, Urban Outfitters – in Britain and America. But while these are now mass-produced across South Asia, in Nasar's village, where there is little electricity, the *khussa* are made by hand, the leather stitched together with thick cotton thread. And in Pindi Bhattian, *khussa* manufacture has never been a lucrative business, nor a prestigious job (when Nasar first told me his family's trade, he made me swear not to tell a soul in the office). The shoes, each requiring hours of work, sell for 80 rupees a pair (cheaper than a can of Coca-Cola). When Nasar was only three, however, even this meagre source of family income dried up. Long hours of fine needlework in bad lighting had left his father near blind, unable to work.

The walls of Nasar's family house were bare. There was no running water, electricity or gas. Nasar's mother cooked over a wood fire. And as children, Nasar and his six siblings all worked to bring in a wage, helping at home and labouring for the local *zamindar*, or landowner. Having suffered at its hand, *khussa* manufacture was not the life Nasar's father wanted for his sons. He encouraged their ambitions. The two eldest boys joined the army. Nasar would become a *munshi*.

Nasar's first job, like Sarah's, was found through family connections. When he was a young boy, his father took him further away from home than either of them had ever been before. They were to visit Haji Muhammad Yusuf, Nasar's father's cousin, who lived in Lahore. Haji Muhammad Yusuf had worked as a *munshi* for twenty-five years when he took his young cousin under his wing. He too had moved to Lahore as a teenager. When his father presented Nasar, Muhammad Yusuf engaged him in a brief conversation. He agreed to take him on for a month. If Nasar worked well, Muhammad Yusuf would find a lawyer to pay for his education. He should speak legal Urdu and some English if he was to work in Lahore, and he needed to learn his way around the court. To become a *munshi*, like becoming a lawyer, is to undertake almost a decade of apprenticeship.

Because the best of them must know the biography of every judge in forensic detail, every lacuna in a lawyer's knowledge, *munshis* in Lahore start their training young. They loiter by white plastic tables under the large banyan tree at the entrance to the court, looking for piecework from resting clerks. Literacy is important, in English and Urdu, and is learnt either though elementary schooling or by immersion, running errands through the court's corridors. But the most important characteristic is a canny street sense and a keen intuition. Encyclopaedias of court practice, clerks are the custodians of the legal profession.

Fifteen years on, Nasar is well established at the Lahore High Court. Barely in his thirties, with a self-assurance verging on arrogance, he tells me that he is regarded as one of the ten best of the Lahore High Court's 12,000 clerks. He is a member of both the Supreme Court and Lahore High Court clerks associations – clerks, like lawyers, have associations both to represent their interests and to provide a common room in the court, which Nasar dominates like the most popular boy in a classroom. He comes with recommendations from many of Lahore's senior lawyers and some High Court judges. Since arriving at Haji Muhammad Yusuf's house, Nasar has spent almost every day at the Lahore High Court. His first 30-rupee-a-day salary paid for his schoolbooks. His boss paid for his exams. As he studied, his salary increased with the seniority of the lawyers who employed him. After a few years, he developed exacting expectations of the lawyers he worked for. His two favourite teachers – Maloo Qureshi and Rana Anwar – he remembers with reverence. They knew the provisions of the penal codes and the procedures of the courts by heart.

Before Sarah, Nasar worked in the Supreme Court for one of Pakistan's best-known criminal lawyers. But when his boss was made governor of the Punjab, Nasar was out of a job. He came to the attention of one of Sarah's previous bosses – a man of some influence at Pakistan's criminal bar and a board member of Sarah's new organisation – who put the two of them in touch. Sceptical as he was of her ramshackle office and all-female staff, Nasar nevertheless accepted Sarah's offer. Now he was stuck teaching a foreigner how Pakistani law worked, and was not particularly enjoying it.

'*Aftab ke muqadime mem kia hua?*' What happened in Aftab's case?

'*Pecheeda heh.*' It's complicated.

'*Us ko thane mem, kia hua?*' What happened to him at the police station?

'*Aap nahin parh sukti heh?*' Are you unable to read?

A case file always begins with the first information report. If properly organised, it then proceeds through the case chronologically: supplementary statements from the injured party, *zimnis* (daily police diary entries recording the custodial conditions of the accused), the magistrate's orders, the *challan* (charge), the Sessions Court judgment, the High Court judgment, the Supreme Court judgment, and any number of orders and applications in between.

As one reads on, the case rises through the institutions of Pakistan's criminal law: police station to Magistrates' Court to Sessions Court to High Court to Supreme Court. The judgments become easier to read. Handwritten notes are replaced by typewriters, typewriters by computers. But legibility does not mean accuracy. Whilst handwritten, narratives are negotiable. As they are typed and retyped, false accusations can calcify into facts.

Judgments of the Sessions Court – Pakistan's court of first instance for capital crimes – are still drafted in English, quickly hammered out on tired black typewriters by the court stenographers and scribes. These drafters dot themselves through the courtrooms: at a small desk in a corridor, outside a judge's chambers, in a windowless records room. During the summer's electricity shortages, a candle lights the page in the building's stifling warmth. In the Karachi Sessions Court, the stenographers' study is abandoned, piled prohibitively high and deep with documents. Scribes gather instead around a table at the gates of the court; a discarded tablecloth stretched over poles above their heads provides a shifting square of shade, like the awnings shielding Lahore's roadside barbers and fruit sellers. Judgments are written so quickly – often within hours – that mistakes invariably creep in. Sometimes whole paragraphs are missed out. Corrections are made by hand; biro markings, like editors' notes on a proof, amend the smudged type.

In the High Court – where parties can appeal Sessions Court judgments – scribes are dignified with offices. In Lahore, they are based in the old British carriage house and bicycle shed, where files, typists and typewriters have replaced horses' tack and Royal Enfield bicycles. Rooms built to house judges' horse-drawn coaches are now packed with paperwork. Clerks weave between the crammed and cluttered desks, always hopeful that their friends in the filing room will allow a quick glance at a court order before it's published. Shouts – commands and questions – bounce between one table and the next. These judgments are drafted with greater care than those of the Sessions Court. But with this slightly better administration comes administrative delay: a person can wait weeks for an order to be handed down from the High Court.

Islamabad's Supreme Court, a utopian building that pays architectural homage to Fritz Lang's *Metropolis*, is far removed from handwritten judgments and bicycle-cum-record rooms. Within its 1960s-built geometric walls are computers and fully staffed offices. Its judgments, set out in neat type at the back of the file, come as a blessed relief to a young pseudo-*munshi* like me.

From Nasar's brief tutorial I got the impression I annoyed him, but I also started to learn some of what had happened in Aftab Masih's case. Firstly, his surname (in Urdu, Masih means 'Messiah') meant that Aftab Masih was a Christian, a fact I bore in mind as we read through his story. According to the papers, Aftab Masih and his co-accused had been found guilty of brutally murdering a mother and her two sons at a house in Lahore – their throats were slit, the house covered in their blood and littered with their dismembered bodies – and stealing a VCR and some jewellery. The evidence against Aftab Masih and Ghulam Mustafa appeared strong: an eyewitness account, their fingerprints in blood on the walls. The alleged motive was robbery. But Aftab Masih had never confessed to the police, or a magistrate, and Sarah speculated that the woman's husband had arranged the murders as a result of some infidelity or family dispute – the egregious violence, she said, suggested a crime of passion. The brutality was tragically disproportionate to the gain of a second-hand VCR.

Like Sarah, Nasar was convinced that Aftab Masih was innocent. Using the case file, he talked me through Aftab Masih's version of events, and set it against the prosecution's case.

We began with the first information report. The husband and father of the deceased persons, a textile merchant, had left home at 9 a.m. on a Saturday morning. Home was in an affluent housing estate, built in the late 1970s and named after Pakistan's national poet, Muhammad Iqbal. A town within a city, the estate enclosed parks, several high schools, a university, a boating lake, a hospital, a church, a number of mosques, a Pizza Hut and a McDonald's. The house was by the park ('*a successful man, the park has nice houses,*' Nasar said). The bathroom needed some work done on it, and plumbers were to arrive to complete the job that day. The doorbell rang at about 2 p.m. An elderly servant opened the door to two plumbers: Ghulam Mustafa and Aftab Masih ('*Aftab wasn't there*'). They were invited in by the textile merchant's wife, who directed them to the bathroom. She and her children then left to collect prescriptions from the local hospital: her father-in-law was ill. They returned. ('*From here nothing is true.*') The servant was sent by the mother to deliver the medicine to her father-in-law. When he returned, at about 4 p.m. (having been gone for at least an hour), he found the doors locked from the inside and heard cries. Through a window ('*look at the floor plan – he couldn't have seen anything through that window*'), he saw Aftab Masih strangling and assaulting the mother and Ghulam Mustafa, covered in blood, dragging one of the deceased boys into a cupboard before slitting the throat of the other. ('*Ghulam Mustafa pulled* churi *around the neck of deceased,*' the report read. I knew *churi*, the Urdu for knife.) The servant, the only eyewitness, left to get help but fell unconscious on the way. At 10 p.m. – six hours later – the police found him lying in the park, about 250 metres from the house. ('*This is a lie, it makes no sense.*') A VCR, some cash and some jewellery were missing.

Nasar quickly flicked through the following pages and I tried to keep up: the police send the bodies for post-mortem and chemical examination. Then there is a piece of paper with something sketched on it. ('*This is a plan of the room.*') They take fingerprints ('*false – Aftab Masih was taken to the house much later and forced to put his fingerprints on the walls*'). We move to the next day: 6 September. There is a statement from Ghulam Mustafa, who has spent a day with the police. A medical report: Ghulam Mustafa has an injured hand ('*from the police*'). A statement from the elderly servant, now resuscitated ('*he was drugged or kidnapped that afternoon*'). On 12 September (after six days in police custody), Ghulam Mustafa makes a second statement, telling the police that they can find the VCR in his home. A recovery memo from Ghulam Mustafa's house in the Anarkali bazaar: the bloodstained *churi* is under Ghulam Mustafa's bed, as is the VCR, one watch and two suits ('*the police put them there; there are no witnesses to the discovery of those items*'). 14 September: Ghulam Mustafa's fingerprints.

'*Aftab kahan heh?*' Where is Aftab? I interrupt.

'*Wo Lahore se gia.*' He left Lahore.

'*Kab?*' When?

'*Qatlon ke bad.*' After the murders.

Nasar continues. On 19 October: a note of Aftab Masih's arrest. 1 November (after thirteen days in custody): a statement, in which Aftab Masih tells the police where to find the weapons ('*they beat him until he said what they told him to say*'). A recovery memo: the wire used for strangulation is found in a fence. A second recovery memo: two gold rings ('*the police put them there, Aftab Masih had never seen them before*'). Fingerprints. Magistrate's approval of certified match of fingerprints ('*this is fake: the Magistrates Court doesn't use that stamp*'). Finally, the *challan*: the formal charge against Ghulam Mustafa and Aftab Masih. This is typewritten, signed by a judge, dated 10 April 1993, seven months after the murders. Murder on three counts, attempted murder and robbery. Aftab Masih and Ghulam Mustafa plead not guilty.

Next in the file are the judgments. They are in better condition than the police notes: more recently printed and easier to read. But the court's reasoning was wanting. Guilt did not appear to be established: there seemed to be cause for reasonable doubt.

Fingerprints. When giving evidence, Ghulam Mustafa told the court: '*I was taken to the spot where the blood was found and my hands were smeared with that blood and then my fingerprints were got fixed on the wall in the house of the complainant by the police.*' Independently, Aftab Masih claimed something similar: '*I was taken to the house of the complainant and asked to put my finger impression on the cupboard. I refused. The police beat me until I did it.*' The judge dismissed their defence: '*I have no reason to disbelieve the senior police officer.*'

75

Eyewitness. The man who is said to have seen the murder take place through the window is the family's septuagenarian servant. There were several possible problems with his account. First, the floor plans show that he couldn't have seen the bodies from the window, although they may not have been drawn precisely to scale. Second, it is highly coincidental, though of course not impossible, that the servant should return to the house, by chance, at exactly the moment that the murders were taking place and then witness each of these murders in turn. Third, Aftab Masih told the court that the complainant was trying to protect the identity of the real murderer. The complainant denied this and Aftab Masih didn't present any evidence in support of this theory, but if there was any truth to it, then it's possible that an elderly servant, anxious not to lose his job, might give a false account on the instructions of his employer. Fourth, as to the servant lying unconscious in the park for six hours, Nasar told me that this was absurd: late in the day, late in the summer, in the middle of the weekend, that park is busy with people taking a turn in the evening's comparative cool; one of these walkers would have noticed an unconscious old man. The court hesitated when considering this part of the prosecution case, but concluded that if a passer-by had seen the servant, they would merely have thought that he was asleep. The court held the servant's eyewitness account to be the lynchpin of the convictions:

> I have minutely examined the oral as well as documentary
> evidence produced by the prosecution. Large number of
> witnesses is not required to prove a case. Conviction can
> validly be based on the statement of even a solitary disin-
> terested witness if found correct. The most material
> witness in this case is the servant . . . He is keeping a

beard. He was having a mark on his forehead indicating
that he had been offering prayers regularly since long time.
I noticed the mark and enquired from him if he was
offering prayers regularly and he answered the query in
affirmative. I cautioned him that it was a murder case
in which death sentence is provided and he should not
make false statement.

The servant's religious observance was taken to guarantee his sincerity.

Torture. Exhibiting a familiarity with police violence, the judge found Ghulam Mustafa's injuries not sufficiently serious to amount to torture: '*I cannot agree with the accused that those injuries were the result of police torture. In case the police had tortured him, injuries would have been found all over the body.*' The medical report found that Ghulam Mustafa's injuries were sustained at some point between 5 and 7 September, whilst he was in police custody. The court held that the injuries were sustained as a result of the murders.

Motive. The prosecution cites theft of money, jewellery and household goods as the motive for the murders. Such a motive, however, doesn't fit the narrative of premeditated murder given by the prosecution: on the prosecution's facts, the plumbers waited for the servant to leave so that they could murder the mother and her children; but if they had been looking to commit a robbery, why didn't they wait until the house was empty? In its judgment, the court does not interrogate the prosecution's alleged motive. Ghulam Mustafa and Aftab Masih's baffled defence is mentioned in all of the judgments. When asked by the court to respond to the prosecution's case, Ghulam Mustafa said '*that he did not know the reason as to why he was implicated. He conceded that he had been working as a plumber from time to time in the house for the last 5/6 years. He stated that he had no other link with the complainant . . . Almost to the same effect is the statement made by Aftab Masih.'* Aftab Masih maintained that he had not been at the house at the time of the offence and did not know why he had been charged with murder, as the trial court noted: *'the accused was asked to explain as to why the case was made out against him. He stated that he was getting training as a plumber from Ghulam Mustafa accused and for that reason he was involved in the case. He added that he was innocent.'*

When making his first statement to the police, Ghulam Mustafa had given Aftab's name as accomplice. Once the police had his name, Aftab Masih says that they requested he attend the police station for questioning on 7 September, which he says he did voluntarily (although the police say that he was not questioned until his arrest, on 19 October). During that week, however, Aftab Masih left Lahore, staying with an aunt in a village in the northern Punjab. He doesn't explain this flight to the court: it could fairly be read as evidence of guilt. But it may also demonstrate a young man's fear of the police, a fear that many, even within the police force, would say was justified: when interviewed by a human rights organisation, one Pakistani police officer admitted that *'unfortunately, there is little doubt that we proceed from the suspected criminal to the crime, rather than from the crime to the criminal. But you have to understand that we are pressed for results, so we have to deliver and make arrests, at almost any cost.'* During his absence, Aftab Masih's two brothers, teenage cousins and father were detained by the police. They all say that they were tortured, and that they ultimately told the police where Aftab Masih was. In mid-October, he was arrested.

Illegality. Finally, a footnote to the above: Aftab Masih's sentence was potentially unlawful. Birth certificates are not issued in rural Pakistan, but by most accounts – his mother's, her sister's, his three cousins' (two older, one younger), his schoolteacher's, his brother's – Aftab Masih was fifteen when sentenced to death. Under both domestic and international law, it is illegal in Pakistan to sentence a juvenile to death. But Aftab Masih cannot prove his age. At the time Nasar and I read the file, he was thirty-five and had been on death row for nearly twenty years.

Reading through the case file in 2011, I realised that I was not the first to wonder at how long Aftab Masih had been on death row. Towards the end of the file, dated May 2009 (sixteen years after the murders), was a bundle of High Court orders. These were typed, in Times New Roman, and in English. I presumed they were incorrectly filed: the parties to the case were *'The State' v. 'Central Jail, Lahore'*. If Aftab Masih wasn't involved, why were these orders in his case file?

I read on. On 2 May 2009, the Chief Justice of the Lahore High Court, the Chief Justice of Pakistan (Iftikhar Chaudry, the man who had been impeached in 2007) and a Supreme Court judge (whose nephew had once given Sarah a job in his law firm) had visited the jail. The first order I read opened with a note about the visit: *'During that trip they met a condemned prisoner namely Aftab Masih who was awarded death sentence on three counts by Lahore High Court and they learned that said condemned prisoner is in death cell since 1993. His lordship is shocked to know as to why this condemned prisoner has been in the death cell for the last 16 years.'*

A letter showed that the Chief Justice had demanded to see Aftab Masih's case file. It had disappeared. The next few orders showed the *'hectic efforts'* made by police officers, prison wardens and superintendents to search for the papers that would explain how this man had come

79

to be on death row. Aftab Masih has been in jail longer than most of the officers who worked there: none remembered his arrival. The prison warden made enquiries at the police station: '*the first information report only has the result of the trial court, it is silent about further appeals*'. On 9 May 2009 (things happen fast when the Chief Justice is involved), the superintendent found some record of the trial. '*The total sentence of the above said condemned prisoner is <u>death sentence on three counts</u> + 45 years + compensation 10,000 rupees + fine 15,000 rupees + 6 years rigorous imprisonment. Twice the condemned prisoner approached jail authorities to file appeal before the Honourable Supreme Court through his relative but till today no appeal has been filed.*' In his defence, the Advocate General had claimed that Aftab Masih had hidden the appeals in order to escape execution. Outraged, the Chief Justice confronted police and prison: '*Under the circumstances, I take notice of the matter myself and direct the superintendent of Lahore Central Jail to appear before the court on 11 May 2009 . . . I would like to know whether Aftab Masih after dismissal of his appeal by High Court has filed any petition for leave to appeal in the Supreme Court of Pakistan.*' 26 May 2009: there was no record of an appeal. The Home Secretary was summoned to court the following day. He knew nothing of Aftab Masih's legal history. The Chief Justice himself filed Aftab Masih's appeal.

The file Nasar and I were reading had thus been pieced together by panicked police officers during those weeks in May 2009. Before that, Aftab Masih's detention had been undocumented. Neither prison warden nor policeman knew the status of his appeals. Aftab Masih had had no lawyer and, an illiterate teenager himself, had forgotten how many times he'd been in court and what the status of those courts was. Once he had entered the legal system, no one cared enough to track his trial. The police had satisfied their mandate, making an arrest for three brutal murders. Aftab Masih's family were poor, powerless and perhaps relieved: his criminality had only brought them police threats, periods of imprisonment and beatings. He had no money to pay lawyers, and none – until Sarah picked up his papers in 2010 – were willing to act for free. And so he had stayed in jail for decades, with no execution date and no prospect of release. The Chief Justice retired. Aftab Masih remained on death row.

To the Chief Justice, the delay in Aftab Masih's case was an aberration. But, taking tea with a Lahore High Court judge one afternoon, I learnt that Aftab Masih's case is just one of 140,000 cases currently pending at the Lahore High Court. Fifteen thousand of these are criminal. Every day, almost a thousand new ones are filed. The ever-expanding backlog is not necessarily heard in chronological order. Rather, it is a clerk's connections, a judge's disposition or a lawyer's influence that determines which of the 140,000 is next in line.

It is perhaps not the court's fault. Built in the late 1870s as the chief court of northern India, the Lahore High Court has tried to grow with its caseload, but has failed to keep up. Following Partition – the boundary lines between India and Pakistan decided by four judges sitting in the Lahore High Court itself, overseen by an English judge on his first trip to the subcontinent – Lahore's became the chief court of Pakistan. And since that time it has been completely overwhelmed. Over the years, a host of wings have been added to what was once a simple quadrangle: judges' chambers, jury rooms, libraries, lavatories, translators' rooms, refreshment rooms, English and Persian records offices, verandas, servants' quarters, fountains, carriage houses and a vast complex of *munshis'* bicycle sheds. The monumental and once symmetrical architecture – originally designed to express the power of imperial justice – is now an overgrown maze, a dense ecosystem of alliances, loyalties and jealousies.

Aftab Masih, while in prison with neither execution date nor release date, needed someone who could navigate that world and get his case back to the top of the pile. Fortunately for him, in Nasar he had one of the Lahore High Court's most cunning operators – a man steeped in the protocol, symbols and codes of court life. And fortunately for me, Nasar was forced to take me with him as part of my own apprenticeship in Lahore legal society.

We went to the Lahore High Court on Sarah's orders. Her latest plan for Aftab Masih was to try to get the court to recognise and record his age and to acquit him as a juvenile. It was unlikely to work: Aftab Masih had no birth certificate, and all Sarah had were witness statements from a schoolteacher and family members who remembered helping with his birth. Nevertheless, Nasar and I left the office one sweltering afternoon and took a car over to the court.

Driving along the Mall – British-built and nostalgically named in 1851 – was laborious. Traffic policemen stood under white umbrellas, dressed in pristine blue uniforms with whistle, truncheon and radio hanging from their belts. They directed heavily congested traffic with white-gloved hands. As we inched our way towards the court – Nasar irritated and wishing, with characteristic impatience, that he had been able to whizz through the traffic on his motorbike rather than take the foreign intern by car – I stared into a mass of orange tuberoses, carefully planted at the foot of the lofty thick-trunked trees that marked the central reservation.

The High Court was at the far end of the Mall, separated from the road by black wrought-iron railings and a stretch of fine green lawn, rimmed with palm trees. Standing tall in front of the building was a statue of King-Emperor George V, with a plaque – large and legible from the road – commemorating his establishing the building as a High Court of India in 1919. The British saw India's High Courts and legal codes as the Raj's crowning glory: in this building was consecrated justice, vigour, certainty. And like the Gothic cathedrals of medieval Europe, the High Courts of India were built to inspire awe. Designed by English architects and engineers, the Lahore High Court was said to have been built in imitation of a fourteenth-century South Asian palace. Behind the smooth lawn rose a medley of minarets and Mughal mouldings set on to a formidable fortress-like framework. Situated opposite a busy mess of shopfronts and advertisements – Baba Gee Garments, AMB Nice Shoes, AT Alfa Mobile Phone Accessories – the Lahore High Court commands this section of the Mall. Its red stone, offset by the greenery of its gardens, flared in Lahore's sun.

The court's entrance is not grand. Penguin-like crowds – men dressed in black suits, bright white shirts and black ties, women in white *shalwar kameez* and black jackets – gathered, everyone holding a file or two. All of Pakistan's lawyers wear this uniform, excruciating in the high summer. For security reasons – there were several bombs in the court during the lawyers' strikes of 2007 – few cars are allowed to drive through the gates. Instead, lawyers are dropped like schoolchildren and walk through the security checks into court. But our car was different. The guards, stepping from their rickety box, circling and noting our number plate, were suspicious. One stood high behind a khaki-green blockade, his AK-47 cradled in a concrete niche and aimed directly at us. Nasar banged impatiently on the window. Hands off his gun, the guard smiled and threw him a comic salute. They were clearly good friends. We were waved through; no weapons checks, no metal detector scans, no questions.

A fierce light flashed off the windscreens and painted white metal barriers of the car park. Nasar strode towards the large banyan tree under which clerks and lawyers sat on scuffed plastic chairs, drinking tea outside the members' room of the Punjab Bar Association. As his gold-beige *shalwar kameez* billowed in the breeze, and his shiny shoes struck the pavement, he was met by waves and nods. Like a celebrity, he acknowledged his admirers with a palm pressed to his chest, occasionally walking over to shake someone's hand. Trotting to keep up, I followed in his wake, spinning my head to take in the buildings we passed through. The court's quads, turrets and verandas were a deep magenta, accentuated by white marble facings. A filigree of light terracotta trelliswork cobwebbed across ogee arches and dark entrances to form passageways of comparative cool. Benches, doormats and swinging wooden signs, hand-painted with judges' names, marked the entrances to courtrooms. Ceiling fans chopped the air. An AC unit poked incongruously from the window of a higher-ranking office. Opposite, behind the resting tea drinkers, were the garages, bar common room and administrative offices that had been added throughout the twentieth century in the court's desperate scramble to accommodate its caseload.

Our destination was the objections room – deep in a warren at the back of the building – where we were to file Sarah's application to have Aftab Masih's age certified. Nasar took a short cut. The room was cool, painted in the light mint green of doctors' surgeries. A man sat at a cheap pine desk, on which balanced a cumbersome computer. Nodding at Nasar, he noted our application and gave us a ticket. As in a local council office in England, or an embassy's visa-issuing section, the *munshis'* applications are ticketed. Each waits their turn. But although the room was full of people, our ticket was called first – I suspected another friendship had bumped us up the queue. Nasar winked at someone as we walked towards a wall of counters. Registrars sat behind Plexiglas screens and in front of a bookcase whose carefully labelled shelves were packed with pale yellow court folders. Our registrar was another old friend of Nasar's; they had been raised in the same village and embraced one another warmly before we sat down. He was neatly dressed in a light blue shirt, synthetic black trousers suspended by a black belt with a large Hermès 'H' glinting as its buckle, thin-rimmed spectacles and polished black leather shoes. Sitting opposite him, hot and flustered despite my loose lawn cotton clothes, I wondered at his temperature. I couldn't imagine how he coped outside. He had worked this same job for thirty-five years, since he was fifteen.

Registrars are the gatekeepers of the courts. Theirs is a difficult and painstaking job, requiring concentration and precision throughout long, busy days. Without registrars, the 'honourable judges' (as all court staff deferentially refer to them) would be presented with unworkable cases, and no dispute would reach resolution. Paperwork is their province, and in the court it is peculiar. Everything must be submitted on a special size of paper, curiously thin and long. Each application – bails, appeals, injunctions, reviews – has different filing requirements and different possible objections (usually as many as forty-five) that the registrar can make. If a registrar objects to a lawyer's mistake – the wrong signature, stamp, date, fee, authorisation or certificate – the application will be thrown out. But most applications are immaculate, presented on pristine white paper to which are affixed coloured court stamps, exactly like old postage stamps. *Munshis* provide multiple copies, which the registrar distributes throughout the building. When examining files, a registrar will cross-refer with a checklist of requirements, detailed on a thin page of grainy paper, its font Times New Roman and written in English but smudged through years of zealous Xeroxing. As I looked at it, many of the requirements were illegible – I couldn't make out numbers 1–26 – and there were numerous spelling mistakes and typos. Lahore was spelt 'Lahroe' on the title page. But Nasar and the registrar knew the sheet's contents by heart.

In theory, a lawyer knows how to draft an application, but Nasar refuses to take anything to the objections room unless he has checked it first. No one knows the filing room and the fastidiousness of the High Court's registrars better than he, and whilst he's happy to fudge security checks and jump queues through his connections, professional pride bars him from ever submitting a sloppy application. Walking to the car with me before we left the office, he had quickly flicked through each page of the application before loudly cursing the lawyer who had drafted it and spinning around. The application wasn't certified, it incorrectly stated Aftab Masih's name and designation, and there were handwritten amendments to the contents page. Nasar, for whom the professional was deeply personal, was outraged, and corrections were hastily made. There were no objections to the amended application that he handed to the registrar. (Turning to me as I sat beside them, Nasar and the registrar joked about Nasar's always being right.)

Once past the objections room, a document works its way through the court machinery, winding up two flights of stairs and into the writ records room. With Aftab Masih's application filed, this records room was our next destination: Nasar wanted to check the progress of one of Sarah's writ petitions, which was buried away in the back of a filing cabinet somewhere in the court – a careful custodian of Sarah's clients, Nasar rarely visits the court without tending to a couple of cases. Overwhelmed by filing rooms and new terminology, I dredged my memory for the definition of a 'writ'. I was too embarrassed to ask Nasar. An archaic legal term, the writ is part of English common-law history, adopted into India's laws in the nineteenth century. Writs begin cases: through filing a writ petition, a person asks the court to hear their claim. The term is now an anachronism in English law, but it remains central to India and Pakistan's legal systems. On the bookshelves in Sarah's office, several four-inch-thick spines read 'WRITS' in large capital letters.

The long corridor leading to the writ records room was dark and filled with people, filing cabinets and, for some reason, old wardrobes. There was a mingled smell of warm wood, damp piles of paper, leftover lunches, and stale sweat. Groups of men sat on the corridor's sole bench or crouched on the ground, waiting for offices to open. Muttered conversations, hurried footfalls and the rushed rustle of court papers used as fan and fly swat echoed down its length. Rooms led off the corridor and swinging black signs with hand-painted white text detailed the offices' incumbents: 'Additional Registrar (Human Rights)' caught my eye. I wondered what that was.

At the foot of a staircase, in a pool of light at the end of the corridor, was a security guard with a metal detector. My laptop triggered wild beeping, but although it shouldn't have been let into the court, Nasar's familiarity eventually persuaded the guard to let me through. Up the stairs, the landing on the first floor was dense with old filing cabinets. Their backs were to the staircase and along them were posted fliers advertising the mobile numbers of court stenographers. The stair traffic was relatively heavy, with clerks and registrars all heading somewhere in a hurry. Nasar nodded hello to most, brisk and businesslike. At the second-floor landing, he ducked left, out of what I had presumed to be a window.

This window, leading on to a veranda running the length of the records rooms, was in fact a doorway. The veranda's arches, once open to the elements, were now filled with coloured glass, plain glass, cardboard and wood. The walls were whitewashed, the woodwork green. This, Nasar told me, was one of the court's writ records rooms. A desk was wedged behind the window-cum-door, allowing it to open only six inches, and Nasar and I were forced to squeeze through awkwardly. At this desk sat an initially suspicious record keeper: few are allowed to roam through these rooms. There was a second desk at a midpoint of the room, just behind another pair of one-time French windows. Red fabric had been slung across the panes of glass and cardboard, providing patches of shade and casting the men and their records in an ancient red glow. With this scant shade, the room remained green-house hot, fully exposed to Lahore's climate of tinder-dry Junes and 100 per-cent humidity Augusts – I couldn't imagine the damage caused to documents here. Unsurprisingly, the two men at the desks knew Nasar well and greeted us warmly. Waist-high open filing cabinets lined the walls, receding to a vanishing point. Between them was a narrow path strewn with paper detritus and file debris. In the cabinets, countless hundreds of hanging files were tightly packed. More were piled on and around each man's desk. 'Pending files,' the man by the first doorway said to me, gesturing with a sweep of his arm down the length of the room.

Around the corner was the filing room for these pending petitions. Another narrow room, but this one built for purpose rather than reclaimed. Again, filing cabinets lined the walls – dark grey and full height, their doors swinging open into the back of registrars' chairs and files erupting from them like stuffing from a sofa. In front of the cabinets was a row of dark-brown wooden desks: a medley of styles and sizes with an assortment of office, dining and garden chairs behind them. At each desk sat a registrar with an overflowing inbox and a records book spread open like a great medieval chronicle. Between the desks ran a very narrow channel. Shared by all the registrars, a few phones and computer monitors were scattered throughout the room. It was busy with men, most wearing light-blue *shalwar kameez* and gesticulating with files. Two fans beat on the ceiling, troublesome for stray papers and near useless in a room so full of bodies and direct sunlight. There was little on the walls but for a Lahore High Court calendar, with a photograph of a judge for each month, the Chief Justice elaborately framed on the cover. Men and their files blocked the central aisle but parted for Nasar – who passed them shaking hands like a visiting dignitary – and the curious white girl in his tow. I was an awkwardly conspicuous presence anywhere in the Lahore High Court, but particularly so here, in the heart of the court's bureaucracy.

Crossing the room, Nasar greeted a thirty-something man wearing a tight short-sleeved purple-striped shirt and black trousers. Another old friend. He found us each a chair, and cups of *qahwah* (green tea) appeared. With little encouragement, he launched into his life story, telling me how he had grown up near the court and, watching lawyers busy about their work, had longed to become an advocate. Here in the records room, sweat rolling down his face from hairline to shirt collar, he was working toward that ambition. Once he had mastered the record system – an insurmountable task, it seemed to me – he would complete his legal training.

Watching the room while Nasar's friend talked to us, I began to see something of its logic. The registrars, through intimate knowledge of their files, formed a human filing system. Shouts rang through the room: one registrar asked another the number of a file, another double-checked a date. Each registrar commanded the filing cabinet behind his desk, and by shouting information to one another, they cross-referred files and made coherent what I had first read as chaos. Once dealt with, a file was unceremoniously tossed back into the cabinet or on to a pile. The room's two computers were largely ignored.

Nasar's visit to this room was part of his pastoral care of case files. Several of Sarah's cases sat in the filing cabinet behind us, and Nasar wanted to check on them. As I looked around the room of bundled papers and shouting men (and knowing what I did of Aftab Masih's file), I appreciated his anxiety. From the cabinet behind us, the registrar pulled a huge, tattered bundle. The file's appearance told of its journey through the court – it was bound in the light yellow folder and white canvas straps that files first get in the Objections Room, but the folder was now bursting, dog-eared and splitting at the spine. Petition after petition had been filed and grouped with those that went before it. New petitioners had been added as the litigation grew. And beneath it were several other similarly battered bundles. Each would determine whether a man lived or died. It was little wonder that Nasar kept a close eye on them.

The room that held these petitions was only one section of the writ petitions' storage space, Nasar told me as we left. There are three sections in total, and three winding records-rooms to match. One is for *kaccha* petitions (literally, 'unripe' and here meaning incomplete). Another is for *pukka* petitions (literally, 'ripe' or 'proper' and here meaning complete). The final section is the largest and is for urgent petitions. It is for their storage that the court houses such a plethora of wardrobes, filing cabinets and record rooms. These petitions come from throughout the court's near-60,000-square-mile jurisdiction (an area two-thirds the size of the UK), and a close eye needs to be kept on them if they are to stand any chance of swift and fair resolution. Nasar can recite the petition number and month of filing for each of Sarah's cases; illustrating the volume of cases that comes before this court, and his attention to detail, he told me that one of her cases that was filed in March was numbered 13,072; another, filed in June, was numbered 27,773.

When I suggested that the paper-filing system must cause chaos, Nasar was quick to correct me. In the Lahore High Court, he said, files are relatively well organised. Instead of using hard drives, intranets and internal email systems – difficult to manage with irregular electricity supplies – the court relies on informal, intimate knowledge and trust. Sarah depends on Nasar, and Nasar depends on his friends within the court. The court's 5,000 employees possess a detailed knowledge of how their jobs relate to those of the men in the room next door, downstairs and on the benches of the courts themselves. Without these registrars, who spend their whole careers in the same room, the Lahore High Court would grind to a halt. But with their dedication, the enormous building and its tons of paperwork possess a certain functionality underneath an appearance of dysfunction.

If, as one nineteenth-century jurist put it, the life of the law has not been logic but experience, the Lahore High Court offers a striking illustration of this point. At first sight, the court and its filing rooms seem to be a place wholly lacking in logic. But walking through its corridors with Nasar, I came to see that in fact it has a logic that one can only understand through experience. Nasar relies on a childhood apprenticeship and a thirty-five-year-long friendship to file an application in a case like Aftab Masih's. Experience, therefore, creates its own brand of logic: the registrars of the writ filing room and objections room have systems in place that keep track of cases. And through Nasar's experience of the court and Sarah's growing experience of the law, they were able to understand that logic and to manipulate it to their clients' advantage.

But a legal system that relies on such experience is not necessarily just. It remains true that Aftab Masih's case file lay forgotten for well over a decade. In a case like this one, where the prisoner has no lawyer, and no connections to manipulate the workings of the court, the legal system's complex web of relations can work to his profound disadvantage – and the plight of those abandoned prisoners, in such a busy system, is easily forgotten. Overcrowded prisons, an overburdened, underpaid police force, the privileging of one religion over all others, the alienating language of law (English statutes and judgments, technical legal Urdu), the price of lawyers, the absence of employment protections and social security, the social, psychological and philosophical distance between jail warden and judge all conspire to create an underclass in Pakistan's prisons. Aftab Masih is emblematic of that underclass: a poor petty criminal, from the wrong village, with the wrong witnesses, of the wrong religion.

By mid 2012, Sarah had built up a team of trusted staff. Since my arrival the previous year, I had got to know Sarah and Maryam well. Late-night drafting sessions often involved reading bedtime stories to Sarah's daughter. Maryam's family practically adopted me when I was struck down by the inevitable food poisoning. Through following them in their work, I had also got to know Arthur and Nasar somewhat. But there was one staff member who proved much harder to pin down. This was Sohail, a tall, broad-shouldered man in his late thirties, clean-shaven, with hair cropped at the sides and longer on top, who wore a uniform of nondescript grey jeans and a loose plain T-shirt. When Sohail was in the office, he sat silently in front of the bulky grey computer that Sarah and Maryam had taken with them from the factory headquarters. But he kept irregular office hours: sometimes I wouldn't see him for days or weeks at a time, then he would reappear, planted back in front of the monitor, silently typing up scrawls from a notebook.

Sohail, I was told, was an investigator. My only knowledge of investigators was of PIs in 1940s Hollywood noirs – Bogey, braces and broads – and I could not reconcile this image with the quiet, rather anonymous young man who sat across from me. Sohail's long absences meant that for weeks I had little contact with him. When we spoke, while waiting for a kettle to boil, or sitting outside waiting for the electricity to come back on, we were both polite and reserved, neither enquiring too much about the other. He seemed a kind person, often smiling, and he was carefully considerate of those around him. He spoke quietly and appeared to me to be overly deferential to his bosses. It came as a shock, therefore, to learn that Sohail had spent ten years in prison charged with the murder of a young man.

In 2011, Sohail was living in the same small house that he had been born in: just off Jail Road, Lahore. His parents had had five children in that house – two girls and three boys – and as the youngest, Sohail had grown up adored and spoiled. Their family house was part of a *mohalla*, or neighbourhood, composed of a crowded complex of rooms that hosted a spectrum of Lahori life: Christian, Muslim, migrant, local. The men of the *mohalla* were employed as cobblers, fruit vendors, shop assistants and salesmen. Sohail's father, Emmanuel, worked as a motor mechanic. Salaries ranged from ten to twenty thousand rupees per month (£120–£240), just enough to put a vegetarian meal on the table every day. The families of this *mohalla* were poor. And Emmanuel's household, as his name suggests, was Christian.

While serving in the British army during the Second World War, Emmanuel had been trained as a heavy machinery mechanic, expert at fixing tanks. After Independence, he retired from the army and returned home to Lahore. It was difficult for him to find work. During Partition, and for several decades afterwards, he fixed cars and motorbikes. But when he married and started a family, he looked abroad in the hope of more lucrative work. In doing so, he followed a path familiar to many millions of South Asians since the early nineteenth century. Through migration as indentured labourers, they built plantations in the Dutch East Indies, farmed sugar cane in Mauritius and, more recently, constructed the skylines of Dubai and Doha.

In the late 1970s (as for such workers in Pakistan today), Emmanuel's only means of accessing a foreign employer was through the *kafala* system, an agency mechanism by which migrant labourers are sent from South Asia to the Persian Gulf. The *kafeel* is the migrant's local sponsor, organising visas and work. But like its nineteenth-century forebear, the system is notorious, a form of modern slavery. Emmanuel's *kafeel* took his passport and paid him no salary; Emmanuel spent several years in Abu Dhabi whilst his wife worked as a maid and seamstress to feed their children. When he finally came back to Lahore, he returned, with relief, to earning petty cash for fixing carburettors. Although the family, like their neighbours, were poor, the children remember a happy, loving childhood. Sometimes, sitting on the edge of the household's only bed, Emmanuel would relive his past career. Stories of his travels and exploits abroad and at war thrilled his children as they lay curled around him, ready for sleep. His youngest son's favourites were those from his time in Chittagong: swashbuckling tales of Japanese invaders, night-time ambushes and jungle marches.

Most of Emmanuel's small income was spent on school fees – with Pakistan's state school system unable to keep pace with the country's rapid urbanisation, even the poorest families have to pay. As children tend to care for their parents in old age, this investment is as close as many come to a pension plan. Aware of what it had cost their parents, Emmanuel's children clung proudly to their literacy and worked hard. But Emmanuel never saw the results of his labour or his carefully saved earnings. He died in 1990, when his youngest child, Sohail, began secondary school. His wife followed him within the year.

Aged thirteen, Sohail was an orphan. His older sisters had married, converted to Islam and joined their husbands' families. In Pakistan, a new wife often lives with much of her husband's extended family – parents, brothers and sisters-in-law, grandparents, aunts and uncles. And it helps if families are compatible in terms of religion. The reasons for this are logistical as much as spiritual. Religion determines what a person eats, drinks and wears, while prayers structure their day, week and year. Sohail's older brothers had also married, and had their own wives and children to support. Stuck in the same matrix of poverty in which they'd grown up, his siblings had neither the time nor the money to look after their younger brother. Unable to pay the fees, he left school without any qualifications and took a job in a carpet factory.

Of the factory's forty employees, Sohail was by far the youngest. As a 'knotter', his job was to tie threads at the edge of carpets. This was a job, like many in the cotton mills of nineteenth-century Britain, for which children, with their sharp eyes and nimble fingers, were highly prized. Once knotted, those carpets would find their way, through the port at Karachi, to street markets around the world, 'Made in Pakistan' emblazoned across their backs. The work was hard, and Sohail's fingers bled from it, but he lived cheaply and saved his wages. At work, he imagined schemes for self-improvement and education – he wanted to leave the labouring classes, maybe to teach. He studied part time, between shifts. In 1997, aged twenty, he passed his secondary school exams (the equivalent of GCSEs). The same year, he took a job at a company that exported textiles (accounting for almost half of Pakistan's exports, textiles form the backbone of the country's economy) to America and Canada. Three years later, he landed a job at a computer college, where he was allowed to study part time for a diploma in information technology. He would later look back on this as the decision that transformed his life, for better or worse, depending on his mood.

At the time, the IT diploma promised to take Sohail from textile warehouse to office desk. For an orphaned carpet factory worker in Lahore, this was real progress. These colleges and their excited advertising are everywhere in Lahore: painted on walls, on banners hung from the gates of houses, on posters and business cards in the photocopying shop, on home-made roadside billboards. Most of the signs are in English, with more details given in Urdu below, in colourful blocks of script. *4 in 1 Bundle offers: IT Basic. Discounted fee! Unique Computer College: Unique tools for unique talent! Xtreme Computer College. Star College of Informatics. Career Plus: Tools for success! Good Luck Computer College.*

Sohail worked and studied at Infovision, whose packed office was above a café in Lahore's cacophonous mini-market. His desk was in a room at the top of a narrow staircase; hot from the busy café below and fetid from the many sweating students. Conditions there were in many ways tougher than in the factory. He was a 'marketing executive', his salary earned on commission, which forced him to work overtime. The environment was stressful and insecure, his boss encouraging competition between employees, reminding them of the thousands of recent IT diploma graduates eager for their jobs. But Sohail liked his colleagues. His closest friend was Raju. At barely five foot tall, with a slight frame and a dark head of thinning hair, Raju was a comical contrast to Sohail – by then a broad-shouldered young man who stood well over six foot. But the two shared a sense of fun, and despite all that subsequently happened, Sohail would look back fondly on their time as colleagues.

One evening, after two years at this job, Sohail and Raju were working late when Raju received a phone call. His father, who suffered from heart problems, had fallen ill and had been admitted to hospital. Sohail and Raju borrowed a friend's motorbike and drove straight to the hospital. They sat in the waiting room for several hours, during which time Raju was intermittently called in for private conversations with the doctors. At about 3 a.m., some police officers walked into the waiting room, approached Sohail and handcuffed him. They told him nothing, except that he was under arrest. (Sohail still has no idea why he was targeted.) None of the hospital staff questioned the police. No one else who witnessed the arrest intervened. Raju, for his part, had disappeared. In Pakistan, an encounter with the police is another person's problem: given how little it takes to find oneself in prison, people learn quickly to look the other way.

Sohail was blindfolded, placed in the back of a police van, and driven to a suburb of Lahore called Model Town. Conceived in the 1920s as a utopian, cooperative garden town of meticulous geometric urban planning, Model Town is nowadays home to affluent Lahoris – judges, lawyers, professors, politicians. It's the last place you would expect to find an informal police lock-up. It was only after three days here that Sohail found out where he was.

The lock-up, Sohail told me, is a mechanism by which the police dodge ordinary procedural and penal protections. As I had learnt through Zulfikar Ali Khan's case, the police have twenty-four hours at the police station with an accused before they must apply to a magistrate for an extension. When they drafted this provision, British India's legislators had imagined, reasonably enough, that twenty-four hours is not long enough to make a false case convincing. But the twenty-four hours only begin at the police station. Taking a detainee to an informal lock-up, Sohail said, buys the police time to gather evidence.

Sohail was told that he had been arrested for unlawful possession of a weapon. This relieved him slightly. Of all the possible false charges, it was one of the better ones: the sentence wouldn't be heavy, he might not have to go to jail. Poor as he was, he might even be able to afford the bribe. Ignorant of sentencing procedure, he had been told that every police officer, every charge, had its price, and that this price rose steadily with the gravity of the offence. Sohail could never afford to escape a murder charge, but he might be able to scrape together enough to cover unlawful possession of a gun.

He was eventually taken to the police station. After twenty-four hours, he was duly brought to the Magistrates' Court, where he stood, handcuffed, as the court reader read out the charge against him. But now there was no mention of unlawful possession of a weapon. The magistrate was told that Sohail had been arrested for the murder of a young man. He had no idea who had been killed, or how, or why. Murder carries the death penalty.

These early stages of a criminal case are very much under the control of the prosecutors and the police. The defendant can only answer the case when it is put to him, once the charge has been framed. Sohail was given no chance to protest the mysterious murder charge. The magistrate returned him to the police station for a week. From there he went to Kot Lakhpat Central Jail, Lahore, for one night, before being transferred to Sahiwal, one of the largest prisons in Pakistan.

When Sohail first arrived in Sahiwal, he thought he had been brought to a village. He stepped out of the police van – flanked by officers and handcuffed – and looked around. The jail buildings were grouped together in a large expanse of agricultural land, the boundary far out of sight. Like the Pakistani villages he knew, many of the buildings looked incomplete: their walls half-built or half-ruined. They were low buildings, slotted next to one another and constructed simply from brick or mud. For Sohail, villages were places where life was hard, and poor: the sight of Sahiwal worried him. In Lahore Central Jail, you could see the walls and imagine life beyond them. In Sahiwal, he knew nothing beyond the prison. He had never before been to this district, two hours south of Lahore. The day he arrived, the sun was high and hot.

As Sohail was taken to his prison barracks, he was transferred from police to prison warden custody. His papers were handed over. Names, in Pakistan as in many places in the world, describe as much as they identify. 'Sohail son of Emmanuel' told the prison wardens that he was a Christian, which determined how they were to treat him. Christian prisoners are nicknamed *chura* – a reference to Pakistan's roadsweepers, the lowest form of manual labour and a job largely held by Christians – and rank lowest of all prison inmates. They are placed in the smallest, most crowded cells; given the filthiest food and the most menial jobs. They are threatened and harassed – other inmates, like school bullies, see them as obvious objects on which to exercise their own anger and frustration. Such routine discrimination, Sohail later told me, makes Christians feel more like the rodents that scurry between the walls than the men they share their cells with. Many Christians convert to Islam whilst in prison, or try desperately to hide their religion. But Sohail's name was transparent. Marked as a Christian, he settled into the routine of life in Block 3D-1, his home for the next decade.

*   *   *

The jail population of Sahiwal is informally classed in three groups, with the cells ordered accordingly. The first group is of those sentenced to death, 'the condemned' – described thus in English even by those who speak only Urdu, such is the influence of the English-drafted criminal statutes. Second are the prisoners on a sentence of anything between five years and life. Third are the *jutti*: prisoners whose cases are still pending in the trial courts. Whilst Sohail was in Sahiwal, 1,500 of the approximately 4,500-man (most of Pakistan's inmates are men) prison population had been condemned to death. The prison having been built when death sentences were exceptional rather than routine, condemned cells in Sahiwal suffered from overcrowding. Rethinking jail policy to ease these accommodation pressures, Sahiwal's authorities decided that prisoners charged but not yet convicted of capital crimes would be held in the life-prisoner barracks and moved to condemned cells at the termination of their trial.

Sohail's cell was roughly ten foot by twelve. He shared it with seven others, who all looked exhausted and sickly – their muscles etiolated, skin pallid, frames thin and eyes sunken. There was a rudimentary bed, and a toilet bowl in the corner. The various illnesses that plagued prisoners – dysentery, typhoid, rabies, skin disease – coloured the unpleasantness of those 120 square feet. The close living conditions made for constant recontamination. As prisoners rotated between cells, they were frequently re-exposed to new variants of the same infections. The water supply was dirty – rumours spread that it was contaminated with arsenic. It tasted salty and was light brown, the colour of weak tea. Food was of poor quality. Prisoners were fed twice a day: tea and a small chapatti in the morning, *dal* and *roti* in the evening. Once a week they were given rice. This diet remains largely unchanged since the late nineteenth century – the 1850s British jail manual provided for the following meals: *'early morning meal: half bread, half oil, dal; midday meal: parched or boiled gram [chickpeas]; evening meal: half bread, half oil, vegetables.'* Inmates beg family members to bring salt, spices and chillies during visits. The prison authorities scan these foodstuffs – often including basic groceries and whole bags of rice – like hand luggage at an airport, checking for anything illegal. Packages are then numbered and delivered to the prisoners. In many cases, requests for food and other small gifts – irresistible for close family members – make the costs of jail visits so high (as much as several thousand rupees, a third of a low monthly salary) that poorer families can only visit once every few months, if at all. Gifts from family members are often pooled, and groups of cellmates render the jail food edible by illicitly re-cooking it over a choking coal fire in the corner of their cell.

Sahiwal operated as a grand ecosystem, largely self-sufficient. Not only was the food re-cooked by prisoners in their cells but it was prisoners who staffed the kitchens, cooking for the whole prison population. Prisoners cleaned the kitchens and the cells, and tilled the fields and gardens, growing the vegetables – including cabbage that when cooked, Sohail joked with me, smelt worse than anything he'd ever known – that went to the kitchens. In the nineteenth and twentieth centuries, prisoners were also responsible for the lime orchard beside the jail garden, and for planting mango trees along the roadsides, and tamarind trees where necessary. These trees provided *'agreeable shade if planted within the jail enclosure but must not be planted so thickly as to interfere with free ventilation'*. Prisoners also worked in the jail's jute and carpet factories, ultimately making the money through exports that allowed the purchase of seed and farm tools. Prison cobblers made boots for inmates. Prison tailors made their uniforms. This labour economy followed the nineteenth century British model of the prison, which made of the Punjab's petty criminals a formidable labour force: basket makers, blacksmiths, blanket weavers, bookbinders, brick makers, carpenters, cooks, fan bearers, gardeners, hairdressers, hospital staff, masons, paper makers, potters, sweepers, tailors. In the early nineteenth century, some theorists saw labour as inherently beneficial to both prisoner and society: carefully structuring a prisoner's day allowed them to sleep well at night, and the years of routine prepared a prisoner well for employment upon release. Others saw penal labour as further means whereby the prison asserted power over the prisoners, forcing them to labour in submission, or merely made practical use of such a large population of unemployed men. Sohail didn't much care either way; he just did what he was told.

In theory, a prisoner's sentence determines what sort and how many hours of work he will do. Khurshid's sentence, for example, included ten years of 'rigorous imprisonment': manual labour or other prison work, always of the 'hard labour' category unless an illness or infirmity prevented it. In practice, however, Sohail explained, those who can afford it do no work and those who can't do double. The jobs are deeply resented, the lumpy division of labour emblematic of a corrupt prison administration. Condemned prisoners are treated differently from all other inmates. Locked in their cells for twenty-three hours a day, they are not allowed to work. For diversion they have one hour a day in which they circle the caged concrete space outside their cells.

The pacing ground of the condemned cells at Sahiwal backed on to a large expanse of rich agricultural land. Benefiting from the sunlight and rainfall of the late summer, vegetables grew well in Sahiwal, and it was the deputy superintendent's responsibility that they should continue to do so, tended by a prison workforce. Every morning, prisoners were marched on to these fields. As had been the case for over a century, the routine began with the morning count, after which columns of prisoners were walked to their work, unshackled except for those convicted of robbery, who remained cuffed at both wrist and ankle. Working days in prison are long, and for some prisoners the physical exhaustion was a blessing, draining them of their capacity for anxiety. Others were not so lucky, and it was to them that Sohail was drawn.

Acclimatised to life in the prison, immunised from some of the more common illnesses, he spent his time learning about the spiritual and intellectual lives of Sahiwal's prisoners. He began by doing some research. Sahiwal had one large mosque – the *juma masjid*. But as with everything in the prison, the official institution was supplemented by informal ones; small Islamic places of worship were dotted about the complex. Sohail counted as many as twenty-six of these informal mosques, roughly one for each barrack. They might cater to different denominations of Islam, but, reflecting the population of Pakistan, the majority were Sunni, with some Shia. The jail also housed a large Islamic library, known as the 'Qur'an complex', and a general library that all prisoners except the condemned technically had access to. Most of Pakistan's prison libraries are composed of donated literature, making them an odd medley of Urdu and English books, magazines and pamphlets. There is little logic to the catalogue, but prison wardens carefully scan everything before it gets to a shelf. Offending or unsuitable pages are torn out. Sahiwal sponsored a system of education where prisoners would train as teachers. Teaching tended to be religious. There were about thirty Muslim teachers and one Christian one – an illiterate man who had bribed officials to give him the job, and who used his position to wander around the prison demanding that inmates give him massages. Of the jail's four and a half thousand prisoners, about seventy-five were Christian. There was no church. Having experienced the discrimination Christians faced from wardens, Sohail wasn't surprised that this was reflected in the prison's institutional architecture. But it shamed and disturbed him that there was no place to pray.

Sohail learnt that education in Sahiwal came in many forms. Just as the bland prison food was supplemented by illicit spices, teaching was supplemented by black-market knowledge. Prisoners traded legal information through discussing their cases or hearing about other people's. A basic understanding of criminal procedure emerged from compared anecdote and experience. The fact that most of the men he spoke to had been held in police custody for fourteen days told a prisoner of the maximum length of custody a magistrate would grant. That the Multan High Court murder trial of a factory workmate took two years to complete, but the trial in Lahore of another man had taken seven told a prisoner of the administration of provincial and urban justice. That it had cost one man's father Rs. 25,000 to effect a false charge of murder and another's uncle Rs. 30,000 to overturn a similar charge told a prisoner of the economy of justice. A legal lexicon of phrases like *judicial remand*, *cognisable offence* and *writ petition* became a part of prison vernacular, along with detailed references to sections of the Pakistan Penal Code. Many prisoners learnt archaic English legal terms before basic English vocabulary, pronouncing them with slight hesitation and a strong accent – *'peteeion'* rather than 'petition'. Muddled into this learning was a share of rumour, conspiracy and hypothesis.

Nevertheless, after a decade in prison, men knew the practicalities of criminal procedure better than some lawyers.

As well as delivering a crash course in criminal procedure, the prisoners pooled and spread a shared, folkloric knowledge of the history of Sahiwal. For many, this prison complex had been their home longer than any other place in Pakistan. There was a hint of pride in Sohail's voice as he told me that Sahiwal was Pakistan's oldest and largest prison. (It is not actually Pakistan's oldest prison, although it is, by area, the largest.) Most prisoners agreed that the British had built Sahiwal, although there was some debate over when: 1863, 1867, 1873, 1876 were all mooted. General consensus was that the *ferengi* (a derogatory term for foreigner, and here implying British) had built the prison as a place to lock up freedom fighters. Sahiwal's prisoners were sharing these cells with memories of the men who had fought for India's independence and had ultimately created Pakistan.

After hearing Sohail's story, I later learnt that Sahiwal jail was founded in 1876. It was named – after Sir Robert Montgomery, judicial commissioner of the Punjab, advocate of penal reform and grandfather of Viscount Montgomery of Alamein – Montgomery Jail and was built as an instantiation of an ideal. Victorian morals and *'reformatory principles'* – as Major Hutchinson, Inspector General of Police, proudly referred to them in a speech on 'Treatment of Criminals in the Punjab' – made for a jail that had large fields and factories. Criminologists from Ireland to France to Calcutta noted the fine moral benefits of labour. A vast number of sleeping cells were built to ease the *'contaminating effect'* of overcrowding – criminality, as well as disease, was deemed contagious, and the success of prison discipline in India was deemed to depend on more square feet between bunks.

Knowledge of the prison's rules, like knowledge of its history, was acquired informally. Aware that breaching an unknown Sahiwal by-law could mean beatings or bribes, Sohail tried hard to be unimpeachable. Rules were passed down from older or longer-serving prisoners, like the oral transmission of an epic poem. Rumours were traded about what wardens were and were not allowed to do. This partial knowledge meant that prisoners were often confused by the contradictions between the supposed rules and the guards' actual behaviour. Sohail therefore supplemented his learning with careful scrutiny of the tattered copy of the jail manual he found in the prison library. He was a diligent student, his early career in the carpet factory having prepared him well for long hours straining his eyes in poor lighting, and his after-school study training him for late nights in the library. Learning his duties also taught him something about his rights. He began to challenge prison wardens when he saw them acting beyond their powers. The guards became wary of him and started to allow him more freedom within the jail: he was given extended access to the library and he borrowed books – mostly fables and moral tales, Victorian and improving – to take to other prisoners. He spent longer in the cells of the condemned than anywhere else, sensitive to how restricted their lives were. He also knew that he was likely to join them.

As it turned out, it was in jail that Sohail's dreams of working in education came to be realised. During his first two years in Sahiwal, he volunteered to help the illiterate Christian teacher, giving basic literacy lessons whilst the official teacher dozed off in the corner. He loved the work, and it kept him busy, but he soon realised that he depended on the job as much as his students did on him. The purpose and structure that teaching gave to his days allowed him to cope with the vast, life-shattering horror of being imprisoned for a capital crime he hadn't committed. He needed the distraction. It wouldn't be until the beginning of his trial in late 2002, more than a year after his arrest, that Sohail found out any significant detail of the case against him.

While Sohail learnt to live in Sahiwal, his case had been slowly moving through Pakistan's criminal justice system. Finally, he learnt more of why he had been arrested. He was one of four accused men, all unknown to one another. The complainant was the uncle of Kashif Hussein, a twenty-nine-year-old man who had been shot dead in northern Sahiwal at midday on 22 January 2001.

Sohail's case file challenged even the most diligent reader. It comprised a deep pile of annotated judgments, witness statements, court orders, adjournment notices, certificates, charges, medical reports, applications for suspension of sentence, notices of appeal, writ petitions, and reports in English and Urdu, handwritten and typed. Dense narratives, counter-narratives and non sequitur statements of motives, suspicions, defences and complaints added to the names of multiple witnesses, accuseds, accusers and their extended families to create extraordinary confusion. Over tens of pages, lawyers had scored out whole judgments with a biro, for no apparent reason. I was instantly overwhelmed. But by the summer of 2012, when I felt I knew Sohail well enough to ask to see his case file, my several months' training under Nasar had paid off. I had learnt not to be fazed by incomprehensible stacks of paper. Abandoning my law school methodologies and literal analyses, I searched the story – like a post-modern literary critic – for fissures, fragments and ruptures.

As I read, the bizarreness of the situation quickly emerged. Sohail had somehow been caught up in the private debt dispute of two expat Pakistanis, as well as a police plot to arrest some troublesome student political dissidents. The two expats lived in Saddle Brook, New Jersey, two members of America's 700,000-strong Pakistani community and Pakistan's seven-million-person diaspora. A dispute had arisen between them: one of the men owed the other $92,000. At some point in 2000, they had had an argument about this money – the details are opaque, but the family of the debtor say that he was threatened with violence by the creditor. The creditor says that he merely asked for prompt repayment of the debt.

A few months later, in January 2001, the debtor flew to Pakistan both to attend his brother's wedding and to get married himself. His family home was, by novelistic coincidence, in Sahiwal, 500 yards from the prison. Throughout the week of the weddings, the house was a place thick with activity. Sons, uncles and brothers revved motorbikes to bazaar and bus station, buying vegetables and meat for the women to cook, collecting ever more rounds of relatives.

On 14 January, the debtor's brother was married. The following week, he was shot dead by four assassins. When they heard gunfire, members of his family had rushed outside. They saw four men running away from the house and getting into a white car with no number plate. The debtor's brother lay on the ground, bleeding in a sprawling mess of fruits and vegetables he had just bought in the bazaar.

The primary eyewitnesses were the debtor's uncles. Crouching by the debtor's brother's body, they hailed a rickshaw and took him to the hospital on the edge of town. Shortly after they arrived, the debtor's brother died. They then went to the police station in the centre of town, where they filed a first information report (FIR). Their report didn't mention any of the four gunmen by name, and only vaguely identified them:

1. *gandmi rang mazbut jism, darmiane qad, umr jawan*: brown-coloured [skin] (literally, 'swarthy', 'wheat-coloured'), strong body, middle height, young age
2. *gandmi saf rang, mazbut jism, darmiane qad, umr jawan*: brown-and-white-coloured [skin] (literally, 'clean', 'pure'), strong body, middle height, young age
3. *gori rangat, mazboot jism, daraz qad, umr jawan*: fair-coloured [skin], strong body, tall, young age
4. *gandmi rang, darmiane jism, darmiane qad, umr jawan*: brown-coloured [skin], medium-strength body, middle height, young age

This list – capable of describing many millions of Pakistani men – was the beginning of Sohail's troubles.

Colloquially, an FIR where none of the alleged assailants is mentioned by name is referred to as an 'unknown FIR'. It is something Sohail and many others have learnt to fear. The unknown FIR leaves the police unfettered discretion over who to arrest, and the vulnerable poor are often locked up in exchange, many maintain, for large fees from richer complainants or suspects. In such cases, the police act as mercenaries: for the right fee, they'll pick off an enemy, business rival, inconvenient landlord or irritating neighbour. The legal system can then be put to work, rubber-stamping the misfeasance. Lacking proper defence lawyers, the poor often have little to say other than 'I am falsely accused' – a plea common to guilty and innocent alike and one, therefore, that tends to fall on deaf ears. Relying solely on the prosecution case – defendants generally receive such poor legal representation that witnesses are rarely called and little evidence is brought in support of a plea of innocence – judgments tend to find the unknown guilty. Those judgments both validate police malpractice and make it difficult to appeal the most glaring factual inconsistencies, such as Sohail not being in Sahiwal at the time of the alleged offence. On 22 January 2001, he was a hard-working, badly paid marketing executive in Lahore. His combination of height (six foot four) and dark complexion make him incompatible with any of the four descriptions. He knew nothing of the deceased man and little of Sahiwal (a city three hours from his home). But Sohail was a nobody. He had no family and no influence: there was nothing he could offer the police beyond his innocence.

After sketching the gunmen, the FIR mentions the creditor, the only person named in the document. The debtor's family claimed that he had orchestrated the shooting and sent the four gunmen as assassins. According to them, the creditor had threatened to follow the debtor to Pakistan to kill him. The creditor denies this.

Four months later, Sohail appears on the case record. Suspected to be one of the unknown assailants, he was arrested in early May 2001. '*On 8.5.2001 the police of . . . Model Town Lahore apprehended the present accused persons on suspicion while on patrol duty and on their personal search firearm weapons were also discovered.*' During the trial, Sohail remains unknown. He is often referred to just as one of the 'accused persons'. Where he is named, it is rarely with any consistency. For the poor in Pakistan, second names are mercurial. Where Pakistan's rich have names that situate them historically – ruling dynasties such as Bhutto and Sharif, for example – the poor are named merely to identify them in the immediate present: during a court case, dispute or arrest. During his trial, Sohail was variously identified as his father's son (*Sohail son of Emmanuel*), by his address (*Sohail resident of Lahore*), and by his religion (*Sohail Maseeh* or *Masih*: Sohail the Christian). Two other young men were arrested. The fourth, tall, fair-skinned unknown is never mentioned.

In finding the three unknowns guilty, the judgment simply states that '*the accused persons disclosed during investigation that they had committed the murder of [the deceased man] dated 22.01.2001*'. Sohail says that he was kept, blindfolded, in police custody for three days. This is not mentioned in the judgment. He also says that he was detained in Sahiwal police station the night before being taking to Sahiwal jail. That night, he says, some people who were friendly with the police visited his cell. They took a long look at him, 'examining me like an animal in a zoo'. Looking back, he thinks these visitors were the deceased man's family, making sure they remembered his face for an identification parade that would be held the next day. With a tone of resignation, he reminded me that this was against the law. It was not raised at his trial. During the trial, no question was asked about how Sohail and his co-accuseds had 'disclosed' their guilt. As all oral evidence taken in police custody (including confessions) is inadmissible unless it leads the police to material evidence, the judgment was unlawful in relying on these 'disclosures'. Not one defence lawyer made this easy procedural point.

Guilt is the given of a Pakistani police station. The clear binary nature of the criminal trial – guilty, not guilty – collapses under police investigation. Once they have a person in their custody, the police are under pressure – financial, reputational and organisational – to find them guilty. Information and evidence, therefore, is gathered in order to prove guilt, not reveal truth. For the police, it is perhaps a belief that a person cannot be both an object of suspicion and completely innocent that justifies such lopsided investigation. Either way, as more evidence is found or fabricated, an accused progresses from slightly guilty to more guilty. When the police picked him up in that hospital, Sohail was already sliding towards his conviction.

Three days after their arrest, Sohail and his two co-accuseds entered Sahiwal jail. This was the first time that Sohail had seen the other defendants. On 21 May 2001, the investigating officer of Sahiwal City police station, as he swore to the court when giving evidence, lined up the three co-accuseds with a mix of other prisoners. According to the investigating officer's evidence, the victim's uncles immediately, and correctly, identified Sohail and his co-accuseds. Having listened to Sohail, and having read the case file and eyewitness accounts, it is difficult to imagine how these uncles could identify with any precision those men whose backs they had seen running into the distance.

From their statements to the court, it is clear that Sohail's co-accuseds had some history with the Model Town police. The two were members of the Muslim Students Federation of Government College, Lahore – the Lahore student wing of Nawaz Sharif's Pakistan Muslim League. In 1999, during Pakistan's third successful *coup d'état*, General Pervez Musharraf overthrew then Prime Minister Nawaz Sharif, suspended Parliament and the constitution and declared a state of emergency. Nawaz Sharif was tried for treason by an anti-terrorism court in March 2000. Like Prime Minister Zulfikar Ali Bhutto before him – ousted by General Zia-ul-Haq's military *coup d'état* of 1977 – Sharif was held in Adiala jail, sentenced to death.

In October 2000, whilst Sharif was in jail, the president of the Muslim Students Federation was killed. Sohail's co-accuseds claimed that they were eyewitnesses to this murder. Following the murder, the police failed to arrest anyone. In November 2000, the two men agitated for prosecution of the murderer and called a strike across Lahore's colleges. They said that the police of Model Town had *'apprehended and tortured'* them during these strikes, and claimed that *'the then government became hostile'* towards them. The present case, they told their trial court in March 2003, was the culmination of this political argument: the assistant sub-inspector of Model Town police station had deliberately embroiled them in a false case.

The court dismissed the dissidents' tale as uncorroborated conspiracy, and they were tried together with Sohail. Standing beside the dissidents, ill-advised and intimidated, Sohail gave no defence evidence and his lawyer called no defence witnesses. It was held that his case, *'not supported by any defence evidence, has no bearing on the prosecution case'*. Accordingly, the judge came to the *'irresistible conclusion that the prosecution has proved its case beyond reasonable doubt'*. But *'as motive has not been established beyond reasonable doubt'* and *'it is not clear from the evidence whose fire proved fatal to cause death of the deceased'*, he decided not to award the death penalty. Instead, he sentenced Sohail and his co-accused to imprisonment for life and a payment of Rs. 25,000 (£250) each to the heirs of the deceased. By now unable to summon the energy for indignation, Sohail merely felt relief that his sentence was not one of death.

By the time his trial ended, Sohail had spent nearly three years in Sahiwal, busying himself with his education project. As a result of his sentence, he was given formal employment for the first time (prisoners who have not yet been sentenced by a court to labour cannot be put to work inside the jail). He was taken from his teaching and made a jail secretary, responsible for the oversight of Sahiwal's carpet knotting factory – a role that his years of child labour well qualified him for. This abrupt conclusion of his teaching was almost more than he could bear. Later in 2003, however, the Christian pastor – who visited the jail to give sermons every Sunday and had been impressed by Sohail's teaching – recommended him to the prison authorities. Sahiwal's illiterate Christian teacher was sacked and Sohail was promoted in his place.

On 20 May 2003, Sohail had applied through the prison authorities – by himself, with the knowledge learnt from hours with Sahiwal library's statute books – to have his appeal heard. He was given a hearing date in 2009. In December 2004, one of the student dissidents applied to the court to have his sentence suspended. Courts in Pakistan, as in many jurisdictions, have the power to suspend a person's sentence. On a suspended sentence, a person leaves prison on probation; any crime committed during suspension will usually result in a return to prison and perhaps a further sentence. It is generally only for relatively minor offences, committed by first-time offenders, that a court will suspend a sentence. In granting suspension to a person found guilty of murder, the court as good as admits that there was next to no evidence against that person. In such circumstances, suspension could be read as something of an official apology. The following year, the student dissident's sentence was suspended: *the evidence against the petitioner requires reappraisal*. In December 2005, the second student dissident applied to the court to have his sentence suspended. He too was released from jail: *the evidence against the petitioner requires reappraisal*. Sohail learnt of their success in court and was buoyed by it. He made several applications to have his own sentence suspended, but each was refused. In a painfully ironic twist, his diligent obedience to criminal procedure was working against him. He was told that whilst his appeal was pending (this would take four years), the court would not consider suspending his sentence.

Upset by his trial, but safe in the knowledge that he wouldn't be executed, Sohail taught fellow inmates with renewed vigour. Increasingly, he spent his time with condemned prisoners. Sahiwal's death row consists of five wards, or barracks, of around forty-five cells. Although built for one man, each of these cells now houses as many as three – making a total of between 400 and 600 condemned prisoners in Sahiwal, roughly five hundred times the prison's nineteenth-century death row population. The cells are grouped five in a row, each group sharing a twenty-foot-square caged concrete veranda where the condemned can walk for an hour a day. The cell doors are simple iron bars, facing the veranda. Behind ward number one are the gallows: they sit at the edge of the agricultural land, in the centre of a large parched field. At the back of each cell is a square ventilation shaft. By standing on their toes, on a bucket or on one another's shoulders, prisoners can peer out of the shaft at the expansive prison grounds. And so those in ward number one, whilst Sohail was in Sahiwal, watched all executions.

Sohail got to know the condemned through bringing them library books. He was motivated by Christianity, but his teachings were not evangelical. His faith taught him simply to help those who were vulnerable, and he believed that inculcating literacy was a good place to start. Although condemned prisoners were barred from the library, the jail manual allowed them to read any books that were brought to them. In bringing him close to the condemned men, Sohail's educational programme made him a natural volunteer for one of the jail's hardest jobs.

Executions need careful preparation. The week before an execution, the British jail manual requires prison wardens to test both gallows and rope. The rope (*'manilla, one-inch diameter, 19 foot long, well twisted and fully stretched, of equal thickness and capable of being passed readily through the noose ring and sufficiently strong to bear a strain of 280 lbs with a 7 foot drop'*) is taken from the storeroom. A sack of sand or cement equal to one and a half times the weight of the condemned man is tied to its end and dropped the required length. Such testing is important: if the ratio of body weight to rope length is wrong, the accused will die of suffocation or decapitation rather than a broken spine. The tested rope is then securely locked up until the eve of the execution. A few days before the execution, the prison wardens ask for volunteer *negran*, or caretakers, from the prison population. Sohail always volunteered. The night before the execution, the *negran* carry the condemned prisoner from his cell to a special, higher-security death cell, or *kalkothri*, where he is kept in solitary confinement. The fear of death is so great that very few condemned are able to walk unaided. The morning of the execution, they carry the prisoner to the gallows. Where a prisoner is too heavy, he is dragged. At the gallows, the executioner puts a black mask over the man's face and ties his legs together. The noose is then hooked over his head.

Sohail performed his role with sombre sincerity. After taking a man to the solitary cell, he stayed with him, talking through the long hours of his last night. He kept up his words of comfort until the moment the condemned man began the seven-foot drop.

The morning after an execution, the atmosphere in the prison is nervous and subdued. Silence weighs over both the guards and the guarded. The execution jolts the prison from its routine. It was on such days that Sohail's quiet comfort was most in demand. He would read to groups of prisoners, passing through the jail like a nurse on a ward, supported in his teachings by another life prisoner the wardens had allowed him to employ as his deputy.

The years passed as Sohail and his deputy ministered to the condemned. When he wasn't teaching, Sohail was fund-raising. In 2004, with a small pot of money raised, he asked the prison authorities to allow him space for a Christmas party. By now trusting and respectful of Sohail, the prison authorities granted his request: one disused barrack was given over to the three-day-long event. Through the prison guards, Sohail's pot of money bought gallons of Pepsi and tea, big bowls of fruit and sweets and one enormous Christmas cake. Invitations were extended to every barrack; all prisoners, of any religion, were welcome. The party was a great success. Muslim and Christian prisoners chatted to one another as equals, and Sohail became popular throughout Sahiwal. When the month of *Muharram* came around, he was invited as a guest of honour to the Shia celebrations, where, as he stood at the front of the room, the collected prisoners prayed for him and his good work. Those first incarcerated days, when he felt worth little more than the prison rats, were far away. After the success of his party, he raised enough money to have Sahiwal's first church built.

In 2009, Sohail's appeal date came and passed: it was never heard and never argued. He applied to the court once again to have his sentence suspended. This time, the Multan High Court found that his case for suspension *'was on better footing'* than that of his student co-accused's, who had been released five years before. That is, the court found there to be even less incriminating evidence against Sohail than against his fellow accused. And so, having served half of a life sentence in jail, Sohail was released from Sahiwal prison in 2010.

Having lost his adolescence to accelerated adulthood and his twenties to imprisonment, Sohail emerged from jail at the age of thirty-three a very unsure young man. Throughout his imprisonment, he had been helped by an older sister, Rubina, who worked as a schoolteacher in Lahore, and the girl he had been dating at the time of his arrest, Shazia. When he left Sahiwal, they were the only people he knew; the rest of the world seemed utterly foreign.

Life outside was as difficult as it had been in jail. Rubina died of cancer the year after his release, and with her went the last link to his close family. A decade in prison leaves its mark on a person's CV, and it was proving impossible for Sohail to get a job. He and Shazia soon married, and her wage from a local beauty salon was their only income. They lived wherever they could rent a room, or a corner of a room. Shazia's family had cast her out, embarrassed by her association with an ex-convict accused of murder. Sohail's family were not much more supportive, nervous about what their ties to him could bring. His appeal was pending, despite his release, and the complainants still wanted someone in jail for their nephew's death. If the police unearthed new evidence he could be re-imprisoned and life made difficult for those close to him.

Sohail's unemployment and lack of family commitments decided what would otherwise have been a difficult choice. He would continue the work he had begun in prison. Looking back, he now repeats his motivation like a chant: 'What I learnt in prison was that I should speak for those who cannot speak for themselves, I vowed to become the voice of the voiceless.' Unclear how to begin, he turned to the only community he had: St Andrew's Church, on Lahore's Empress Road. There he met Arthur Wilson. The first stranger who had shown him kindness in almost a decade, Arthur became something of a mentor to Sohail. At that point, Arthur had just started working with Sarah, who was looking to expand her staff. It would be difficult work and she wanted committed employees. She didn't care about their background. Arthur Wilson introduced her to Sohail, and she hired him, despite the fact that he had never done any investigating before.

Investigators plug a hole in the legal system. Since policemen can be paid not to investigate a case and a false account or confession can form the basis of a conviction, defence lawyers need to hire their own investigators. Without them, a trial court has no evidence before it other than that presented by the police. With a private investigator, a rival narrative can enter the record and bring with it an accused's chance of acquittal. Where a clerk pulls apart the police file, an investigator pieces it back together.

In incorporating investigators into her firm, Sarah was attempting to revolutionise the practice of defence lawyers in Pakistan. In large part, the injustice suffered by many on Pakistan's death row owes more to the failings of their defence teams than to the corruption of the police or prosecutors. It is almost unheard of, for example, to call a defence witness in a murder trial – court transcripts will list as many as twenty prosecution witnesses in a case without a single defence witness (often not even the defendant himself will give evidence at his own trial for murder). The reasons for this are primarily financial. Employed by the government on meagre rates, defence lawyers simply cannot afford to spend several days of unpaid work tracking down witnesses and preparing their statements. In working for free and providing investigators (following the model of her by then most trusted adviser, Clive Stafford Smith), Sarah was, therefore, doing something extraordinary for Pakistan's poor.

Sohail loved his job, and his shoestring salary (at around 5,000 rupees a month, about £30, he earned little more than a road sweeper) allowed him to make his life with Shazia more comfortable. After several months, using money borrowed from Sarah and earned by selling Shazia's jewellery, he bought a Honda 70cc motorbike. Symbolic as well as practical, this sign of upward mobility impressed his brothers, who were cautiously allowing him back into their lives. Within six months of his employment, Shazia fell pregnant. Employed, married and soon to be a father, Sohail began to relax. There had been no word from the police or the Multan High Court for over a year. It seemed that bad luck had finally stopped chasing him.

Sarah's fledgling organisation was starting to feel like a real grown-up office. Everyone now had a job title, detailed in an email signature – I was 'Case Worker, Death Penalty', proud to no longer be called a volunteer, with a salary of £260 per month. We had headed notepaper. And an IT manager. Sarah wrote grand-sounding applications to international donors about our mission and strategic objectives. She gave a TEDx talk. There were weekly meetings, where all the staff sat around a long table pooling the previous week's work and scheduling the next's. At the centre of a long white wall in the room that Arthur Wilson and I worked in was an eight-foot-by-four-foot whiteboard, a handful of primary-coloured marker pens on a table by its edge. Spidery diagrams and colour-coded columns (according to the case name and member of staff's duties) set out strategies for the office's workload. Timelines counted down to hearing dates, next to which Nasar had scrawled the details of time, judge and courtroom (which he invariably managed to obtain from the registrar in advance of the published court lists). Evidential gaps were flagged up on the board, and a schedule of investigations and interviews (Sohail's job) ran alongside the court dates (Sarah's job). We felt proud, and a little surprised, to be so organised.

At one such meeting, in early 2012, 'RAZA HAYAT' was written in capitals and underlined at the top of the whiteboard. Raza Hayat was the only eyewitness in Aftab Masih's case: he had been the servant of the family that had been murdered in their house. He was also perhaps the only man who stood between Aftab Masih and the gallows. Nasar and Sarah's attempts to get the court to recognise Aftab Masih's age had not been successful. All they could now do was speak to Raza Hayat and try to work out what had happened that afternoon. Sarah tasked Sohail with finding him.

Sohail took the bus from Lahore, reaching Raza Hayat's village early one weekday morning. Arriving by bus is never ideal for an investigator's first meeting with a witness. People are impressed by a car and a driver. The display of wealth reassures them that the newcomer is a man of some position, who may have the resources to help them. Taxis, rickshaws and buses hold little promise. But for quasi-undercover trips like this one, a low-key approach made sense. With a notebook hidden in his back pocket, wearing his uniform of jeans, a loose T-shirt, trainers and a baseball cap, Sohail strode past the village shop – which he would later learn was owned and run by Raza Hayat's nephew – past a collection of benches, with a roof for shade, where some old men dozed, and up to the door of a two-storey house where he and Sarah had guessed Raza Hayat lived. Behind its rickety metal front door, which was swinging slightly ajar, he could hear children running, doors slamming, women shouting, pans clattering. Over the cacophony, he announced himself to be the son of an old colleague of Raza Hayat's from Lahore. Continuing the deception, he said that his father was keen to enquire after Raza Hayat's health. Would Raza Hayat take a walk with him outside; they could get *chai* nearby? Although this was one of his first assignments, Sohail knew that busy households and prying daughters-in-law made for unsatisfactory interviewing conditions.

In his early nineties, five foot six tall and crooked with old age, his face deeply lined, Raza Hayat did not like to dwell on his regrets. He had spent the latter part of his working life in the employ of a middle-class Lahori merchant, working for 9,000 rupees (£108) a month, as a general servant and odd-job man at the merchant's family home in an affluent suburb of Lahore. Long-standing and loyal, he was a trusted employee. Every day, the merchant would drive to his shop, leaving his wife and children under the guardianship of Raza Hayat, who ran errands, sat guard at the gate, cleaned, cooked. When money was tight, the merchant would lend Raza Hayat small sums or pay for his medical treatment. But when Sohail met him, Raza Hayat had been retired for over a decade.

Only too pleased to get out of the house, Raza Hayat showed Sohail to his usual *chaiwallah*. He then asked Sohail about his father: 'What was his name?'

Sohail prevaricated: 'Oh, I don't know if you knew his name. He worked with you at the Lahori merchant's house. He was the one who sometimes worked at the merchant's cloth shop, and sometimes ran errands at the house.'

The gamble paid off: 'Ah, you mean Muhammad Hussein?'

'Yes, Muhammad Hussein.'

His father, said Sohail, was anxious about Raza Hayat's health and had sent Sohail to check on him. Raza Hayat told Sohail that he was well and should send Muhammad Hussein his regards.

This first meeting was brief. Apologising for such a short visit, Sohail told Raza Hayat that he was travelling to Islamabad and really must be getting on, for he had a lunchtime meeting to rush to (this too was a lie – Sohail returned to the office after their meeting). Work would take him to Islamabad for three days, he said, but he would be passing through Raza Hayat's village again on his way home. If Raza Hayat needed anything, Sohail could buy it and drop it off on his way back.

Sohail returned to Lahore by bus. Walking into the office a few hours later, he sat at his old desktop computer and wrote up his meeting, as Sarah had said he should do. He included a 'strategy note', resolving to follow up with further meetings over the next few weeks, until he thought the old man was ready to talk about the case. Sohail had been briefed about strategy: it was important to know what each meeting led to, what the ultimate objective was. This was what would be reported back at the small weekly meeting; Sarah would use this information to work out what applications to file, and when.

Three days later, Sohail returned to the village. He was laden with 'gifts from Islamabad' – warm clothing and several shawls – and he again expressed concern for Raza Hayat's health. He did not find lies problematic in this context. His mission, he explained to me, was discovering the truth and saving Aftab Masih's life, and in pursuit of this noble goal, committing fraud was fine. For Sohail, the ends of Truth and Justice justified the means of deception. Over the next fortnight, he and Raza Hayat had four more meetings and became friends, of a sort. Sohail was excited by how well his first big assignment was going, how quickly he could win friendship, and how easy he imagined it would be to get to the bottom of this case.

Sohail knew that success in his job depended on sensitivity and good timing. During his meetings with Raza Hayat, he practised both these attributes. The fifth time they met, he asked Raza Hayat for some advice. 'You are an aged and wise person who understands the world,' he said. 'What is the most important value for me to live my life by?'

Raza Hayat replied: 'Always be honest and true to others.' Sohail couldn't have hoped for a smoother segue to what he had to say next.

He reminded Raza Hayat of an incident that had taken place almost twenty years earlier, at the house of his previous employer. His employer's wife and two sons had been murdered, gruesomely. On the police file, Raza Hayat was the only eyewitness to the event. His evidence had identified two young plumbers – Aftab Masih and Ghulam Mustafa – as the murderers. Sohail now identified himself to Raza Hayat as an investigator working for a legal charity that represented prisoners on death row. He told the old man that his client was Aftab Masih, who had been on death row for more than twenty years. He and his bosses, he said, had pored over Aftab Masih's file for weeks, following up every contact to find out whether Raza Hayat was still alive and, if so, where he might be living. Earlier that month, they had finally discovered his address and Sohail had come to meet him, hoping that he would tell them more about the case. 'I am here for the sake of humanity,' he explained. 'Due to your witness, two innocent men have been behind bars for twenty years, and both will be executed. Aftab was only fifteen when he was arrested.'

Raza Hayat, Sohail later told me when recounting the old man's response, had gazed silently into the distance. The revelation had caught him off guard, and for a moment, Sohail thought, he looked distressed and deeply sorry. He had had no choice, he blurted to Sohail. His job had depended on doing what he was told; he didn't want to be a burden on his children, who themselves had young children. He told Sohail that he had seen the dead bodies, but only at 10 p.m. that night. And he added that he had also seen the plumbers at the house, much earlier that day. Late that night, he said, the police had forced him to sign a blank sheet of paper. He didn't know what he had agreed to. He told Sohail that he had given evidence at trial because he was scared of being put in jail. But he expressed remorse, telling Sohail that he was a religious man and didn't know how to reconcile this act with his God, or how to atone for it.

Sohail comforted him: 'You merely made a mistake; you can still fix it.'

This was familiar territory for Sohail. His nights consoling prisoners on the eve of their executions had prepared him well for encouraging cathartic confessions. The truth, he pleaded, would save both Aftab Masih's life and Raza Hayat's soul. But anger then coloured Raza Hayat's despair. Sohail had lied to win his friendship; perhaps he was still lying? As a Christian, Sohail might himself be related to the defendant. And even if Sohail was telling the truth, Raza Hayat was anxious that he could be charged with perjury (which, in a capital case, is punishable with a life sentence or, where an accused has been sentenced to death and executed as a result of that perjury, execution of the perjurer himself). Raza Hayat's fear of the police, Sohail observed, turned out to be greater than his fear of God. Nothing Sohail said could convince him to retract his statement. He remained adamant that he had told the truth.

Sohail was upset. He had failed to make Raza Hayat see that 'my intentions were very clear and very noble: I just wanted to get the truth'. He resolved to go home, before remembering that he had been asked by Sarah and Nasar to meet other members of Raza Hayat's family. He thought the village shop might be a good place to make enquiries about the family, and so he dropped in on his way to the bus stop. The shop's owner, Hamza, considered Raza Hayat his 'uncle', and although that word is very imprecise in Pakistan – 'uncle' and 'auntie' are terms of respect for both a close older family friend and a parent's siblings – it meant at least that Hamza was close enough to Raza Hayat to remember his return to the village after the murders in Lahore. The murders had apparently changed Raza Hayat profoundly. Hamza told Sohail that he might be able to meet with one of Raza Hayat's sons, Khizer, who had long been worried by the impact the incident had had on his father's mental health.

Hamza told Sohail that immediately after the murders, Raza Hayat himself had been arrested for several days, and though he was soon released, terror of the police station combined with anxiety about the paper he had signed and the evidence he had given had deeply affected him. When he returned to the village (he retired a few years after the murders), his family noticed that he had become depressed and prone to fits of anger. A fury overcame him if the incident was ever referred to – as it had been during his conversation with Sohail. A devout man, Hamza said, Raza Hayat prayed five times a day, but if someone mentioned the murders he would not go to the mosque for several days. He was once a gentle father, but now he shouted at, and sometimes struck, his children.

The meeting didn't improve Sohail's mood; neither Hamza nor Khizer was willing to speak to Raza Hayat about making a new statement. Disheartened, he returned to the office, a feeling of failure hanging heavy around him. But reporting back to the next case-management meeting, he was surprised at the reaction to his news. The mere knowledge that Raza Hayat was alive came as an enormous relief to Sarah and Nasar. That he lived with an extended family, who remembered the effect of the murders and who were friendly and willing to talk to Sohail, delighted them. Raza Hayat's willingness to discuss the case at all was something they hadn't even dared hope for. It seemed almost insignificant to them that he wouldn't yet sign a statement. Even if it couldn't be used in court, this information would be helpful in drafting a mercy petition to the provincial government and the President. Quickly, Sohail became central to all of Sarah's cases.

In April 2012, Sohail was preparing for his son's birth. Worried about complications – and unwilling to take risks – he agreed with Shazia to book a Caesarean at the local hospital. His colleagues all donated money to pay for the procedure. Sohail began to get excited about being a father, and his enthusiasm was infectious. Conversations at the office became dominated by the logistics of parenthood: advice for the first few days with the newborn baby, plans for leave, visits, donations of other children's outgrown clothes. I told Sohail stories of my boyfriend's sister, who was also about to have her first child.

When the big day arrived, Sohail absented himself from work. The following day, he didn't come in either. Arthur Wilson explained that there had been a complication. The doctors had begun the operation but Shazia's heart was weak, and she suffered a heart attack. The traffic had been so bad that an ambulance from the Institute of Cardiology hadn't been able to reach her in time. Shazia had died. Their baby boy had died with her.

On the day of the funeral, Sohail's neighbours, friends and family sat with him, forming a circle of chairs and cushions on the concrete courtyard outside his home. Sohail was ravaged with grief, his eyes raw, his face wet. Sitting silent and embarrassed in that cramped courtyard, exposed to the searing midday sun, with sweet wrappers and dry leaves curling at my feet, I was viscerally affected. I had come to think of Pakistan as a place where people were resilient and uncomplaining, with a capacity for enduring untold tragedy and shattering misfortune. That afternoon, I realised that I too had hardened myself to misery. Immersed in the complex horrors of Pakistan's legal system – where innocent men can be imprisoned and face execution for more than twenty years – I had too often shielded myself behind technicalities. I found codes and rules easier to grasp than messy, indecipherable lives. During the gathering, I bit my lip hard. In the car on the way home, I sobbed uncontrollably.

But from this tragedy came some small consolation. The funeral had brought Shazia's and Sohail's families together. Neither side had attended the wedding, but both clearly felt more compulsion to share grief than joy. And although so much of his new-found happiness had just been obliterated, this sad gathering was evidence to Sohail that he had rebuilt something after his decade in prison; that he had friends, family and a job that mattered. Out of pity, his brothers invited him to live with them once again – and immediately after the funeral, Sohail returned to work.

As Sarah's chambers grew in size and experience, it also grew in notoriety. Sarah knew she was under surveillance. The office received suspicious phone calls. One anonymous caller claimed to have been following her, and knew of her recent travel plans, home address and young daughter's name. In late 2011, Sarah decided to move offices. No staff were allowed to mention the new address to anyone. Meetings were to be conducted elsewhere. Potential clients and interns were scrutinised. The headed paper was shredded. At the same time, Sarah's work was becoming increasingly controversial within the legal profession. Lawyers and judges queried her court manner, trial strategies, training and experience. Others doubted her motivations and pursuit of foreign funding. A junior lawyer working in a similar field saw her work as nothing but a 'shameless act of self-promotion'.

But this did not stop her tackling increasingly difficult work. And in taking on the case of Altaf Rehman, a man charged with blasphemy, Sarah began to grapple with perhaps the most inflammatory issue in contemporary Pakistan.

It was a Thursday evening in mid June 2009. The raiding team travelled south through Karachi to a quiet, affluent residential district on a thumb of land that jutted into the water where the Malir river meets the Arabian Sea. Altaf Rehman, his wife, Sameena, and their children – aged six, eleven, thirteen and fifteen – were at home. The six men and one woman fast approaching their house in a convoy of cars were all senior investigators and inspectors. They had been planning this trip for a fortnight.

Forcing the front door, the raiders found the Rehmans in their ground-floor sitting room. They announced themselves as officers of the Federal Investigation Agency – a government intelligence and security agency – and began to search desks and bookshelves. They were looking for computers, particularly ones with an internet connection. From the sitting room and the adjoining bedroom they collected a desktop computer, its hard drive and accompanying cables. They were led to Altaf Rehman's office in the basement. They documented a Dell laptop, some external hard drives, a USB stick, a Samsung phone, three bottles of locally brewed brandy, the family's passports and the contents of a bookshelf:

The Life of Muhammad by Ibn Ishaq, translated by A. Guillaume
Islam – A Short Introduction by Karen Armstrong
The Geometry of God by Uzma Aslam Khan
The Qur'an translated by Abdullah Yusuf Ali
The Story of God by Robert Winston
Three Cups of Tea by Greg Mortenson
Descent into Chaos by Ahmed Rashid
Nineteen Eighty-Four by George Orwell
Dude, Where's My Country? by Michael Moore
Rogue States by Noam Chomsky
The Clash of Fundamentalisms by Tariq Ali

The books, bottles, passports and computers were taken to the police station. Altaf Rehman was arrested.

On a Tuesday morning two weeks before the raid, an editor at a prominent Pakistani newspaper had arrived at work in Islamabad and sat down at his desk. In his inbox was a message from someone calling himself Jalal al-Din Muhammad Rumi – a pseudonym inspired by the famous thirteenth-century Persian poet. Under a subject line reading: 'Your recent article', the author made a series of blasphemous remarks about the Prophet Muhammad. The email quoted lines from the Qur'an. A few hours later, the editor received a second, very similar email and phoned the police.

Cyber crime is taken seriously in Pakistan. To commit a crime using a computer is to extend the maximum sentence for that crime by an additional two years. And cyber crimes have a sophisticated team of investigators quite separate from the police. The National Response Centre for Cyber Crime was founded in 2007. Its website offers answers to 'FAQs' and boasts of its expertise in *digital forensics, technical investigation, information system security audits, penetration testing*. Cyber crime investigators publish typed reports of their findings, in contrast to the Urdu scrawl of their police-officer counterparts. They descend on crime scenes like characters in a US cop drama, collecting tangles of electronic equipment, labelling it and carting it off in vans. Once the editor had made his complaint, therefore, a report was sent to the 'Cyber Crime Circle', who traced the email to an address in coastal Karachi, and authorised a raid to secure the computer equipment. Once the cyber investigators had done their work, the police had a relatively easy job. When asked if he had sent a series of blasphemous emails, Altaf Rehman replied that he had. He gave the investigators his computer password, so that they could check his sent items. He was then moved from the police station to a solitary cell in Karachi Central Jail, where he would spend the next five years awaiting the determination of his trial. He was charged with blasphemy, which in Pakistan is a capital offence.

The decision to take on a blasphemy case is not one that lawyers make lightly. An accusation of blasphemy is so highly charged that any association with it – such as acting as defence counsel for an alleged blasphemer – is life-threatening. In 2011, the governor of the Punjab, Salmaan Taseer, was shot dead by his own bodyguard because of his public opposition to Pakistan's blasphemy laws. The same year, the Minister for Minorities was assassinated for publicly supporting the defence of a Christian woman charged with blasphemy. In 2014, gunmen entered the office of a senior lawyer who was working on the defence of a university professor accused of blasphemy, and shot him dead at point-blank range.

The corruptibility of blasphemy trials in Pakistan is the result of historical accident. When the British were drafting the Indian Penal Code in the 1850s, religious strife and sectarian violence preyed heavily on their minds. India's population was, and is, composed of Hindus, Buddhists, Sikhs, Jains, Parsees, Muslims and Christians – sectarian violence, the British law commissioners noted, *risked the dissolution of society*. Concerns about law and order were only heightened as revolt and rebellion spread across the subcontinent in 1857. Filled with utilitarian enthusiasm for the legal code, the British drafters guarded against religiously motivated violence by criminalising it. Into the penal code, hastily published in 1860, three years after the 1857 Mutiny, they inserted Chapter XV – *Of Offences Relating to Religion* – Section 295 of which made it an offence, punishable by two years' imprisonment or a fine, to *'destroy, damage or defile, any place of worship, or any object held sacred by any class of persons with the intention of thereby insulting the religion of any class of persons'*. But they did so with some hesitation. Studying the code, English barristers noted concern over how the court would *'ascertain whether the intention of the person was deliberately to wound religious feelings'*. And the drafters made clear how important they thought it to *'distinctly [prove] that there was an intention on the part of the accused to insult the religion of a class of persons'*. The section, barristers scrawled anxiously in notebooks, risked 'unsafe' judgments. Section 295 remained relatively unproblematic for over a hundred years.

Legislative change was its undoing. Following General Zia-ul-Haq's military coup in 1977, the colonial blasphemy laws were amended. In 1986, crimes of blasphemy under Section 295 were made a capital offence, and in April 1991, the Federal Shariat Court made execution the mandatory punishment for blasphemy. (Curiously, although this judgment changed the law, and was authoritative from the date it was handed down by the court, Pakistan's criminal statute remains unamended, and inaccurately reflects the law to this day.) The broad British code was narrowed from a provision that prevented all blasphemy against any religion to one that prevented only blasphemy against Islam: under Zia's new law, only insults to the Prophet and the Holy Qur'an were punishable. And where in 1860 a person had to intend to insult religious feelings, today they can do it by accident. Zia's Section 295-C reads: *'Whoever by words, either spoken or written, or by visible representation, or by any imputation, innuendo or insinuation, directly or indirectly, defiles the sacred name of the Holy Prophet Muhammad (pbuh) shall be punished with death, or imprisonment for life [this alternative sentence has been unenforceable since the 1991 Federal Shariat Court judgment], and shall also be liable to a fine.'* With no requirement of criminal intent, Zia's law lay open to abuse.

But more than the wording of the new Section 295, it was the efficiency of Zia's legislators that caused the ultimate harm. Where most of Zia's new Islamic criminal offences fell under the direct jurisdiction of the Federal Shariat Court, the blasphemy laws remained part of the British-drafted secular legal system. Most of the High Court judges who sit on blasphemy cases were trained at Lincoln's Inn, not at madrasas. The High Court itself, ostensibly secular (and known for adopting a less Islamic stance when sitting in judgment), cannot command the religious respect and deference owed to the Federal Shariat Court. High Court judgments, therefore, are much more vulnerable to the influence of local religious pressures than the Federal Shariat Court. Moreover, by not falling under the Federal Shariat Court's jurisdiction, those accused of blasphemy do not benefit from the court's generally lenient sentencing. By 1998, the Federal Shariat Court had fully upheld only 19 per cent of the cases that came before it, resulting in a surprisingly low conviction rate for most of Zia's Islamic offences, and had announced itself loath to apply severe penalties: *'not only the maximum benefit of every reasonable doubt will be extended to the accused, but an effort, too, will be made not to inflict [fixed penalties] as long as it may be avoided by all legitimate and established means'*, the court wrote in a judgment of 1986. Denied the protection of the Federal Shariat Court, however, blasphemy convictions and sentences of death continue to increase.

Sarah took on Altaf Rehman's case in 2010. The injustice of these laws was too great to ignore. There was, as well, a certain allure to the danger.

In 1958, nine years after the creation of Pakistan and a week before the country's first military coup, Altaf Rehman was born in Karachi. He was the last of his parents' eight children, and the family was poor. He grew up between the simple, crowded households of his parents and their siblings – the responsibility and cost of child-rearing shared amongst the family. He loathed his aunt and uncle for their hypocritical rules and unrelenting punishments, but he was close to his parents and brothers and remembers them fondly. At primary school, he was a quiet student: hard-working, solitary, shy, not especially brilliant. As a teenager, nurturing ambitions to become a businessman, his school record improved. He did well in his exams and showed promise. After two years of secondary school, he went to a specialised government college of commerce, enrolling on a BA in business when he was sixteen. But he was tired of Pakistan. He had already lived through the country's first war with India, East Pakistan's fight for independence, and his father's death: life, and success, in other countries looked easier. Aged seventeen, he emigrated to Bradford, England.

One time powerhouse of Britain's Industrial Revolution, when Altaf Rehman arrived Bradford was no longer booming. In the nineteenth century, fuelled by tremendous quantities of locally mined coal, the city had become one of Britain's capitals of textile production. Wool, silk, alpaca and mohair made it rich, and big. But it also brought poverty, particularly for the Irish and German immigrant populations. With the decline of Britain's industry in the late twentieth century, much of Bradford's wealth moved on. But the factories remained, and following India's independence in 1947, Bradford, like Birmingham, became a site of South Asian, particularly Pakistani, immigration – young men were willing to travel far for a much-multiplied daily wage and relative political stability. So when Altaf Rehman arrived in 1975, he moved into an area with a large Pakistani population and took a job in a textile mill.

Witness statements attesting to Altaf Rehman's good character, religious piety and local standing show him to have been popular in Bradford. He quickly made friends in his new home town and, despite its strangeness, began to enjoy some familiar aspects of life. Bradford had a strong Muslim community – today, almost a quarter of the population are Muslim, and there are over eighty mosques in the city – which was largely composed of Pakistani émigrés. Altaf Rehman soon became a familiar face at the local mosque, observing Friday prayers and Ramadan, travelling to Mecca on Hajj and often leading Eid celebrations. Within four years he had met, and fallen in love with, an English girl from a nearby neighbourhood. She converted to Islam and they married in 1979. Their first child, a boy, was born four years later, just as Altaf Rehman was given indefinite leave to remain in the UK.

With a home, a wife, a son, and – almost – British nationality, Altaf Rehman was embarrassed by his labouring job. Rekindling a teenage ambition, he enrolled on a two-year course for a diploma in business studies. Through a patchwork of part-time employment and late-night shifts, he supported his family while he studied and his wife gave birth to a second child. After graduating, he saved enough money to buy a small restaurant. A keen entrepreneur and natural manager, he was soon buying more restaurants. His food became well known and much loved. He only hired Pakistani chefs – his patrons, almost all Pakistani, wanted food that tasted like their grandmothers had cooked it. Before long, Altaf Rehman had moved his young family into a bigger home. But he had also begun to miss Pakistan, his mother, siblings and cousins. His marriage was no longer happy, and shortly after the birth of their third child, the couple separated. In 1993, Altaf Rehman went to Karachi to visit his mother – who had long had her eye on a Pakistani girl, Sameena, for him. Aged thirty-four and already a father of three, he remarried.

The Pakistan to which Altaf Rehman returned was quite different from the country he had left. Whilst he had been in Bradford, Zulfikar Ali Bhutto had attempted democracy, been ousted by General Zia's military coup (Pakistan's second) and hanged. General Zia himself had then mysteriously died in a plane crash after a decade of rule by martial law. Bhutto's daughter, Benazir, who was governing the country as Pakistan's first female prime minister in 1993 when Altaf Rehman came back to see his mother, would be assassinated fourteen years later. Life in Pakistan felt unstable – the year after Altaf Rehman's return was the most violent Karachi had ever seen – but hopes still seemed to rise and fall with politicians' promises.

Throughout the 1990s and 2000s, Altaf Rehman and his new wife, Sameena, were torn between Karachi and Bradford. Not long after their wedding, they left Pakistan for Yorkshire. By this point, Altaf Rehman was a British citizen, and Sameena soon became one. They were happy. Business prospered. Over the next decade, they had four children. But it was partly these children that prompted the couple's final commitment to Karachi. After the birth of the fourth, Altaf Rehman bought the house that would be raided five years later. He imagined the move to be good for his children, and – although he would later look back at this with bitter, heartfelt irony – it was primarily religion that drove him. The children would grow up in an Islamic country, surrounded by grandparents, aunts and uncles. It was 2003, two years after 9/11, and relations between British-Pakistani Muslims and the British government were tenser than they had been in 1975. Altaf Rehman returned to Pakistan excited, quoting optimistic statistics – an economy growing by 7 per cent a year – to validate his decision.

But events turned against him. In 2004, a year after returning to Pakistan, Altaf Rehman was in a near-fatal car crash. He suffered severe head injuries. Four years later, the financial crisis decimated his property portfolio. Houses and offices in Pakistan and the Gulf that had been bought with the proceeds of selling his business in Bradford were now worth a fraction of their purchase price. As Altaf Rehman plunged into depression his family worried about his mental health. Once a sociable man – when they first moved to Pakistan, the Rehmans' house was filled with family and friends most days of the week – he became reclusive and shy. He was haunted by hallucinations and controlled by obsessive-compulsive desires. All those close to him felt the change. In late June 2009, during another long period of study in his basement office, Altaf Rehman, under the pseudonym Jalal al-Din Muhammad Rumi, sent an email to the editor of a national newspaper.

Sarah and I were terrified, convinced that we were moments from death. Our stomachs were left thirty feet above us as the plane plummeted for the second time. The cabin filled with the blurted prayers and curses of other passengers. It was late July and we had left Lahore in a monsoon. Upon landing, we vowed never to do so again.

Driving through the gates of Karachi High Court two hours later, we were light with relief. The sky was a bright, unblemished blue. A gentle breeze jostled the makeshift awnings that sheltered teams of shoe-shiners, booksellers and letter-writers from what would soon be an unbearably hot sun. The car park and pavements around the court were becoming busy with opportunistic beggars and aged, anxious litigants. The court rose behind them like a Victorian school behind its playground. To its left, a row of tall, greying sixties office blocks, banks, billboards and stacks of breeze-blocks at their base, lined the street. To its right, glimpsed through a lattice of leafy fronds and brightly coloured flowers, rose the soft pink domes of something Indo-Saracenic.

Sarah and I were dressed for court – a less punishing uniform away from Lahore's clammy heat. But being away from Lahore also meant being away from the support of our office. We had no Nasar. Our desk was the back seat of a yellow Toyota Corolla taxi. The driver looked baffled as we opened ring binder after ring binder and rehearsed Sarah's arguments out loud. Through the gates and car park we climbed stairs to a first-floor veranda – wide, with heavy masonry painted a scuffed white to waist height, quite different from Lahore's elegant balconies. A lawyer sat on a shaded bench, busy with a phone call, a pile of documents at his side. At the end of the corridor gathered a group of court readers at a registrar's desk. All wearing white *shalwar kameez*, they had paused to chat on the way to a courtroom. Large thermoses of tea, perhaps destined for a judge's chambers or bar room, stood at their feet, as did several piles of paper, waiting to be filed. The fans were off: cooling, salty sea air passed through this cavernous passageway. The atmosphere was relaxed. It didn't feel right. The High Court of a provincial capital should be thronged every day of the week. Many of the large, panelled doors to courtrooms were bolted shut. Double-checking the list we had downloaded the week before, we peered around the doorway of our allotted court.

It was pitch black, the darkness intensified by a blinding square of light that projected through an open window high on to the back wall. As our eyes adjusted, a near-empty courtroom came into view. Opposite us, on a plinth three feet above the ground, sat a desk, and at it a man wearing spectacles, a baggy white shirt and a quizzical grin. Leaning against his chair, at ground level, was a second man, dressed similarly but with a line of pens clipped over his shirt pocket. He was of middle height and middle age, with the beginnings of an expanding gut and receding hairline. Hand on hip, he turned to us and smiled: 'So no one told you about the strike?'

This was Altaf Rehman's prosecutor. Sitting behind him at the high desk was the court's reader. On the floor around him was spread an arc of Karachi High Court applications. He appeared to be using the quiet day to organise his crowded desk. Our hearing, said the reader, wasn't going to be called until the following week: the judge was on holiday and the court staff on strike – something we would have known had we had a local clerk. On three sides of the courtroom, facing in toward the raised plinth, were long wooden benches, simply carved and slotted together like pews in a Scottish Presbyterian church. On hearing this news, Sarah and I slumped on to the benches, dropping our files with a thud on the floor.

Never one to waste an opportunity, Sarah began to chat, engaging the prosecutor and reader in what appeared to be casual conversation. She had long hoped that Altaf Rehman would be acquitted on the basis of insanity, and she wanted to gauge the likelihood of the judge giving such an order. The prosecutor and the court reader were talkative, friendly, even helpful. On a normal day, Karachi's High Court is even busier than Lahore's. The building sees defendants, witnesses, claimants, victims, police, medical officers and lawyers pour through the gates from the moment they open. Perennially over-burdened, the prosecutor and court reader seemed to have been mellowed by their unrelenting workload, like sharp rocks worn to smooth pebbles in a rapid river current. They were laid-back and unhurried. As we talked, they both expressed some sympathy for Altaf Rehman, and surprise that Sarah was still arguing the case – they remembered her from two years before, when she had been more pregnant than many thought decent to travel, let alone argue a blasphemy case in a Sessions Court. As far as the legal teams are concerned, it's in everyone's best interests to dispose of blasphemy cases as quickly and quietly as possible. Everyone knows what association with blasphemy brings, and although it's not a dangerous job for the prosecutor, he would not want to be seen lingering over a conviction. So the men were cooperative. As we chatted and joked, Sarah asked them if they knew of Altaf Rehman's mental illness, and whether they thought the court had kept records of the medical documents she had filed earlier that year. The reader was unsure but told us where we could find Altaf Rehman's file, to check that the medical reports were still in it. As it was a quiet day, we should have the filing room to ourselves.

A lawyer wandering through the passages and filing rooms of an empty court building feels like a schoolchild walking through classrooms at night. Our footsteps echoed. Padlocked metal filing cabinets lined the corridor, posters, or their remnants, striping their sides. Small rooms and offices to our right and left were filled with similar cabinets, paper stacked three feet high on top of them, two or three desks jammed between them. Inside one of the rooms we found a record keeper. He had grey hair and a neatly trimmed moustache. He wore a collared lilac *shalwar kameez*, black leather sandals and wire-framed spectacles. The room was warm and he was dozing. A radio burbled quietly. A rotating fan ruffled some papers on his desk. When we woke him, he smiled at us. He knew where the file was. From behind a packet of Camel cigarettes in his shirt pocket he retrieved a rattling bunch of keys.

Back in a yellow taxi, heading north through Karachi, Sarah and I were feeling positive: Altaf Rehman's medical report had been in his file, and we had other expert opinions with which to augment it at the next hearing. All of them found Altaf Rehman to be extremely unwell, both at the time of committing the offence and during his imprisonment and trial. Sarah was confident that this gave him a strong defence. Driving away from the port, through the centre of the city, we left Karachi's old town and headed towards the new. As we travelled past the cantonment and Civil Lines built by the British, towards twentieth-century housing cooperatives, the streets became less busy, the roads wider. We took a detour to avoid a protest. After half an hour, the taxi stopped outside the castellated guarded gates of Karachi Central Jail.

The superintendent of Karachi Central Jail was a kind man who tried hard to run a model prison – a lonely mission in one of the world's harshest penal systems. His office was near the jail gates, in a simple bungalow that sat in the relatively open grounds of the complex. Patches of tended flower beds surrounded it. Trees with shiny green leaves, splendidly bright against the ochre yellow of the heat-baked ground and square buildings, swayed gently. Through his window we could see an audience of men squatting under a coloured awning that was blowing animatedly in the wind. It was a reading and writing class. This jail encouraged literacy and other lessons, the superintendent said. Sarah and the superintendent had first met two years before, when she took on Altaf Rehman's case and began visiting the jail regularly. But he had known Altaf Rehman since his arrest almost three years ago. When Sarah asked him about her client, he spoke with compassion and concern. Altaf Rehman's hallucinations had apparently got worse. He was desperate to spend time with his children, he longed for books and seemed increasingly depressed.

Sitting just behind Sarah, bag on my knee and notebook balanced on top of it, I listened eagerly. I knew a great deal about Altaf Rehman's life: the names and ages of his children, details of his marriage, home, parents, work. I knew every aspect of his legal case. I knew the contents of his bookshelf and the layout of his house. I even knew a lot about his state of mind, having catalogued his medication and filed his medical reports. But I had never met him. As the superintendent and Sarah discussed his mood, I was unable to imagine his face. For me, the man at the centre of countless trips to court, discussions, arguments, documents, analyses, expert opinions and accusations remained completely blank.

From his office – through the grounds of the jail, past the open-air classroom, a cordoned-off car park, groups of two or three uniformed guards perched on pastel-coloured plastic stools, chatting over cups of tea and cigarettes – the superintendent led us to a meeting room, guarded by a prison warden. Sarah and I perched on a low springless sofa while a pair of prison guards smirked and whispered in the corner, perhaps amused by the sight of two female lawyers, one blonde and pale, the other wearing tailored trousers, heels and no headscarf. A door opened, and through it, led by the elbow, entered a short, kindly-looking man wearing a light brown *shalwar kameez*. He smiled at us weakly. Sarah introduced me to Altaf Rehman.

With a head of thinning grey hair, eyes distant and melancholy, feet that shuffled rather than walked, Altaf Rehman was misery made manifest. Sarah, so naturally exuberant, was trying her hardest to improve his mood. She cast our near-wasted trip to the court in its most positive light – 'the judges are all sympathetic, they'll help us' spoke about her plans for a bail application – 'we're really positive about this, you could be home within six months' – and that morning's meeting with the prosecutor – 'we'll file another medical report at our next hearing, we hope the insanity defence will work.' But Altaf Rehman's responses were limp. His shoulders drooped in a lifeless shrug. He told Sarah that the judge had frequently visited him in the middle of the night, in his jail cell, announcing his death sentence personally to him. Sarah reassured him that these were just nightmares, while privately worrying that they were hallucinations. Altaf Rehman received no medication whilst in jail. She told him about his family: that they were happy, and healthy, and that they missed him. She brought him another book, and asked what else would improve his time here. We talked about our day at court and told him of our flight: for the first time during our meeting, he laughed, thinking our fears unfounded and silly. But any talk of the law plunged him back into despondency. Then we had to leave, to return to Lahore. He embraced each of us tearfully.

Viewed from afar, the meeting might have looked like a family visit. In the face of such profound terrors – execution, injustice, years of solitary confinement – lawyer–client intimacy, Sarah had found, was as important as it was inescapable. Her clients often developed an emotional as much as a formal dependency on her, one that has sometimes inspired the jealousy of wives. But where the stakes were this high, she felt her duties to be broad and weighty. Pastoral care, overseeing a delicate complex of fear and hope, was paramount. To pull a person through the unpredictable, unimaginable ordeal of death row, Sarah felt that friendship was at times her foremost function.

Sarah had walked into a trap, and she knew it. But it was only as she handed over the document to the court reader that she was sure of her mistake. And by then it was too late.

Things had been looking up for Altaf Rehman since our visit to see him in Karachi jail. The Karachi trial judge in his case had made Sarah a promise: if Altaf Rehman submitted a full written apology to the court, he would be acquitted. She had initially been suspicious. The lower courts rarely acquit on blasphemy charges: with the risk of assassination by Pakistan's relatively few but unforgiving supporters of the blasphemy law so great, a lowly-paid Sessions Court judge is rarely willing to chance it. But as contrition was a central tenet of Islamic law, the promise was plausible. Sarah had been carried away by the prospect of an easy way out. She submitted Altaf Rehman's apology. But at the following hearing, the judge thanked her for her client's *full written confession*. As she had realised only too late, he intended to read the 'apology' as a full admission of guilt. Since he now had this detailed confession – written and signed by the accused (Altaf Rehman), and witnessed by his lawyer (Sarah) – he informed Sarah that he would proceed straight to sentence. There was no need for a trial, no need to call witnesses or examine evidence. His motivation was clear: the confession would expedite the trial, allow the court to sentence Altaf Rehman quickly and the judge to move on from this dangerous, time-consuming case to the hundreds of other applications that awaited him. To a degree Sarah was sympathetic to the judge's personal predicament. But she was still stunned at the deception, and seething. She went to the Supreme Court.

It was 4.30 on a morning in late July 2012, and rain was beginning to speckle and darken Lahore's dust-caked roads. Having splashed some water on my face and blindly packed my computer, notebook and pens into a bag, I was standing on the doorstep when Sarah phoned. As her headlights flashed the undersides of trees and the white walls of neighbouring houses, I opened the gates (snoring guards oblivious) and slipped out. In good weather, the journey to Islamabad takes three to four hours, but our progress was now slowed by sheets of horizontal rain, falling too fast for the windscreen wipers and bouncing several inches on hitting the tarmac. Sarah's driver was racing – perilously weaving between lanes of traffic – to get us to the Supreme Court by 9 a.m.

Nasar had travelled to Islamabad the previous night. Before grudgingly taking the job with Sarah, he had been a Supreme Court clerk (the downgrade to the Lahore High Court was another reason he resented the job, quite apart from the change to a female boss). He knew the place well and had gone ahead to file documents and, more importantly, have his old friends in the court's administration tell him who was going to hear our application, and what they were likely to decide. Along roads perfectly perpendicular, we skirted the edge of Islamabad's large national park before turning into the regimental Constitution Avenue. Embassies stretched back from the right-hand side of the road – French, Japanese, Australian,

German, Spanish, Turkish, Indian. We passed the offices of the World Bank, Ministry of Foreign Affairs, State Bank and National Library.

Islamabad is a city of decisions. Its street plans imply logic, certainty, simplicity – an aesthetic attempt to force the messy complexity of Pakistan's domestic politics into a grid. Created by martial law in 1959, designed by a Greek modernist architect and urban planner in 1960, the new city had replaced Karachi as the capital. A committee had chosen its location, this northern position preferred by Pakistan's then military ruler as being nearer the Punjab (Pakistan's politically and militarily most powerful province) and troubled Kashmir (should military intervention be necessary), and close to the army headquarters in Rawalpindi. It also had the advantage of being far from Karachi's increasingly turbulent social and political movements. It was named 'Islamabad', the 'Abode of Islam', in February 1960 by an ambitious young Information Minister (who would one day become prime minister), Zulfikar Ali Bhutto. A high-modernist utopia, the city was meant to be functional, a machine of the state.

Driving down Constitution Avenue was slow work – the road was heavily guarded, and our passports were checked several times. My attention was divided between nervous glances at the dashboard clock (we had fifteen minutes before being late) and sweeping stares at the landscape around us. Islamabad's surroundings looked cool, wet and hilly, a palette of greens, greys and cobalt blues wholly different from the dusty, roseate warmth of Lahore. Designed by a Japanese architect who cited Le Corbusier as his abiding influence, Pakistan's Supreme Court is a simple, imposing structure, its interiors and exteriors grey, white and of soaring scale. Inside, like a troupe of mime artists, the building's employees gesture in uniforms of black and white.

While a person's trial is ongoing in the lower courts, discrete points of law or procedure can be appealed up to the Supreme Court, with the result that lawyers can end up arguing different aspects of the same case, near simultaneously, at opposite ends of the country. And that was why Sarah, whilst Altaf Rehman's trial was being heard in Karachi, was filing an application in the Supreme Court in Islamabad. She was there to challenge the trial judge's reneged promise, to ask the Supreme Court if they would enforce it.

Entering the building in a rush, Sarah, Nasar and I were channelled through a series of X-ray machines, via a lofty atrium, into a solemn, silent courtroom. The room was wider than it was deep. Opposite the entrance, raised high above the floor of the court, was a long, dark wooden desk, with seats for up to nine judges. It stretched the full width of the room. We sat to the left, in chairs that folded down like cinema seats. The court-room was cavernous and discouraged speaking above a whisper. There were three other people there, who sat in the opposite corner and ignored us. Clerks and court readers swung soundlessly in and out of subtly disguised doorways.

Modernist design suited the building well, for supreme courts are places for minimalists. There were no distrac-tions in this courtroom, no sagging bookshelves, no leaning piles of paper, no queues of applicants, accuseds and accusers. The cases, too, are less cluttered than in lower courts. It is single questions that go to the Supreme Court, not dense disputes. Facts are focused and the argu-ments increasingly abstract. The judges have time to think. Speaking in Pakistan's Supreme Court is a privilege, which Sarah, a young and relatively inexperienced barrister, had not yet earned. This, however, was a blas-phemy case, and people with anything to lose – such as the standing that comes with a Supreme Court licence – don't often argue them. So Sarah had been given special permission, because she couldn't find anyone else to do the work for her. Her hand shook as she turned the pages in her bundle of previous cases and religious opinion. As she made her submissions, the judges unhurriedly asked her a range of careful, interrogative questions. Standing in that colossal, empty courtroom, her voice wavered as she answered.

To appear in front of Pakistan's Supreme Court was to face a very different aspect of Pakistani justice from that which Sarah encountered day to day in the lower courts. Pakistan's Supreme Court was first empowered to enforce fundamental rights by the Constitution of 1956, and although its constitutional status has had a turbulent history (to list just a few instances, its power to protect fundamental rights was suspended by Zulfikar Ali Bhutto in 1971, by General Zia in 1981 and by Nawaz Sharif in 2014), it has been a remarkably active site of political opposition, championing its independence from the government. Besides upholding the rights of individuals, the court has charged prime ministers with contempt, vetoed laws and constitutional amendments, and disqualified politicians from holding office. Sarah was all too aware that she stood before powerful, intelligent, principled men.

The judges were sympathetic to her client. His was a sorry story, they agreed. One muttered disapproval of the blasphemy laws. Another asked, almost conversationally, if her client had really written those emails. Was he mad? Politely, Sarah referred to Altaf Rehman's medical records. But the judges had no interest in finding fault with Altaf Rehman's trial judge. Judicial misconduct is a serious, career-destroying reprimand and – particularly in a country where corruption and torture routinely go unnoticed – they were willing to forgive indiscretions on a case as pressured, scary and volatile as this. In any event, Altaf Rehman, to the minds of these three Supreme Court judges, had an easy way out. And so they dealt with Sarah quickly and instructed her simply: file his medical reports in the trial court and he'll be acquitted for insanity.

Insanity is an ancient legal principle that has long affected findings of guilt. First cited in Babylonian legal codes, it is less a defence to a crime than a status that renders a person incapable of committing a criminal act. The insane, in legal phraseology, 'lack capacity'. And incapacity renders a person incapable of criminality. As a result, a finding of madness strips the law of its power to punish. In Britain, Pakistan and most of the world's legal systems, however, legal and psychiatric insanity are completely different things. Like many words, 'insanity' loses its common-sense meaning when it enters a courtroom, where it is re-dressed with a legal definition. Some long-recognised psychiatric conditions do not amount to legal insanity; while some illnesses that psychiatrists hold to have no bearing on mental health, such as diabetes, do. This improbable situation is the result of the attempted murder of Sir Robert Peel, then British Prime Minister, in 1843. Commenting on the trial of Peel's would-be assassin, Daniel M'Naughten, judges held that a person was insane – in law and regardless of psychiatry – if he, 'because of a disease of mind, did not know the nature of his act or he did not know that it was wrong'. A 'disease of mind' is anything that can affect your mind, not a mental illness; hence, a hypoglycaemic attack in a diabetic can amount to legal insanity.

Pakistan's mental health and criminal procedure legislation, drafted in the mid-nineteenth century and passed into law in 1860, reflects the spirit of its times and the trial of Peel's thwarted assassin. There are two moments in a criminal case at which the accused's psychiatric condition has a bearing on his guilt. First, at the time of committing the offence. As Section 84 of the Pakistan Penal Code reads: *'nothing is an offence which is done by a person who, at the time of doing it, by reason of unsoundness of mind, is incapable of knowing the nature of the act, or that he is doing what is either wrong or contrary to law'*. Where the accused presents evidence that they were of unsound mind at the time of committing the offence (or the court thinks that they may have been), then the court will enquire into the accused's mental health. If the defence can prove unsoundness of mind, the court should order acquittal. Second, at the time of standing trial. The Criminal Procedure Code – Section 465: *'Procedure in case of person sent for trial at Court of Session or High Court being a lunatic'*, to be precise – provides that where the court considers the accused to be of unsound mind, the trial must be stayed and the accused should be acquitted and either detained in a hospital or released. A lunatic, according to Section 3(5) of Pakistan's 1912 Lunacy Act, is *'an idiot or person of unsound mind'*. For a brief period in the early 2000s, a Mental Health Ordinance supplemented the law and gave a glimpse of much-hoped-for reform. It provided definitions – of, for example, 'mental disorder', 'mental impairment', 'severe personality disorder' – that were both broad and in keeping with contemporary international understandings of mental illness. But the Ordinance was never passed into law. When it lapsed, three years after its drafting, the British-drafted Lunacy Act of 1912 came back into force.

Determining whether the person before him is 'an idiot or person of unsound mind' is no easy task for a judge. Sometimes he will begin his enquiries by asking a series of basic questions, like 'Who is the President of Pakistan?'

and it is only if the defendant gives suitably 'insane' answers that the judge will order a psychiatric assessment. It is often difficult, therefore, for defence lawyers even to persuade a judge that their client requires a medical examination. But it can be even more difficult for defence lawyers to establish the accused's state of mind at the time of committing the offence; given the delays in Pakistan's justice system, the trial is often held several years after the offence, and illnesses may have gone undiagnosed for decades.

The medical examination itself, once sanctioned by the judge, is conducted by a medical board staffed by court-appointed psychiatrists, the employees of government hospitals. In considering the accused's state of mind, the board may take into account evidence presented by both the prosecution and the defence, and this can include independent psychiatric assessments. But the board has the ultimate discretion over what finding to make, and on the basis of that finding the court will reach a conclusion on the accused's state of mind either at the time of committing the offence, at the time of trial, or both (depending on which defences are relied on). The predominance of this court-appointed, government-employed medical board is potentially problematic. It risks bias: the experts may be influenced by a desire to secure further employment and may give opinions, therefore, more favourable to the prosecution (the state) than the defence. (It is largely for this reason that in countries like England, when questions of the defendant's 'fitness to stand trial' are raised, both prosecution and defence will call their own expert witnesses – although all psychiatric experts must be of a court-approved standard, they need not themselves be court-approved.) But in a blasphemy trial, quite apart from career concerns and the difficulties inherent to these assessments, a variety of additional pressures comes to bear on the role of medical officer.

In Pakistan, the significance of a finding of insanity in a blasphemy trial varies according to your perspective. For the defence lawyers, it would be a quick, legally sanctioned and relatively uncontroversial way out of a difficult case. For the judge, with the right evidence from a medical board, it might allow them to wash their hands of a case they had come to dread. But for the medical officers, it could be a death sentence: where an acquittal is based entirely on a psychiatric report, the psychiatrist may find themselves the object of threats and possible attacks. And so the government medical officers have a strong disincentive to find a blasphemer insane.

Sarah argued that Altaf Rehman was both of unsound mind at the time of committing the offence and unfit to stand trial. She had psychiatric reports confirming this. But the court was not persuaded, and although a medical board was constituted, they were taking a long time to come to a conclusion.

Nevertheless, Sarah was persistent in arguing the insanity plea, and her attempt did in the end save Altaf Rehman's life, just not quite in the manner she had expected. The delay caused by the medical board meant that Altaf Rehman soon became eligible for bail: in Pakistan, where a person charged with a capital offence has been detained for over two years without their trial being concluded, they may be released on bail.

Altaf Rehman's first bail application did not get far in Karachi. But, true to form, Sarah appealed the refusal of bail up to the Supreme Court, which granted her application. The superintendent of Karachi Central Jail had Altaf Rehman released so discreetly that none of the other prisoners noticed (thereby reducing the risk that people in Karachi would learn of an alleged blasphemer walking the streets). The next day, he left Pakistan, taking a flight back to Bradford – where he, Sameena and their four children now live together.

Breaching bail is a criminal offence. Bail is granted in return for a person's promise to return to prison, police or court when requested. The court will take an accused's good word as guarantee of their return, and won't grant bail where there's a high chance of that accused absconding. But by this point, Altaf Rehman had lost all faith in Pakistan's legal system. He did not find it difficult to break his promise.

Altaf Rehman's blasphemy charge and his decision to breach bail raise many questions about Pakistan's blasphemy laws. Unlike many blasphemy cases – where there are often factual disputes over whether or not the accused actually blasphemed, and what amounts to blasphemy – Altaf Rehman's situation was not evidentially or legally complicated. Within moments of his arrest he admitted that he had blasphemed. Alongside his apology/confession, a wealth of evidence proved his blasphemy. But many would argue that his arrest remains wrong and his trial unfair. Not because either was unlawful. They weren't: sentencing Altaf Rehman and even executing him would have been entirely lawful under Pakistan's laws as they now stand. But because the laws themselves might be wrong. Blasphemy laws (particularly those that carry a death sentence) seem obviously unjust to proponents of secular legal systems, but Pakistan's blasphemy laws are even anathema to some Islamic religious scholars. Based on a statutory provision drafted by British colonial lawyers in the nineteenth century, which was then amended by a series of Pakistan's rulers in the twentieth, Pakistan's blasphemy laws are not directly modelled on a single school of Sharia jurisprudence. There is no requirement of intent in Pakistan's blasphemy laws, an element central to Sharia jurisprudence (a point that Pakistan's Federal Shariat Court made when reviewing the laws). Persons accused of blasphemy are not given the full evidentiary protections of Sharia – which, in many schools, bar circumstantial evidence and require the testimony of four adult male witnesses or a repeated, voluntary confession. And secular lawyers, not Islamic scholars, sit in judgment on their acts. Furthermore, the courts have lost control of these laws. So great are the external pressures on a judge that he can barely call judgment in a blasphemy case his own. These laws are now beyond the law, enforced by a small but deadly minority and easily abused to settle scores and instil fear.

In Pakistan, the decision to oppose or flout the country's blasphemy laws is one that can end in death. But this death is not imposed by law. More than 1,200 people have been charged with blasphemy since General Zia's amendments – a striking number compared to the mere fourteen cases of blasphemy reported during the previous thirty-nine years. Many of those accused have been sentenced to death. But these executions are never carried out. In a quiet, subtle act of objection, the higher courts of Pakistan find ways of overturning convictions, and as yet, no one has been executed for blasphemy in Pakistan. The real danger of a blasphemy charge lies instead in the legal system's delay. During the many long years spent in prison awaiting appeal, those accused of blasphemy are at high risk of being killed by the country's passionate supporters of the law – poisoned to death in jails, stabbed to death in hospitals, tortured to death in police custody, shot dead outside courtrooms, mauled to death by mobs. Likewise, those who publicly oppose the law risk not judicial execution but extra-judicial violence, threats and probable murder. This puts the person protesting these laws in a precarious place, where traditional methods of opposition are both dangerous and futile. And so Altaf Rehman, instead of fighting an appeal, ran away from the country he was born in and vowed never to return.

The case of Yasir Ansari – a newsagent from Manchester who had been born south of Multan in Pakistan's Punjab – was perhaps the most dangerous of Sarah's career. If Altaf Rehman's case had largely taken place behind closed courtroom doors and in relative secrecy, the case of Yasir Ansari, a man also charged with blasphemy, played out, very visibly, on the streets: crowds gathered outside the jail where he would be tried, waving placards demanding his death. A fatwa was issued in his name. Videos on the internet encouraged a campaign for his execution. In this extremely threatening environment, Yasir Ansari's initial defence lawyer had backed out. With no one else willing to take the case on, Sarah stepped in.

Yasir Ansari was not well. But although the British NHS possessed a decade's worth of medical records detailing his ill health, the court held those records inadmissible as evidence early on in his trial. As in Altaf Rehman's case, therefore, most of Sarah's energies went into trying to prove Yasir Ansari's mental illness to the court. As a volunteer in London, I had spent several weeks deep in Yasir Ansari's medical files, typing and mistyping charts of the eight-syllable-long names of myriad medicines. In Manchester, I had driven to the houses of his doctors, psychiatrists in local surgeries and hospitals on the outskirts of the city who had never before been called to give evidence in a death penalty trial, collecting their signed affidavits before couriering the papers to Pakistan. These documents made an extraordinary connection between a world I knew so well – the NHS, local GPs and Britain's rainy suburbs – and one that was so alien – a trial court in the southern Punjab, a death sentence and blasphemy. But for a Pakistani court, the papers were treated as entirely unconnected to the case; the affidavits were useless. They were from a foreign jurisdiction: the Pakistani court would only trust their own psychiatric assessment of Yasir Ansari.

In keeping with the Criminal Procedure Code, the judge's inquiry into Yasir Ansari's mental state was cursory. He asked him some general knowledge questions in court – *What government is in power? What date is it? What is your name?* – but Yasir Ansari, a man with a tendency to obsessively construct elaborate conspiracies concerning the governments of Britain and Pakistan, did not struggle with general knowledge questions. He appeared quite normal in court. In fact, more often than not his illness came across as merely a bad mood or an obsessive attention to detail. And with an irony that infuriated Sarah, his ability to fashion complex conspiracy theories was something the court considered to be strong evidence of sanity.

Given the volume of British medical evidence documenting Yasir Ansari's mental illnesses, Sarah demanded that a medical officer examine him. Despite his scepticism, the judge allowed the examination. Adept at answering short, targeted questions, Yasir Ansari made a less convincing case for his sanity during longer consultations. Soon after exchanging pleasantries, his conversation often took surprising turns. He might, for example, casually mention the time machine he had recently invented, or his detailed plan to solve Pakistan's electricity supply problems, or his television in England through which MI6 and the CIA often spied on him, or his personal correspondence with the Queen, or President Zardari's plans to assassinate him. Familiar with the tenor of his conversations, Sarah was confident that a psychiatric examination would have him acquitted. But as Yasir Ansari was being tried, the court's psychiatric assessment was plagued with a plethora of conflicting pressures.

The context of a blasphemy trial is all-powerful in its ability to corrupt. And Yasir Ansari's trial was particularly highly charged. On travelling from Manchester to Pakistan in the summer of 2008, he had discovered that he had been duped. A plot of land he had recently bought but had not yet seen had been fraudulently sold to someone else. He filed a claim against the man who had sold him the land. Shortly after doing so he found himself facing a blasphemy charge for insulting the Prophet. He had, it turned out, picked a fight with the wrong man: the seller was a man of significant local influence, and it had not been difficult for him to have the police arrest Yasir Ansari. So broadly defined is the offence of blasphemy and so scary its context, it is an easy charge to make stick. Since Yasir Ansari's arrest, the complainant had rallied the local community and religious leaders against him, promoting protests throughout the town. As a result, in a country where angry mobs have often bludgeoned alleged blasphemers to death, the prison wardens decided to exercise caution. To protect Yasir Ansari from further publicity and the risk of attacks that movement between court and jail would expose him to, his trial was held in the jail complex itself.

But information about trial dates and progress leaked – perhaps a clerk told his friend; maybe a lawyer with influence over a registrar read some of the case documents. And so, when Sarah's driver, Abid – an imposing retired army officer who was always armed – parked at the jail entrance on the day of the first 'secret' hearing, there was a gathering of people waiting there. Sarah, invariably wearing a trouser suit and heels to court, refused to be intimidated. She stepped down from her car and walked across to the prison, not making eye contact and ignoring the jeers from the crowd.

In 2012, knowing little more of Sarah than her appearance, the complainant imagined, quite wrongly, that he could easily intimidate her. While she was in the jail during one of Yasir Ansari's first trial hearings, Abid stood watch outside and noticed the crowd swelling, one or two leaders inciting the group. As he and Sarah returned to jail for subsequent hearings, they became accustomed to the uneasy walk between car and jail. Then Sarah's name and address was leaked to the press. Given that Pakistan is a place where you can be shot for merely publicly criticising the blasphemy laws, publishing the name and address of a blasphemy defence lawyer is a death threat. Any government medical officer appointed to conduct Yasir Ansari's psychiatric assessment would have been aware of both the crowd and the threats.

Following the court's order, a psychiatrist in a nearby hospital had agreed to assess Yasir Ansari's mental health. His was a well-known psychiatric department; people travelled far, from all over Pakistan and Afghanistan, to be treated there. But while the psychiatrist examined Yasir Ansari, a large crowd of protesters gathered outside the hospital. People frequently lobby medical staff in Pakistan. In a country where inequality colours everything – electricity, wealth, opportunity, criminality – universal rights have to be earned: healthcare and a fair trial are only yours if you're deemed to have deserved them. Certain criminals, such as terrorists, rapists and blasphemers, have forfeited these rights. The hospital entrance was heavily guarded while a psychiatrist and two neurologists evaluated Yasir Ansari. Their eight-page report, seven copies of which were counter-signed and delivered to various government departments and the jail authorities, stated that Yasir Ansari was sane. It made no mention of the crowd outside.

Sarah asked the court for permission to cross-examine the medical officers on the contents of other, conflicting psychiatric reports and evidence from the doctors who had treated Yasir Ansari in the UK. But the judge refused to file any further reports or evidence. Sarah insisted, repeatedly. Peeved by her persistence, the judge barred her from his court and appointed a government counsel to act as Yasir Ansari's defence lawyer for the final few hearings of his trial. He told Sarah that he would file a contempt of court charge against her, but nothing came of it.

Meanwhile, devastated by the loss of his wife and child, Sohail tried to focus all his energies on Yasir Ansari's case. His job, piecing together the background to Yasir Ansari's psychiatric report, was to interview hospital staff about the crowds outside and to talk to the protesters who had been there to find out what they had done, and why. Members of the crowd said that their purpose was to intimidate the doctors, and hospital staff told Sohail that they were indeed intimidated by any crowd protesting against blasphemy. But these comments were off the record – he was unable to find anyone willing to sign a statement in a blasphemy case.

At this point, Arthur's involvement with Yasir Ansari's case began to run parallel to Sohail's. It had become clear that whatever evidence Sohail might gather, Yasir Ansari's trial was unlikely to be fairly resolved in the courtroom (where Sarah, in any event, was no longer allowed to represent him). Sarah, in the meantime, had heard a rumour that the complainant was willing to accept payment in exchange for dropping the case. She contemplated a compromise and asked Arthur for help.

A few days after Sarah first suggested communication with the complainant, Arthur and Nasar found themselves on the early-morning Daewoo bus from Lahore to Multan. Arthur needed Nasar for this first meeting. Having accompanied Sarah to almost every one of Yasir Ansari's hearings, Nasar knew the complainant and his lawyer. Whilst waiting for hearings, or for Sarah, he had often chatted to the complainant's lawyer over cups of tea in the jail canteen. They had become friends. And so, over another cup of tea, whilst Arthur loitered on a street nearby, Nasar casually mentioned the possibility of a compromise. The lawyer confirmed that his client, the complainant, was willing to negotiate. Nasar gave Arthur a call.

The lawyer's office was small but well kept. Handsome bookcases, filled with the leather-bound law reports common to most lawyers' offices, lined the walls. Previous or current briefs were neatly stacked in available floor space. The talismanic black-and-white photograph of a handsome and youthful Muhammad Ali Jinnah at Lincoln's Inn, present in the large majority of Pakistan's law courts, hung above the desk. The lawyer's father, also a lawyer and a retired judge, worked from the room next door. The meeting was amicable and polite. Arthur noticed how the lawyer – for this meeting and every one of the many they would have over the next few months – came down to the building's foyer to meet them, and would do the same to see them off. He was reasonable, respectful and cooperative. Facing him across his wide desk, Nasar and Arthur sat in comfortable leather chairs. Arthur introduced himself as an independent 'restorative justice expert', senior in Pakistan's prison fellowship and currently working with Sarah. In turn, the lawyer explained his dilemma. The complainant could be willing to accept three crore rupees – that's 30 million rupees, or about £260,000 – in exchange for his ceasing to participate in the case. All parties must be aware, the lawyer said, that any deal was to be confidential. If that were agreed, the complainant would appease the mullah-led crowds that gathered outside the jail, and he would stop appearing in court. This would give the judge the space he needed to discreetly dispose of the case justly. The dangerous element of this case, the lawyer explained, was not the blasphemy laws themselves but the lengths people were willing to go to in support of them. If the complainant defused the case, it would effectively be dropped. Here the lawyer spoke from a position of some authority – he had worked on the case of a notorious citizen enforcer of the blasphemy laws, the assassin of government minister Salmaan Taseer.

Arthur was surprised by how transactional this proposal was, given the supposedly sacred context. Doubtless, he thought, the complainant had Yasir Ansari's rumoured wealth in mind. (Arthur was aware that the complainant's lawyer had grown up in the same area as Yasir Ansari and knew something of his background.) When Arthur turned to Nasar to ask whether he thought Yasir Ansari would be able to pay £260,000, the lawyer declared that he knew that although Yasir Ansari had been poor, through moving to the UK, raising money in the name of Islam and then using it to fund his own chain of newsagents, he had since made many millions of rupees. Although Arthur knew that this was not true, it appeared to him that the complainant's greed might save Yasir Ansari's life.

But the context of these negotiations was fraught with danger. The complainant's lawyer knew, like Sarah, that Islamic compensation payments – Qisas and Diyat – are not applicable to a charge of blasphemy. Even the President of Pakistan is unable to pardon a person accused of blasphemy. This is because blasphemy is an offence against God. The complainant in a blasphemy case is thus not a victim but merely a witness. According to Pakistani law, to offer such forgiveness in place of God would itself be an act of blasphemy. Realising the implications of the deal he wanted to strike, and Yasir Ansari's inability to pay such a large sum, the complainant withdrew his offer, and thus found himself locked into the blasphemy case. It was a monster of his own making, and he and Yasir Ansari were irrevocably bound to it.

What I had seen of Yasir Ansari's case deeply depressed me. As a recent graduate of Glasgow University's left-leaning law faculty, I had studied Marxist legal theories that understood the law as a tool of oppression, a system that structurally disadvantages the poor and gives more power to the already powerful. Early on in my studies, I had read Jean-Jacques Rousseau's warning that 'laws are always useful to those with possessions and harmful to those who have nothing'. I had been told to be wary of the law. But my attention as a student had been on structures and theoretical observations of legal systems as a whole – the effect whole systems of law had on whole classes of people. Before Yasir Ansari's case, I had never witnessed one man using the law as a weapon against another. What I found more disturbing, however, was the power of a blasphemy charge. Yasir Ansari's case was nothing more than a land dispute. But once articulated as blasphemy, it took on its own horrifying logic. Powered by a climate of fear, the case hurtled out of control and no one – complainant, defendant, judge, prosecutor, doctor, witness – could stop it.

In January, 2010, Karim Muhammad travelled to Quetta looking for water. Over the previous decade, drought and population increase had pushed this city close to the Afghan border into a water crisis. For unemployed labourers with the stomach for unforgiving work, there was money to be made in boring for ground-water reservoirs a hundred metres beneath mountain rock. In debt from his recent marriage to a girl from his village, Karim Muhammad had joined a water-boring team prospecting in the Baluch desert, 500 miles from his home. He phoned his wife, back in his village, as often as he could. One evening in early February, he spoke to her and his mother and said he'd be back home the next day. They would not see him for several years.

It was quarter to eight on a Friday morning in July 2012. I was sitting beside Sarah on a row of straight-backed chairs along the edge of a small civil courtroom in the Lahore High Court. Forgetting the court's dress code when I had packed my bag in London, I was wearing borrowed clothes: shoes that were too small, a *shalwar kameez* that was too big and a jacket that strapped my arms to my sides. Sarah to my right, Maryam to hers, we were a conspicuously female trio, wedged in the middle of a long row of male advocates. It wasn't merely my clothing

that made us look odd. Nasar stood just in front of us –
perhaps abiding by some personal code of chivalry, perhaps embarrassed about being too closely associated with
the all-female legal team – and never sat down. Ring binders were piled on our knees. Sarah gripped a highlighter
pen in her teeth and fiddled with a pack of pale-yellow
Post-it notes. She juggled the files, flagging pages and
re-highlighting paragraphs.

We were there to ask the court to ensure that forty
Pakistani detainees – suspects in the War on Terror – be
returned from Afghanistan to Pakistan and given a trial.
Karim Muhammad was one of those forty detainees. He
had been picked up one evening by US Special Forces a
few miles from Quetta. Handcuffed and blindfolded, he
was flown to Bagram Air Base, a sprawl of aircraft hangars
and hooch containers originally built by the Soviet Union,
sixty miles north of Kabul. This was the holding site for
suspected terrorists. A number of Pakistani men – some
as young as fourteen, and most captured in circumstances
as odd as Karim Muhammad's – had ended up there.

This was not Sarah's usual line of work. She was a
local criminal lawyer, and this was a level of international
law and international profile far beyond anything she'd
done before. It was testament to her growing reputation
that she had been approached by an international human
rights organisation to argue the case. From where I was
sitting, though, she looked tiny and vulnerable.

Sarah's application was one small part of the civil
judge's busy morning. His courtroom was on the western
veranda of the High Court, looking across McLeod Road
and Ustad Allah Baksh Road (an intersection of Urdu and
English common to Lahore) to the crimson General Post
Office building. When we entered, the court was already
thronged. A wave of Nasar's hand had cleared a clutch
of chairs, and we sat in front of a bookcase sagging with

law reports, one of several lining the courtroom. Urgent applications – as Nasar had managed to file ours – were heard before 10.30 a.m., ahead of the scores of applicants already gathering outside. Nasar had been promised that we would be done by 9.30.

Lawyers and the occasional client – conspicuous as the few splashes of coloured clothing in the room – had already filled most of the seats, and sat fiddling with files and conspiring with clerks. There was a swell of hushed voices and rustled papers. By 7.55 a.m., there were a hundred people in the room. The only empty space was at the lectern directly in front of the judge, where pairs of opposing advocates would soon stand. Sarah's eyes darted around the room, down to the files and up to the ceiling.

Having just then returned from the judge's chambers, the reader of the court (equivalent to the court clerk in England) caught Nasar's eye. They had a short exchange. Sarah had, for the past few days, complained bitterly about this reader. He resolutely refused to acknowledge her, and she suspected that he deliberately misplaced papers central to the petition. Thankfully, Nasar's friendship with him survived – and that may well have been the sole reason why the petition itself had not yet been thrown out. Nasar returned to warn Sarah that the judge was not pleased with her application. He did not intend to grant it. Moments later, from a discreet door behind and to the right of his chair, the judge – cloaked in long black robes with bright red lapels – entered the courtroom. Lawyers rose awkwardly while he sat down, gathered his papers and looked up to survey the day's pile of applications and assembly of applicants. Within the hour, Sarah would make her submissions.

After he had been captured in Quetta, Karim Muhammad, and others like him – some captured whilst goat-herding on a hilltop on the Afghanistan–Pakistan border, others whilst taking a family member to hospital in Karachi, others whilst working as labourers in the tribal areas – had been catalogued. They were taken to Bagram and given a number – called their Internment Serial Number (ISN), by which, from then on, they were identified. Karim Muhammad became ISN 20275. As third-country nationals (that is, citizens of a country other than Afghanistan), they were kept together in one cell, separate from the Afghan detainees. These third-country nationals were, as a rule, considered more radicalised, and thereby a greater threat, than the other inmates. Separation was a security measure. Their cell was part of a housing unit that contained three other cells and was manned by a desk of military personnel. A long corridor, stretching the length of each prison block, connected the units. Each cell was identical: about ten by fifteen metres and home to thirty or forty men. Continuously lit by halogen strip lights and chill-blasted by powerful air conditioners around the clock, they had three walls and were fronted and roofed by a strong metal cage. Above and in front were viewing platforms from where army staff could inspect detainees. The men slept on the floor, and at the back of the cell were some toilets and showers. When transported around the complex, the men were pushed in wheelchairs, shackled, blindfolded and ear-muffed. At all times they wore standard-issue *shalwar kameez* – with their ISN written across their chests – beards and white prayer caps.

These men were legal pariahs and any review of their detention conditions was perfunctory at best. In 2009, the year before Karim Muhammad was taken to Bagram, the detainees were granted some procedural protections. Under pressure from US federal courts – which had declared Bagram's previous procedures inadequate – the Obama administration established 'detainee review boards', both as a basic guarantor of detainee rights (the boards were to be something of a substitute for the criminal trial these detainees had been denied) and as an attempt to involve Afghans more closely in the detention process (they would hear from family members and village elders, who they called as witnesses). But at no point whilst Karim Muhammad was there was a Bagram detainee ever permitted direct access to an independent lawyer. Even the International Committee of the Red Cross (an organisation usually granted confidential discussions with inmates about their conditions) was rarely permitted to hold meetings with the detainees in private. Conversations were instead held in an airlock at the front of the cell, or, occasionally, under military supervision in a separate room. In 2010, the year of Karim Muhammad's capture, lawyers had argued in an American courtroom that these detainees deserved the protection of international humanitarian laws, and that the detention facility should be exposed to greater scrutiny. The court held, however, that the detainees were not owed such protection, and that ordering a detailed review of the conditions in Bagram was beyond the scope of a US courtroom. In other words, the detainee review boards were the best legal protection these men would get.

But the detainee review boards, crucially, were not criminal trials. The trial – judgment of a person's guilt or liability – is a communal, socially integrated concept. Under English law, and in former British colonies, such as America and Pakistan, the process of a trial is governed by a number of principles, of which 'open justice' is perhaps the most important and ancient. At its most basic, open justice is a guarantee that trials be seen, that they be public and that judicial decision-making be transparent. Societies have long been aware of this imperative: it is the right to a public trial, not merely a trial, that bills of rights such as the European Convention on Human Rights and the US constitutional amendments protect. But publicity is important not only as a guard against unfairness and arbitrary sentencing. Publicity gives the trial a social context, against which the court can assess the guilt of an accused, the veracity of a witness. And a court's open doors (in Britain, America, Pakistan and many countries in the world, members of the public can freely enter a courtroom and observe most cases) enable the law to serve a very public function. Trial by jury – an ancient legal principle – is at its heart a basic guarantee that a trial be public. In ensuring this public involvement, the jury makes the administration of justice a shared project.

Detainee review boards were different. Instead of a lawyer, Karim Muhammad and the other detainees had a personal representative appointed for them by military officers. Although those representatives were supposed to act in the best interests of the detainees, they were overworked (at times there was only one for every hundred detainees) and rarely able to devote time to the particularities of each case. The personal representative also offered none of the standard procedural protections that govern the lawyer–client relationship in Britain, America and Pakistan: communications between personal representative and detainee were not confidential, as they are with a lawyer, and the representative was employed by (and therefore reported to) the military, not the detainee. From the military reports, it's clear that at least some of the personal representatives were aware of their limitations and wary of the evidence upon which they were asked to base their conclusions. When advising the military review boards, personal representatives were often cautious and circumspect. Uncertainty characterised their findings: *'There is no reporting on this guy prior to the arrest, nothing on him . . . He has a plausible explanation for knowing so many Taliban figures; they are well known. Does it rise to the preponderance of evidence [that is, is the evidence sufficiently reliable]?'*

The detainees were often captured on the basis of a local informant's testimony or American intelligence – which identified, reported on and aimed to detain a list of named targets. But even Department of Defense staff have been known to admit that a detainee was captured on the basis of 'mistaken identity'. Inmates of both Bagram and Guantanamo were often guilty merely of sharing a name with a Taliban commander or militant. In Central and South Asia, names are more fluid than in Europe and America. Birth certificates are rarely issued, and even where they are, a person's name will often change significantly with new occupations and reputations. Honorifics, such as Haji, are added, and career choices or nicknames are translated into surnames (like the nicknames of American frontiersmen, such as 'Groundsluice Smith' or 'Pistolgrip Jim'). Names alone, as the personal representatives sometimes told the military boards, were therefore unreliable identifiers. But wrongful captures were not always the result of innocent mistakes. Rather, local power-brokers in Afghanistan learnt that labelling a rival or enemy as 'Taliban' was an easy way to get rid of them. As one of the detainees said to his detainee review board: *'Maybe my enemy gave wrong information to the US forces. Many people now are just giving misinformation.'* Some US military personnel were aware of this risk: review hearings were scattered with statements questioning the trustworthiness of a source, lamenting the lack of vetted, reliable and proven informants. But this did not stop many innocent men ending up in Bagram or Guantanamo, the surreal product of an international superpower's unwitting entanglement in local feuds.

To rebut the evidence of informants and signals intelligence, the personal representative could call witnesses, interview the detainee (who could himself speak at the board hearing) and guess as to the significance of physical evidence found on the detainee at the time of his capture – most often a cell phone or SIM card with perhaps some money, pocket litter (scraps of paper, sweet wrappers, tissues) and a radio. But witnesses were no easier to gauge than informants, and the detainee review boards had no idea if the witnesses were telling the truth. Likewise detainees. Many gave very similar explanations: they had been mistakenly captured, they had no association with the Taliban, they worked in education, or drove a taxi, or sold vegetables, or shepherded animals. If they had the number of a known Taliban member on their SIM card, it was because they had driven him in their taxi or sold him meat. Some of these stories were genuine, some not. Many of these men were from small rural communities and knew a Talib because he was a neighbour, not a co-conspirator. For the Pakistani detainees, language complicated things further. One detainee complained that he had been asked to sign documents written in *either English, Pashtu or in Dari. None of these three [is] my language. I don't understand them. My language is Urdu.'* With only meagre information and mistranslations to go on, it is difficult to imagine how the review boards could state anything with confidence.

Without reliable evidence, there was little point to the review hearings. Evidence is the bedrock of any legal process, civil or criminal. Laws only operate when applied to a set of facts. As a result, hours, even days, of regular court hearings are devoted to determining what the facts are. It is only with facts established that legal argument has any currency. Evidentiary standards are another of law's safeguards against injustice. Their importance underpins legal systems. In England, in a criminal trial, the prosecution must bring evidence that establishes, beyond a reasonable doubt, a person's culpability. In Pakistan, technically, the standard is the same – although people are frequently sent to their death on far less. Under Sharia law, different standards attach to different crimes, with the most serious (or those with the most severe punishments) requiring the greatest standard of proof. For *hudud* crimes (those with Qur'anically prescribed, fixed penalties), for example, most schools of Sharia jurisprudence require the evidence of either four (independent, adult, male, Muslim) eyewitnesses or a confession (repeated four times by a sane, unpressured accused). Legal systems that allow for convictions and sentencing on the basis of scant evidence are usually symptomatic of dictatorships or deeply corrupt political administrations. High evidentiary requirements are an intrinsic part of the democratic ideal. So it is deeply concerning that America, home to one of the world's greatest democratic revolutions, abandoned laws of evidence in deciding to detain these men.

But in the cases of the detainees, lack of evidence was only a secondary problem. The fundamental injustice of the detainee review boards was not that they were unfair trials but that they weren't trials at all. They were exercises in calculating probability. Where a trial judges past actions, the review boards looked to the future. Little concerned with what the detainee had done, the boards aimed to assess what he was likely to do. And as proof of the past proved elusive and proof of the future impossible, the boards looked to the vagaries of likelihood and potentiality, to 'posed threats' and 'mitigated harms'. Detention for potential future criminality is wrong. But the lack of a trial was not only detrimental for the detainees. Without an open, locally informed and public trial process, the military hadn't a hope of ascertaining who these men even were, let alone what they were or were not capable of doing in the future.

When Sarah had first come across Karim Muhammad's case, in late 2010, it was far beyond the scope and capabilities of her limited legal practice. Its context – the imprisonment of alleged Islamist terrorists picked up by US soldiers on the Afghanistan–Pakistan border – combined the ambiguities of international law, the politics of US-run detention centres and the lives of forty men. If death-penalty cases were complicated, this looked unfathomable. But by the summer of 2012, the Bagram petition took Sarah to the Lahore High Court more often than all her death-penalty cases put together. Although it named a long list of prisoners, the petition was not a criminal trial – these men had had no trial, and for a very long time it didn't look like they were ever going to get one. The Bagram petition, instead, was a piece of civil litigation. Sarah was asking the court to review government action, a request that would come to raise the most fundamental, and ancient, of legal questions.

By the time the case reached Sarah's office, Reprieve and other international NGOs had already tried to run the Bagram petition as a 'habeas writ' in both American and English courts. In 1215, at Article 39, the Magna Carta enshrined the legal principle that *'No free man shall be seized or imprisoned, or stripped of his rights or possessions, or outlawed or exiled, or deprived of his standing in any other way, nor will we proceed with force against him, or send others to do so, except by the lawful judgment of his equals or by the law of the land.'* In order to give effect to this clause, English courts began to order officials to produce prisoners in their custody by granting writs of habeas corpus – which means, literally, 'you shall have the body'. One of the law's simplest and most powerful remedies, the habeas writ commands the court to review a person's detention: if the detention is unlawful, the person must be set free. The writs have been used to astonishing effect: in England, in 1772, a habeas writ ended slavery. Protecting individual liberty in a time of tyrannical rulers, habeas writs – established before torture was prohibited and war crimes conceived of – privileged the right to a fair trial as the earliest and most fundamental of human rights. The forty men that this particular habeas writ was drafted to help in 2010 were then being held in the detention facility in Parwan province – technically nameless, offi- cially referred to as DFIP, colloquially known as Bagram. Like Karim Muhammad, they had been captured in Pakistan and had been neither charged nor tried.

The British and American courts had considered the Bagram prisoners beyond their powers. As a general rule, courts are cautious. Constrained by a constitution, or constitutional guarantees, judges can only be concerned with legality and illegality. Politics and international rela- tions are not their business. This split had posed problems for the Bagram detainees. Memorandums of under- standing, not legal treaties, governed the relationships between the US, UK and Afghan governments. Military protocol, not laws, governed detention at Bagram. As prisoners of war, the Bagram detainees should, in many lawyers' opinions, have received the protection of the Geneva Conventions – four treaties drafted between 1864 and 1949, in response to the atrocities of late nineteenth and early twentieth century warfare, that police human- itarian safeguards in times of war. But President George W. Bush had, in 2004, construed anyone suspected of association with the Taliban or al-Qaeda as ineligible for these protections. Islamist terrorists were not, so far as the US government was concerned, prisoners of war. According to Bush's Attorney General, the Bagram detainees were '*an enemy that lies in the shadows, an enemy that doesn't sign treaties, they don't wear uniforms, an enemy that owes no allegiance to any country, they do not cherish life. An enemy that doesn't fight, attack or plan according to accepted laws of war, in particular Geneva Conventions*'. They were 'unlawful enemy combatants': beyond the ambit of humanitarian law. Initially successful habeas petitions in both the US and the UK courts floundered. The judges held that there was no habeas jurisdiction for Bagram detainees. With no law, there was no place for findings of legality or illegality. The detainees were untouchable.

With protections of international humanitarian law denied them, the only route open to the detainees was through domestic legal systems. It was possible that Pakistan's courts could order the government of Pakistan to request the return, or 'repatriation', of the detainees. And so the petition had come to Pakistan. On considering whether to take on the case, Sarah had reservations. Though she had leapt at capital cases about which she knew nothing, she felt ill-prepared to run litigation that challenged the government. In 2010, she had been practising in Lahore for barely two years and, having largely been educated abroad, still felt distinctly foreign. So she passed the petition to a senior, celebrated constitutional lawyer and began instead to help the Islamabad-based investigator who had been working on the case with Reprieve. Heavily pregnant, she commuted to Islamabad – closer to the rural, northern, borderland communities where most of these detained men came from – where she started to understand the details of the case.

Almost as soon as Sarah began her work, natural disaster struck. In July 2010, monsoon rain flooded the

Indus river basin. Eight to ten inches fell every twenty-four hours. At the height of the flooding, up to a fifth of Pakistan's land was under water. Pools several metres deep lay stagnant over once fertile farmland. Cholera broke out in many places, and there was widespread dysentery, malaria and skin disease. The floods caused more destruction than the Indian Ocean tsunami of 2004. By August, over six million people had been displaced from their homes, the relatives of the Bagram detainees amongst them. The addresses, community links and mobile numbers that Sarah had been given a month before became useless. Finding the families seemed impossible. All government and international attention was focused on the present disaster, which the UN estimated would cost $460 million to put right. The War on Terror was temporarily abandoned; Pakistan's troops were recalled from counter-insurgency operations in the tribal areas and put to work building flood barriers and ferrying food. A handful of nameless men in a foreign cell were no one's priority.

With Sarah unable to reach the detainees' families, the case was impossible. She had no contact with the men themselves: their communications were restricted to the American military and employees of the International Committee of the Red Cross, who monitored prison conditions and arranged as much contact with family members as was possible. As a lawyer's job is merely advisory and representative, this was a problem. Lawyers do not speak for themselves in court, they argue 'on instruction' from their clients; an advocate merely transforms their client's position into legal argument. Far from its court-drama Hollywood portrayal, the role of the advocate is modest, deferential, obedient. *Vakil*, the Urdu word for lawyer, literally translates as 'representative'. To exceed a client's instructions, in most countries, is to risk being forever barred from practice. At this stage, Sarah had no client, no instructions. As contacting the men was impossible, she had hoped that their families would put their name to the case. A mother would have been the perfect petitioner. But grouped with six million others in a displaced persons' refugee camp, the mothers were as good as lost. As it was, the court had no business allowing unconnected individuals, or an altruistic lawyer, to bring a case to court.

Sarah is not naturally deferential, nor is she patient. As soon as she had handed the case over to the senior lawyer, she regretted it. He wasn't running it as she would have done, nor was he willing to follow her suggestions – barely qualified lawyers rarely tell well-established senior lawyers what to do. The flood-induced delays and her impending maternity leave added to her irritation. So she filed the case herself, with her fellow investigator acting as petitioner. Nasar got it through the objections room. It was listed with the Lahore High Court. And within days of her return from maternity leave in early 2011, with a two-week-old baby at home, the senior lawyer had resigned and Sarah took on the case.

As we sat waiting to be heard, I saw that the court functioned like a doctor's waiting room. The sole, chest-height lectern that stood in front of the judge was something of a public consultation area. At five to nine, having disposed of disputes between a pair of feuding neighbours and between an angry landlord and a vulnerable tenant, the judge barked at Sarah. Sarah dashed to the lectern. Her messy folder of notes flopped lopsidedly and she could barely see over the top, despite wearing heels. Apart from Sarah, Maryam and me, there was just one other woman in the court, a quiet commercial lawyer in a white headscarf who had not said a word while her male colleague had addressed the judge. As Sarah – in her sharp suit and cropped hair – began to address the judge, the room of lethargic lawyers woke up.

The week before the hearing had been hectic. For months, the petition had been adjourned, the file tossed by judges back into the mildewy cupboard behind Nasar's friend's desk in the Lahore High Court filing rooms. Unaccustomed to being ignored, Sarah had decided to make an attention-seeking application. These men had been picked up from Pakistan's remote, near-lawless western border. They were in an American military detention facility because they were allegedly associated with terrorism. Sarah suspected the military Inter-Services Intelligence (Pakistan's notorious ISI) of working with the CIA in facilitating these detentions; the two agencies had been strategic allies since Pakistan's founding. And so, from the café of an upmarket hotel – Lahore's only boutique guest house, with constant electricity, Wi-Fi and supplies of club sandwiches – we had worked late into the night for the previous five days, preparing a petition that blamed the ISI. This was an incendiary move. Intelligence agencies never like being called into court. And the ISI, who enjoy vast discretionary powers and are accused by many of responsibility for Pakistan's several hundred 'disappeared' persons, are particularly hostile to scrutiny. An encounter with the ISI is generally something best avoided. Sarah knew that most judges would be unwilling to send the spies a summons – which was precisely why she was making the application. In her opinion, the judge then assigned to the case was hostile to her petition; she wanted him to transfer the case to another courtroom, and hoped that this mention of the ISI would prompt him to do so.

In judicial decision-making, reasoned judgments are arrived at through a process of interpretation and application of either statute or, in common law countries, case law. The idea of the 'rule of law' – overused as the phrase has become – is the foundation of such a system, one that protects against arbitrary decision-making. The 'rule of law' concept was first articulated by Aristotle to guarantee a formal system of government, one where rules are known in advance and binding on all. The rule of law, for Aristotle, was far superior to the rule of men: laws guarded against bestial, whimsical judgment. Much debated since the fourth century BC, the phrase 'rule of law' has been defined variously by philosophers, development agencies and law professors. Most agree, however, that the rule of law at least guarantees the system of legal authority, of regulated decision-making, that Sarah sought to rely on. And to me, the rule of law goes little further than this: it demands that decisions are justified, but it cannot guarantee that they will be just. So where a legal system's aspiration may be 'justice', its operation depends instead on procedural guarantees, upon genealogies – be they from statute or case law – of authority, or justification. Laws are not morals but procedures, formulas that await facts. As a result, many hold that judges do not decide what is 'right', only what is 'correct'. And to reach a 'correct' decision, judges rely on precedent. Sarah's petition, although not made with much sincerity, depended on a 1970s judgment from the UK House of Lords, which the Lahore High Court could plausibly use as precedent in impleading the ISI.

Standing in front of the judge with an obsessively highlighted copy of the case, Sarah argued that the judgment allowed the court to make demands of the Pakistani intelligence services. But in order to consider Sarah's argument, the judge would first need to be persuaded that the case she presented to him was applicable, and that decision depended on interpretation of Pakistan's relatively complicated system of legal precedent. In common-law countries – such as Pakistan, Britain and America – legal authority, known as precedent, is drawn from older decisions of senior courts. Daily negotiations should be governed by rules *'easily learned and easily retained'*, wrote the English judge Lord Mansfield – one of Britain's most celebrated jurists, who practised law in the eighteenth century and is heralded as both the father of modern commercial law and the man who ended slavery. And rules, Lord Mansfield thought, could not be easily learned and easily retained when derived from abstract, academic 'niceties', but were instead most effective when drawn from the 'truth' of individual actual cases. The common law, for Lord Mansfield, was merely a codified, authoritative source of common sense. And it was to this reservoir of common sense that Sarah turned when facing the judge. Pakistan's judges, like those in England, are bound by the previous decisions of their senior courts. But the judge Sarah stood before also had to take into account, in this order of precedence: Indian pre-Partition judgments, Indian post-Partition judgments, UK judgments and US judgments. Sarah's invocation of the UK House of Lords should have carried some weight.

But the judge dismissed her. As far as he was concerned, Sarah's application was inadmissible. He refused it, chastised her for pleading inappropriately and excused himself from the case.

After Sarah's abortive application on that Friday morning, the case was transferred to Justice Khalid Mehmood Khan, a corporate finance and banking expert who had recently been appointed to the High Court bench. As with the judge before him, Justice Khan repeatedly adjourned the petition. He wanted nothing to do with this controversial case and its prima donna advocate.

Once again, as so often in her short legal career, Sarah felt defeated. And so, as she had before, she turned to her family's address book. Her father, a wealthy and influential businessman who had for decades dominated Lahore's textile exports and worked closely with Nawaz Sharif's first government, was a well-connected man. At one of his parties – well-known events in Lahore's busy social calendar – Sarah met a senior commercial lawyer. He had been appearing in front of Justice Khan for several years and had a novelist's appreciation of the judge's character. 'Don't discuss the law with him,' the advocate advised. 'Summarise your case, as though making an elevator pitch. If he's excited and engaged, he'll start to give the directions you want.' So overburdened is the High Court judiciary – many judges hear close to a hundred applications a day and are well aware of the miles of pending files awaiting them – that if a case appears difficult, sensitive and time-consuming, they simply don't have the resources to dispose of it. Rather than dragging every case file into the courtroom and presenting a complex legal argument, one should, the advocate advised, carve up the petition: set the scene in a scintillating sixty seconds and then present the judge with manageable, discrete questions that can be dealt with in five-minute hearings.

Sarah decided to go back to court. But this time she wanted publicity, and so she persuaded camera crews and reporters to cover her case. Winning over the court of public opinion, she had been advised by Reprieve, was far more important than winning a case in a court of law. Public interest would pique the judge's interest and at least make him appreciate the petition's global significance. But creating a press furore over a case is controversial, frowned upon by bar councils and regulators in most legal systems as it risks perverting the legal process. In some cases, such behaviour will attract a charge of contempt of court, punishable with a prison sentence. In others, particularly where a jury is sitting, it may result in a retrial, and be deemed an abuse of the court process. Sarah's behaviour did not go without comment in Pakistan. She was seen as glory-seeking. Courts and colleagues alike threatened a charge of contempt of court. But nothing was filed against her, and she remained confident in her tactics: public, extra-legal pressure on courtrooms has helped overturn ingrained injustices from apartheid rule in South Africa to racial sentencing in America's southern states. And in any event, judges are trained to immunise themselves from such pressures. With no juries (trial by jury was removed from the penal code in the early 1960s), Pakistan's professional tribunals should be less vulnerable to media influence. Either way, Sarah cared little for procedural propriety.

The following week was packed with TV interviews, opinion pieces and reportage in both the international and domestic press – *Dawn*, the *Friday Times*, the *Nation*, the *Express Tribune*, the *Washington Post*, the *Independent*. Within a few days, everyone who read a newspaper in Lahore had heard of the Bagram petition and was following its progress through the Lahore High Court. Sarah, meanwhile, had perfected her sixty-second pitch for Justice Khan. It ran like this: 'Sir, we've filed this petition on behalf of an as yet unknown number of Pakistani citizens currently detained in Afghanistan. The only people who can visit them are officials of the governments of America and Pakistan and the American army. All we ask is that the government of Pakistan visit these men and identify them.' And it fell on sympathetic ears. Justice Khalid Mehmood Khan, a genial soul with an unkempt moustache and wavy salt-and-pepper hair, turned to the government advocate and asked accusingly: 'What's going on, have you forgotten about these men?'

That Sarah was arguing a case such as this in the Lahore High Court said a lot about the courage of the upper reaches of Pakistan's judiciary. Since the Lawyers' Movement and its successful opposition to the Pakistani government, the country's senior judges had been more assertive in openly opposing government policy. So while the lower courts remained vulnerable to corruption, fear and organisational chaos, at the pinnacle of Pakistan's justice system the Supreme Court was often a bastion of rights protection. It rivalled America's in terms of constitutional clout. And this courage and independence at the top had a knock-on effect, emboldening the courts below. High Court judges like Justice Khalid Mehmood Khan felt able to give orders against the government. This in turn allowed lawyers like Sarah to challenge Pakistan's international relations and foreign policy from a small, crowded courtroom in the Lahore High Court. She was asking the court to review the detention of Pakistani citizens in Bagram, and thereby to interrogate Pakistan's Ministry for Foreign Affairs about its arrangements with the US government. Pakistan's courts, therefore, allowed Sarah to bring a petition that Britain's and America's courts had refused to hear. It was Pakistan's legal system that championed fundamental rights where two great Western democracies had denied them.

The arguments Sarah put before the court went to the heart of government, democracy and the rule of law. Simply put, parliamentary democracies place an elected parliament (the legislature) at the centre of the state. The leader of the largest party in parliament usually becomes the prime minister, and the prime minister forms a government (the executive). Pakistan, now a parliamentary republic, also has an elected head of state, the president, who serves for a limited term alongside the head of government. But the president's role, something like Britain's monarch, is largely ceremonial. The third branch of government, the judiciary, is unelected. Where the legislature writes the law and the executive enforces the law, the judiciary interprets and applies the law. As such, political power is said to be shared between these three branches. Each checks the power of the other under what Montesquieu eloquently articulated, in his 1748 *Spirit of the Laws*, as 'the Separation of Powers'. The system aims to promote a rational, impartial rule of law over the arbitrary, tyrannical rule of men.

The Bagram petition tested these elegant distinctions. Like America's, Pakistan's constitution empowers the courts to strike out any law inconsistent with a number of fundamental rights. (Britain's Supreme Court can only declare a law 'incompatible' with fundamental rights; it is able to recommend legislative change but not implement it.) Pakistan's senior courts can also order individual government officials to enforce these rights – which include the right to life, safeguards as to arrest and detention, protection against retrospective punishment, prohibition of torture, right to privacy, freedom of speech, freedom of religion. Applying the law, therefore, Justice Khalid Mehmood Khan was able, even required, to hold the government to account regarding the unlawful detention and possible torture of the imprisoned men. In their defence, the government argued that the case involved issues of national security and as such couldn't be reviewed by the courts. Given the sensitivity of the information, ran their argument, it was proper to have elected representatives, rather than unelected judges, decide a course of action. This situation, they claimed, was properly the province of the executive, not the judiciary. It was, after all, the very basis of a nation's social contract that citizens sacrificed a certain degree of liberty for the sake of collective security.

This is a well-rehearsed argument. In Britain, for example, where a case raises issues of national security, the government can refuse to disclose certain information. There are procedures that allow for material to be immune from public exposure and for hearings to be conducted almost entirely in the ignorance of the injured party, on which only security-cleared barristers can act. The provisions were formulated on the presumption that secrecy is sometimes necessary – for example, in cases involving international terrorism, where exposure would make vulnerable the state, the public and/or the intelligence services – but working out exactly when and to what degree secrecy is necessary is an inherently imprecise exercise. And because mistakes are made at a high cost, there is always a risk that courts will tread too carefully, sacrificing important individual liberties in order to give the government the benefit of the doubt (as the US courts and government lawyers had arguably done in denying the Bagram detainees the protections of the Geneva Conventions). National security cases mark the fraught overlap between executive and judiciary, where each attempts to resist the limitations placed on it by the other.

Such a constitutional context made the judgments that Justice Khalid Mehmood Khan gave from 2011 to 2014 even more remarkable. Taking seriously the court's constitutional powers, he ordered the government of Pakistan to take steps toward the repatriation of the detainees. And one by one, the government had these men brought home.

★　　★　　★

After her first hearing with him, Sarah appeared in front of Justice Khalid Mehmood Khan once a fortnight. In 2013, the detainee review boards concluded that, for Karim Muhammad and all the Pakistani detainees Sarah represented (by that point there were nearly twenty more joined to the petition), continued internment at Bagram was unnecessary. The board recommended that the detainees be transferred to Pakistan for either criminal prosecution, participation in a reconciliation programme or release, depending on the individual detainee. But US policy required that the detainees be sent to Pakistan only after the government of Pakistan had confirmed their nationality and assured the US government that they would not engage in terrorism or be tortured on their return. Repatriation was, therefore, subject to diplomatic negotiations. It was Justice Khan who put pressure on the government of Pakistan to participate in those negotiations, and who required the Ministry of Interior and Foreign Affairs to fortnightly report their progress to the High Court.

The governments of Pakistan and the US have a long, fraught relationship. Pakistan first asked the US for money ($2 billion) mere months after it was founded, in October 1947. Military and economic aid was sent in 1954, and since then, billions of dollars have moved from the US government to Pakistan. From that first bank transfer to today, this funding, and friendship, has been a source of political intrigue and popular anger throughout Pakistan. In a series of fictional letters written in the early 1950s – sent to 'Uncle Sam' from his Pakistani nephew – Sadaat Hasan Manto, Pakistan's first and foremost short-story writer, warned his nascent homeland against welcoming US money and influence. The stories proved prescient. The US–Pakistan alliance had been fragile ever since then, and under US patronage, Pakistan's army gained powers far beyond those constitutionally its due. But since 2000, events such as 9/11, the case of Raymond Davis (a CIA contractor charged with the murder of two men in Lahore in early 2011), and Osama Bin Laden's capture have weakened the alliance still further. It may be that this fraught relationship motivated some of Sarah's detainees to take up arms in Afghanistan. And it may be that it motivated the US to undertake preventative detention and drone strikes. It may also have preyed on Justice Khalid Mehmood Khan's mind every second Friday morning as he addressed various officials and government counsel in his congested civil courtroom.

Officials from the Ministry of Foreign Affairs were summoned to court one after the other. They were told that it was a national embarrassment for Pakistan to leave its citizens at the mercy of the US army. That it was shameful to see how quickly the US government had sprung to the defence of its citizen Raymond Davis compared to the years it had taken the government of Pakistan to aid its own illegally detained citizens. The Pakistani government, said Justice Khan, was apathetic and irresponsible. It was acting unconstitutionally. It was deliberately compromising its own sovereignty. He ordered the Ministry of Foreign Affairs to write letters to the government of the US requesting details of the detainees and the charges against them. He ordered Pakistani officials to make trips to Bagram. And he required them to file evidence of these efforts in court. If the government failed to comply with these orders, it was within Justice Khan's powers to enforce compliance through detaining individual officials in jail, requiring the government to pay a fine, or authorising other punitive action as he saw fit. The exact degree to which Justice Khan's orders effected the return of the detainees may be contested, but the fact remains that by September 2014, a little over four years after the litigation was first contemplated, thirty-nine of the Pakistani detainees at Bagram were returned to Pakistan.

The Bagram petition was the inverse of Sarah's death-penalty cases. As a general rule, crimes and their punishments are particular to places. Sovereign parliaments decide which acts to criminalise and what sentence to award. And people can be punished for breaking these laws (so say social-contract theorists) because we have authorised the state to restrict our absolute freedom in exchange for its promise to protect our collective security. We have chosen to enforce a set of rules by which we will live peacefully together. But these laws are usually limited by geography and nationality. If a French person steals something in Japan, for example, they cannot be prosecuted for that offence by a UK court. Laws ought also to be insulated from politics: enforcement of the law is meant to be a purely legal exercise, not a political act. The arguments in Sarah's death-penalty cases were straightforward: they concerned law and evidence. But the Bagram case turned this understanding of law and government on its head. The detainees were held abroad, beyond the reach of the Pakistani police, in a context of international intrigue and war. They were suspended above or across legal systems. They had been moved into an international sphere, one dictated more by politics than law.

To many law students and practising lawyers, international law is seen as interesting, dramatic, important, sexy. As a student at Harvard, I saw that the law school's most famous professors, with the most oversubscribed classes, were the international lawyers. You could subscribe to their courses on YouTube. But as far back as the eighteenth century, philosophers have spotted the dangers of international law. Immanuel Kant, a thinker who demonstrated extreme hostility towards international lawyers, was convinced that they were mere apologists for power – *'the only conceivable meaning of [international law]'*, Kant wrote in 1795 in an essay on perpetual peace, *'might be that it serves men right who are so inclined that they should destroy each other and thus find perpetual peace in the vast grave that swallows both the atrocities and their perpetrators'*. My experience of the Bagram petition seemed to illustrate Kant's concerns. International laws of war, which are drafted broadly, depend largely for their enforcement on the political will of states. In the case of these Bagram detainees, labelled as unlawful enemy combatants and thereby denied the protection of international humanitarian law, international law had been used to ratify executive action rather than guarantee fundamental rights.

The failure of these international laws to protect men like Karim Muhammad revealed a great deal about the nature of law. Many argue that the most effective laws are those collectively authored by the people they govern, those that are therefore particular to places. In the late eighteenth century, Montesquieu observed that *'laws should be adapted in such a manner to the people for whom they are framed that it would be merely lucky if those of one nation suit another'*. He was clear that laws should be drafted *'in relation to the climate of each country, to the quality of its soils, to its situation and extent, to the principal occupation of the natives, whether husbandmen, huntsmen or shepherds: they should have relation to the degree of liberty which the constitution will bear; to the religion of the inhabitants, to their inclinations, riches, numbers, commerce, manners, and customs'*. In other words, international rules are at best worthless, at worst dangerous. To my mind, international law is at least risky. Laws phrased generally, for all times, all peoples and all places, can end up powerless to prevent the unjust imprisonment of the very people they were drafted to protect.

There is a coda to Karim Muhammad's story. While Sarah congratulated her staff on their success, Karim Muhammad was much more unhappy in a Pakistani prison than he had been in Bagram. He had ended up in Sahiwal, the same prison as Sohail. But where Sohail had found a certain solace and solidarity among the prison community, Karim Muhammad felt that Sahiwal was a hostile, lonely place. In the years since Sohail had left, Sahiwal had undergone significant alteration. Whilst Karim Muhammad was in Bagram, the Taliban had stormed two large prisons in north-west Pakistan, freeing well over 500 prisoners. As a result, the Pakistani government had decided to upgrade several prisons to high-security status. Sahiwal was one of the first to be transformed. In May 2014, as one of Sahiwal's newest high-security prisoners, Karim Muhammad was kept in solitary confinement and closely monitored. He railed against his new conditions – the bad food, high temperatures and rough-handed guards – and his mental health deteriorated. He would throw food, rend his clothes and smash the light bulb, fan and furniture in his cell. He often asked to be taken back to Bagram.

Finally, after a month in Sahiwal, during which time the investigations team failed to find any evidence linking Karim Muhammad to the Taliban, al-Qaeda or any other terrorist organisation, he was released. By this time, he had spent over four years in prison, often in solitary confinement, without trial. On his return home, his wife found him a different man – angry, distant, prone to nightmares and mood swings, difficult to talk to.

When I, as a young lawyer, had first come to learn about Karim Muhammad and the other Bagram detainees, it was the lack of legality, the denial of due process and the blatant flouting of a foundational legal principle that had troubled me. But after meeting returned detainees, I realised that the wrongs were at once more basic and profound. Karim Muhammad didn't care that the detainee review board hearings were not, technically, a trial. Nor did he care, or even know, about the impact on his life of a habeas petition argued over 7,000 miles away in an American courtroom. The real injustice to Karim Muhammad was not that American military officials hadn't charged him with a crime but that they had taken four years of his life, returning him to Pakistan a broken man, forever divided from his family.

Epilogue

This book was born of frustration. In August 2013, the government of Pakistan refused to renew my visa. Soon afterwards, ISI agents entered our office in Lahore and asked Sarah's staff for details of my work. It would be a long time before I was allowed back. I was never told why. An exile in London, anxious and listless, I found some solace in writing. I had long been nagged by questions about Pakistan, Sarah's work and the law in practice, and felt a need to unpick some of these tangled thoughts. Writing also made me feel, in some small way, that I could still be of use. I thought there might be value in documenting the lives of these men, abandoned and forgotten on death row; that there might be value in telling the story of this team, who worked indefatigably on cases that were unlikely ever to be resolved.

But as I came to finish the book, in the spring of 2015, the context radically changed. On 16 December 2014, seven Taliban militants attacked Peshawar's Army Public School, killing 132 children, along with nine of the school's staff. The tragedy left Pakistan reeling. Shops shut, cinemas closed. Crowds of candles lit the country as a wave of vigils were held. In the face of desperate national mourning, the government took steps to avenge these deaths publicly. The day after the school attack, Prime Minister Nawaz Sharif ended the Moratorium on the death penalty in cases of terror. (At the time, there were roughly 800 people on death row for terrorism-related offences, and a further 17,000 being prosecuted.) Executions began within two days. Then, in March 2015, the government announced that all prisoners on death row whose sentence had been finally determined would be executed, regardless of the crime they were convicted of. Executions began to be carried out at a rate of one a day. Before dawn on 6 May 2015, Zulfikar Ali Khan – Sarah's first client and the man who had kicked off her career with a letter to a newspaper – was hanged.

It is impossible to prepare for the feeling of having a client executed. Until the last moment, Sarah's office shut the thought out by focusing on every conceivable route to a stay of execution. But when Zulfikar Ali Khan was given his final date, Sarah knew there was nothing more she could do. The only hope lay with Arthur Wilson. As we lawyers held our breath, Arthur hurried to Islamabad, desperately trying to appease the complainant. But on the eve of the execution, as I was finishing my supper in London, he called me and asked me simply to pray.

Capital defence lawyers in the US usually remember with poignancy their first experience of an execution. In Texas, for example, inmates are killed with relative regularity and this is a formative part of death-penalty practice. But in Pakistan, Sarah had been practising as a death-penalty defence lawyer for six years before she endured her first execution. Working during a moratorium (that many hoped would never be lifted), her team toiled to save clients from lifetimes lost in prison, with the gallows remaining merely a remote possibility. So when Zulfikar Ali Khan was hanged, it hit horribly hard. There was all the incomprehension and sadness of death, coloured by a desperate feeling of failure and responsibility. And overwhelmingly, there was the shock – particularly awful after having worked with Sarah, for whom there was always something else to file, someone else to approach, some new tactic to try – of cold, unarguable finality.

When the government restarted executions, Sarah was not surprised. In 2013, shortly after coming to power, and over a year before the Peshawar attack, Nawaz Sharif's government had attempted to lift the Moratorium. They had been halted by opposition from both the Taliban, who threatened to target government ministers if militants were hanged, and international rights groups. But since that failed attempt, Sarah, and many others, had suspected that the government would renew its efforts to bring back executions. The Peshawar attack provided just the excuse it needed. It was not hard to pick holes in the government's reasoning: it made little sense to suggest that men willing to strap themselves with explosives and undertake suicide missions would be cowed by the prospect of execution. Moreover, given the breadth of Pakistan's definition of terrorism (Zulfikar Ali Khan was tried as a terrorist, remember), many petty criminals would be hanged as dangerous militants.

As the lifting of the Moratorium became a matter of international scrutiny, Sarah offered a key voice of opposition. She gave long interviews on Pakistan's most popular TV talk shows – Geo TV's *Capital Talk*, Capital TV's *Bay Laag*. Broadsheets across the world – from the *New York Times* to the *Guardian* – wanted her opinion on government policy and prisoners' rights. Alongside this media coverage, she was giving increasing numbers of lectures on the death penalty at conferences and workshops sponsored by international donors like Open Society and Reprieve. Harvard University sent law students to her for summer placements.

All this attention nettled her detractors in Pakistan. Sarah was painted as the plaything of foreigners – she was, some claimed, paid by Britain and America to undermine Pakistan's justice system. Prominent newspaper columnists demanded that she be imprisoned for contempt of court. Other human rights organisations began to denounce her. Sarah Belal was *'self-aggrandising'*, *'social media hungry'*, *'reckless'*, *'Bolshevik'*. As the atmosphere became increasingly febrile, she decided to disband the office – it was safer for her staff to work from home. Back at her kitchen table, where she had started out all those years before, she hurled herself into work, fighting frantically for stays as clients were given twenty-four hours' warning of their execution. And then, in May 2015, she received a phone call from a friend who happened to work at the Ministry of Interior. He told her to leave the country immediately.

'I was lucky it was the government that wanted rid of me,' Sarah said jokingly. 'If it had been the military, I'd be dead now.'

It was late May 2015. Sarah and I were sitting in the one-bedroom flat she had rented above the Troubadour Café in London's Earls Court. She had just put her five-year-old daughter to bed and was now curled up in a window seat, chain-smoking, with a glass of white wine by her feet. She looked exhausted. Dressed in a bulky pink fleece and baggy jeans, she was unrecognisable as the haughty trouser-suited lawyer of Lahore. I sat amid a debris of coloured paper aeroplanes that her daughter had been making all afternoon. On the street below, men carrying guitars and amps filed into the restaurant.

It had been three weeks since Zulfikar Ali Khan's execution. Flicking ash out of the window, which scattered in the breeze like confetti, Sarah told me of the personal strain. Over the last few months, she had become short-tempered and emotional. She had continually fought with those close to her. She felt increasingly alienated from her family. In Lahore, she had had more work than she knew what to do with, and not a moment's respite from the thudding pressure of fast-approaching execution dates. There had been little time to think. Now, in London, spending long, empty days entertaining a five-year-old, she felt miserable and guilty. Ultimately, she told me, she was responsible for Zulfikar Ali Khan's death. Besides this, she felt anxious for her staff. The government was likely to revoke her NGO licence, without which she wouldn't be able to withdraw the funds she needed to pay their salaries. And then there was Aftab Masih – the Christian plumber convicted of murder – who had just been given an execution date for the following week.

Work weighed heavily on her, and it was fraught with life-and-death decisions. What effect would media attention have on this judge? Would exoneration in one case make exoneration in another more or less likely? Should she spend the little time she had before the execution trying to appease the complainant or persuade the court? A terrible responsibility enfolded her. So many in Pakistan were against her. Imagining Aftab Masih in his cell or Zulfikar Ali Khan walking to the gallows, she wept. But she didn't weep for herself. Before dawn on 10 June 2015, Aftab Masih was hanged. The next week, Sarah got on a plane back to Lahore.

Acknowledgements

These are true stories. Those characters who are able to have given me their full support and approval for publication. For that I owe them a great debt. Others, through either death or imprisonment, have been unable to read their stories. Those who remain in prison I have fully disguised, or limited any description to information in the public domain. I have also anonymised or disguised several characters for reasons of legal or political sensitivity. The chapter notes make clear which characters I have disguised.

My greatest thanks to Sarah Belal, Sohail Emmanuel, Nasar Hussein and Arthur Wilson. I've learnt so much from my time with you all.

This book couldn't have been written without the support of Reprieve, in particular Clive Stafford Smith and Maya Foa, and all the staff, past and present, at Justice Project Pakistan.

Hassam Qadir Shah, who passed away as I began to write this book, taught me a great deal of Pakistan's criminal legal procedure. For helping me work through the history of Pakistan's blasphemy laws and other aspects of Sharia, I'm indebted to Intisar Rabb. Naveed ur-Rehman taught me all I know of Urdu. Maryam, Rubina, Sahar, Amber and Imtiaz were a second family for me in Lahore. For their help with this project during my time in Pakistan I am grateful to Belal Ahmad, Mansoor Ali Shah, Sameena Belal, Omran Belhadi, Cortney Busch, Lizzie Dorrell, Nawaz Hanif, Sundas Hoorain, Abid Hussain, Toby Landau, Daniel Morgan, Reza Munir, Sultana Noon, John Seward, Hannah Sladen, Liana Wood.

Sadakat Kadri was an invaluable reader early on. Fred Wilmot-Smith provided conceptual clarity and exceptionally helpful comments at a crucial moment. Charlie Wide applied his formidable legal mind to the text in its final stages. Other readers to whom I am very grateful are Adam Begley, Lily le Brun, Ursula Buchan, Edward Charlton-Jones, Emilios Christodoulidis, Tilly Culme-Seymour, Charlie Gammell, Grace Jackson, May Jeong, Scott Liddle, Nick McDonell, Samuel Moyn, Francesca Recchia, Julia Salasky, Xa Shaw-Stewart, Bruce Wannell, Felix Wardle.

My agent, David Godwin, took a punt on an unknown author for which I am very grateful. He has been a wonderful friend and ally since. Chiki Sarkar was an important early backer. My editor, Dan Franklin, has been endlessly patient and a great source of support and insight throughout. And my paperback editor, Beth Coates, has been kind, eagle-eyed and an invaluable teacher of the finer points of punctuation. I'd also like to thank Kirsty McLachlan and everyone at David Godwin Associates and Clare Bullock and all at Jonathan Cape and Vintage who worked on this book.

For their teaching and guidance I am grateful to Daniel Alexander, Lindsay Farmer, Judith McClure, Robert Reed, Emma Rothschild, Johan Van der Walt.

For their love, friendship, or help along the way, my thanks to Charlotte Barker, Susanna Berger, Ann, Hugh, Lily, Christian and Fiona Buchanan, Mark Callcutt, David Buxton, Alex Cole, Fred Darbyshire, Arthur Fournier, William Goldsmith, Tess Gammell, Fabienne Hess, Zara Idelson, Pamela Idelson-Smith, Thierry Kelaart, Fran

Lindesay-Bethune, Mike Lesslie, Jamie Martin, Mark Muller, Paul Myerscough, Hussein Omar, Frances Osborne, Katie Parry, Jack Ream, Daniel Rothschild, Charley Samler, Bella Scott, Charlie Shackleton, Amia Srinavasan, Shoshana Stewart, Rory Stewart, James Strathallan, Anna Della Subin, Nina Subin, Emily Thomas, Miranda Thomas, Mirra Vane, Lucas Wittmann, Kate Womersley, Natalie Woolman.

Finally, my deepest love and thanks to Tommy, obv.

Notes

Prologue

Apart from the details set out below, this prologue is based on my own experience and on the court documents (all public records) available in Naveed Hussein's case. Naveed Hussein is not his real name.

p.3 'single theatre': see G. Packer, 'The Last Mission', *The New Yorker*, 28 September 2009, http://www.newyorker.com/magazine/2009/09/28/the-last-mission.

p.3 'We must recognise that the heart of the threat to [the West] comes from the people in western Pakistan': see G. P. Schmitz, 'Holbrooke on Afghanistan: The New American Determination', *Der Spiegel*, 23 March 2009.

p.5 13,223 people had been sentenced to death in the decade before I began university: Interior Minister Chaudhry Nisar Ali Khan, speech to Senate, 30 October 2013, cited in 'No plans to convert death sentences to life imprisonment: Nisar', *The Express Tribune*, 30 October 2013, http://tribune.com.pk/story/624710/no-plans-to-convert-death-sentences-to-life-imprisonment-nisar/.

p.5 at least 8,000 people detained on death row: see Cornell University Law School Death Penalty Worldwide report for 2011: http://www.deathpenaltyworldwide. org/country-search-post.cfm?country=Pakistan.

p.5 making Pakistan's death-row population one of the world's largest: China's death row is thought to be more densely populated, but Amnesty International, one of the most reliable sources of death penalty statistics, stopped publishing figures relating to China in 2009 (as any numbers were impossible to verify), and as a result, the population of China's death row is unknown. See http://www. amnesty.org.uk/world-executions-death-sentences-2014. See also *Death Sentences and Executions: 2014*, report by Amnesty International Ltd (2015), https://www.amnesty. org.uk/sites/default/files/death_sentences_and_executions_2014_en.pdf; N. Ansari, 'Amnesty International's death penalty report: Pakistan execution pause termed a success story', *The Express Tribune*, 27 March 2014, http://tribune.com.pk/story/687817/amnesty-internationals-death-penalty-report-pakistan-execution-pause-termed-a-success-story/; *Death Sentences and Executions: 2013*, report by Amnesty International Ltd (2014), https://www.amnesty.org.uk/sites/default/files/amnesty_death_penalty_report_2014_final.pdf.

p.5 Pakistan's former Minister for Human Rights estimated that roughly two-thirds of those 8,000 people were innocent: see comments of Ansar Burney (former Federal Minister for Human Rights): Ansar Burney Trust, http://ansarburney.org/death-row-in-pakistan/.

p.6 today almost a quarter of Birmingham's population is of Asian ethnicity (with over half of Birmingham's Asian population of Pakistani ethnicity): see 'Key Statistics' for Birmingham 2011 census at http://www. birmingham.gov.uk/.

p.9 Over £1.2 billion is still sent in remittances annually from the UK to Pakistan, over three times the amount Pakistan receives each year in aid payments from the UK government: for the amount of remittances sent from the UK to Pakistan annually, see figures from Oxford University's 'The Migration Observatory' (which relies on World Bank estimates), http://migrationobservatory.ox.ac.uk/briefings/migrant-remittances-and-uk. For the amount sent by the UK government in aid to Pakistan, see http://www.bbc.co.uk/news/uk-politics-27208964/. In 2010–11, the UK sent around £215m in aid to Pakistan; this increased to around £405m in 2014–15. See also DfID Operational Plan 2011–2015, https://www.gov.uk/government/uploads/system/uploads/attachment_data/file/67373/pakistan-2011.pdf.

p.9 This movement of money is part of a larger global flow: expatriate Pakistanis around the world send over $13 billion to Pakistan annually: research conducted by the Pew Research Centre in 2012 estimated that $14,100,000,000 of remittances are sent to Pakistan annually: see http://www.pewsocialtrends.org/2014/02/20/remittance-map/.

p.9 women, children, the elderly and the infirm have been killed in US drone strikes: see Bureau of Investigative Journalism 'Naming the Dead' project, which documents those individuals lost to CIA drone strikes and identifies them as 'civilian' or 'alleged militant', 'male', 'female' or 'child', https://www.thebureauinvestigates.com/namingthedead/the-dead/?lang=en. See also S. Bashir and R. Crews (eds), *Under the Drones* (London: C. Hurst & Co., 2012).

Chapter 1

Except as set out below, this chapter is based on my oral and written interviews with Sarah Belal and Maryam, and conversations I've had with Sarah, Maryam and their friends, families and colleagues in Lahore since 2010.

p.17 these lawyers joined one of London's four Inns of Court: it wasn't until 1850 that lectureships and examinations were required at the Inns of Court. Before then, the law colleges in India offered a more 'rigorous and systematic' legal education than those in England. See S. Kugle, 'Framed, Blamed and Renamed: the Recasting of Islamic Jurisprudence in Colonial South Asia', *Modern Asian Studies*, Vol. 35, issue 2, April 2001, p.276.

p.17 At Oxford, Sarah studied only English law, and for only two years, not five: she studied law as a graduate student (a BA in Jurisprudence with Senior Status), and was therefore able to complete the LLB in two years rather than three.

p.18 Pakistan was created as a homeland for India's Muslims: although this is not the place for a comprehensive literature review, the books I've found most informative on this topic are: F. Devji, *Muslim Zion* (London: C. Hurst & Co., 2013); A. Jalal, *The Sole Spokesman* (Cambridge University Press, 1994); I. Talbot, *Pakistan: A Modern History* (New York: Palgrave Macmillan, 2005); A. Jalal, *The Struggle for Pakistan* (Cambridge, MA; London: The Belknap Press of Harvard University Press, 2014); A. Jalal, *The Pity of Partition: Manto's Life, Times, and Work across the India–Pakistan Divide* (Princeton; Oxford: Princeton University Press, 2013).

p.18 The name 'Pakistan': in 1933, Choudhry Rahmat Ali, a Punjabi Muslim nationalist who was then a student at Cambridge University, first coined 'PAKSTAN' as the name of the soon-to-be-created country, publishing the acronym in a political pamphlet. See Jalal, *The Struggle for Pakistan*, op. cit., pp.14–15.

p.20 In late 2007, only six months after beginning her abortive career, Sarah, along with many other lawyers in Pakistan, stopped work: in early 2007, Chief Justice Iftikhar Chaudhry attempted to limit President Musharraf's power. Musharraf subsequently dismissed the Chief Justice, which resulted in a mass protest movement across the country. For a discussion of the significance and legacy of the 'Lawyers' Movement', see A. Lieven, *Pakistan: A Hard Country* (London: Allen Lane, 2011), pp.113–18.

p.20 The police tear-gassed protesters and made arrests by the hundred: see 'Lawyers protest against Musharraf', BBC News, 12 March 2007, http://news.bbc.co.uk/1/hi/world/south_asia/6441133.stm; D. Walsh, 'Pakistan lawyers clash with police over judge's sacking', *The Guardian*, 12 March 2007, http://www.theguardian.com/world/2007/mar/12/pakistan.declanwalsh; 'Pakistan police attack protesters', BBC News, 5 November 2007, http://news.bbc.co.uk/1/hi/world/south_asia/7078364.stm; A. Stratton, 'Pakistani police tear-gas protesting lawyers', *The Guardian*, 3 March 2008, http://www.theguardian.com/world/2008/mar/03/pakistan.

p.21 Once referred to, during the Raj, as 'Sharks' Lane': H. R. Goulding, *Old Lahore: Reminiscences of a Resident* (Lahore: Civil and Military Gazette Press, 1924), p.41.

p.23 Sarah and the investigator had drafted a mercy petition: once an accused has exhausted all their appeals, the only recourse is in a mercy petition to the President of Pakistan. Under Article 45, Constitution of Pakistan, the President has the power to pardon an accused. This power has, however, only rarely been exercised and it has been limited by a number of other legal provisions. For a detailed discussion of the limits placed on mercy petitions, see 'Slow march to the gallows: Death penalty in Pakistan', *International Federation for Human Rights* and *Human Rights Commission of Pakistan*, January 2007, pp.31–3, https://www.fidh.org/IMG/pdf/Pakistan464angconjointpdm.pdf.

p.23 the accused: in Pakistan's criminal law, the defendant in a criminal case is referred to as 'the accused'. Throughout the book, I use the Pakistani rather than the British term, although they are synonymous.

p.26 Sarah also managed to salvage some mentors: she cites Azam Nazeer Tarar, Hassam Qadir Shah, Shahid Siddiqui as her foremost mentors in Pakistan.

p.28 In Pakistan, the death penalty is popular: see 'Slow march to the gallows', pp.19–20. See also Amnesty International, 'Pakistan: the death penalty', ASA 33/10/96, p.3, https://www.amnesty.org/download/Documents/.../asa330101996en.pdf.

p.28 gave opponents of the death penalty some hope: moratoriums often lead to abolition: see International Commission Against the Death Penalty, http://www.icomdp.org/moratorium/.

p.28 traditional opposition to execution: following the execution of its founder, Zulfikar Ali Bhutto, in 1979, the PPP has been strongly opposed to capital punishment. In 1988, Benazir Bhutto announced that she would commute all pending death sentences – as a result, all executions were stayed and 2,000 sentences were commuted to life. See Amnesty International, *Pakistan: Legal challenges* *affecting the application of the death penalty,* ASA 33/03/91, p.2. For an account of Zulfikar Ali Bhutto's trial and execution, see Jalal, *The Struggle for Pakistan,* pp.213–22.

p.28 During the League's recent terms in office (1990–3 and 1997–9), Pakistan had one of the highest execution rates in the world, close behind China, Iraq, Iran, Saudi Arabia and the United States: between 1975 and 2005, Pakistan executed an average of 37 prisoners a year. See 'Slow march to the gallows', p.26.

p.28 at a rate of almost one a day: see Cornell University Law School Death Penalty Worldwide report for 2011: http://www.deathpenaltyworldwide.org/country-search-post.cfm?country=Pakistan.

Chapter 2

This chapter is a study of Zulfikar Ali Khan's trial as it unfolded in 1999 – at which Sarah was not the defence lawyer (she came to the case in 2009) – and purposely does not take into account a later investigation carried out by JPP. JPP's investigation sets out another version of events, an account (which is detailed on their website) situated somewhere between the defence and prosecution cases as put at trial. Rather than being investigative, the purpose of this chapter is to interrogate the court's conviction and sentencing of Zulfikar Ali Khan and his brother, Khurshid Ahmed, on the basis of the facts before the court in 1999. Otherwise than as set out below, therefore, it is based entirely on the trial court judgment and evidence.

p.32 As most of Pakistan's police stations have no forensic training . . . no national fingerprint database: see 'Slow march to the gallows', pp.49–51.

p.33 and witnesses – on whose evidence the bulk of police investigation is based – tend to be closer to their neighbours than they are to the truth: the privileging of oral evidence by the police can be deeply problematic for criminal cases. Witnesses are liable, in any country, to make mistakes, particularly over identification. But in Pakistan, a country where many have learnt to fear and distrust the police and government, the accounts of witnesses are especially unreliable: people are easily intimidated by the police or the complainants, and few will give evidence against the state. As there are no witness protection programmes, their fears are perhaps justified. For further discussion of the impediments to police investigation as a result of such heavy reliance on the accounts of witnesses, see 'Slow march to the gallows', p.47.

p.35 On the basis of this report, the police decided that they had evidence enough to justify the further detention of both Zulfikar Ali Khan and Khurshid: Pakistan's British-drafted Code of Criminal Procedure only permits the police to arrest those who – after genuine investigation – they reasonably suspect to have committed a crime. See Pakistan Code of Criminal Procedure 1898, Section 54: 'When police may arrest without warrant'.

p.37 it was illegal for the police to keep an accused for more than twenty-four hours unless approved by a magistrate: see Pakistan Code of Criminal Procedure 1898, Section 61: 'Person not to be detained more than twenty-four hours'; and section 167: 'Procedure when investigation cannot be completed in twenty-four hours'; and Lahore High Court Rules.

p.37 guaranteed by the constitution, a detainee has the right to a lawyer: see Article 10, Constitution of Pakistan 1973.

p.37 The lack of a comprehensive system of legal aid means that few accused can employ ... monthly salary: and where someone is sentenced to death, the fees increase exponentially. See 'Slow march to the gallows', p.54. There are provisions for state lawyers to be appointed when a person is sentenced to death (Pauper Council: the High Court Rules), but these lawyers are often badly paid and inexperienced.

p.37 And particularly in murder cases, the extensions granted by the magistrate – during which the accused has no access to a lawyer and rarely learns of the case against him – are characterised by torture: see police interview cited in 'Slow march to the gallows', p.47. See also Justice Project Pakistan and Allard K. Lowenstein International Human Rights Clinic, Yale Law School, *Policing as Torture: A Report on Systematic Brutality and Torture by the Police in Faisalabad, Pakistan*, June 2014.

p.38 Common techniques include sleep deprivation, heat exposure, rolling heavy objects over a person's limbs, beatings with a leather racket, attaching electrodes to a person's genitals and running a current through them: see *Policing as Torture*, Section III, p.4.

p.38 illegal in Pakistan under both domestic and international law: for an overview of Pakistan's domestic laws prohibiting torture, see I. Buchanan and S. Belal, *Torture in Pakistan: A Lawyer's Handbook* (Islamabad: Pakistan's Parliamentarian Commission for Human Rights, 2012).

p.38 Moreover, the worse a beating, the more someone will pay for it to stop: Pakistan's police are patently corrupt. This is partly owing to very low salaries (on average a police constable earns Rs. 5,000 a month (about £30)).

But police practice is also steeped in a culture of corruption, one that the government is slowly trying to change: in 2005, for example, two-thirds of all Lahore police officers (12,530 out of approximately 19,000) were punished on charges of corruption, misuse of power and illegal detention; 667 officers were dismissed from service; and 109 were given compulsory retirement. See 'Slow march to the gallows', p.49.

p.39 Police torture is pervasive in Pakistan: for instances of reported systematic police torture in Pakistan, see annual Human Rights Commission of Pakistan reports, available at: http://hrcp-web.org/hrcpweb/publications/annual-reports/; Human Rights Commission of Pakistan report by A. Jamal, *Revisiting Police Laws*, January 2011, http://hrcp-web.org/hrcpweb/wp-content/pdf/ff/19.pdf; comments of Human Rights Watch, https://www.hrw.org/news/2009/02/02/uk-should-investigate-role-torture-pakistan, Amnesty International, https://www.amnesty.org/en/press-releases/2014/05/torture-pervasive-across-asia-pacific/; Reprieve, http://reprieve.webfactional.com/investigations/pakistanpolicetorture/. See also *Policing as Torture*, op. cit.

p.39 the country's legislature declared, in 1984: see Articles 38 and 39, Qanoon-e-Shahadat Order 1984: 'Confession to police officer not to be proved' and 'Confession by accused while in custody of police not to be proved against him'.

p.39 Most countries presume confessions to the police to be admissible unless it appears to the court that the police used oppressive tactics: in England and Wales, for example (under Section 76, Police and Criminal Evidence Act 1984), a confession obtained in police custody is admissible unless the accused person claims that the confession was obtained by oppression or in circumstances that might otherwise render the confession unreliable, and the prosecution is unable to prove beyond a reasonable doubt that it was not obtained in such circumstances.

p.39 the part of that confession that relates to the evidence found will be admissible in court, regardless of the fact that the confession was made to the police: see Article 40, Qanoon-e-Shahadat Order 1984: 'How much of information received from accused may be proved'.

p.40 Whoever, to strike in the people ...: see Anti-Terrorism Act 1997 (Pakistan), Section 6: 'Terrorist Act', but note that the current definition of terrorism in the Anti-Terrorism Act 1997 is different from that under which Zulfikar Ali Khan was tried, as the definition was amended in 1999 (under the Anti-Terrorism (Second Amendment) Ordinance) and subsequently. See also C. Kennedy, 'The Creation and Development of Pakistan's Anti-Terrorism Regime, 1997–2002', in S. P. Limaye (ed.), *Religious Radicalism and Security in South Asia* (Honolulu: Asia-Pacific Centre for Security Studies, 2004).

p.41 And all people charged with a terrorist act were tried in special anti-terrorism courts that allowed for rushed, expedited trials, limited evidence: see Kennedy 'The Creation and Development of Pakistan's Anti-Terrorism Regime, 1997–2002', pp.388–96.

p.41 and – where the police had any material evidence (such as Zulfikar Ali Khan's gun) – an inverted burden of proof requiring the accused to prove they didn't commit the act: see *Khawaja Hasanullah v. The State* 1999 MLD 51, and Section 8, Suppression of Terrorist Activities

(Special Courts) Act 1975. For a further discussion of the Anti-Terrorism Act 1997, see 'Slow march to the gallows', pp.40–1.

p.41 Only a year after it was drafted, much of the Anti-Terrorism Act was held to be unconstitutional: see *Mehran Ali v. Federation of Pakistan* PLD 1998 SC 1445, and for a discussion of the implications of this case, see Kennedy, 'The Creation and Development of Pakistan's Anti-Terrorism Regime, 1997–2002', pp.389–91.

p.41 poorly paid: state-appointed lawyers are not paid well – the fee is around Rs. 200 (less than £1.50) per hearing. See 'Slow march to the gallows', p.55.

p.43 Under the Act, for example, any police officer who conducts a defective investigation is liable to two years' imprisonment: see Anti-Terrorism Act 1997, Section 27: 'Punishment for Defective Investigations'.

p.43 Both prosecution and defence appealed this decision: the brothers were given leave by the anti-terrorism court to appeal to the High Court. The appeal had to be filed within seven days of the trial court judgment.

p.45 Even Somalia, Colombia and the Democratic Republic of the Congo are more open to humanitarian visits: see the International Committee of the Red Cross website, https://www.icrc.org/en/where-we-work.

p.46 between 2006 and 2012, in one district of the country, doctors found that 76 per cent of those alleging abuse by the police had certainly been tortured, while the remaining 24 per cent showed 'signs indicating injury': see *Policing as Torture*, p.1.

Chapter 3

This chapter, except as set out below, is based on my interviews with Arthur Wilson and his family (particularly his son and daughter, Aroon and Aroona), and on the time I have spent working with him and visiting the families he works with and members of his church congregation in Lahore.

p.49 resulted in the largest and most rapid movement of people in the world's history: see P. Bharadwaj, A. Khwaja, A. Mian, 'The Big March: Migratory Flows after the Partition of India', in *Economic and Political Weekly*, 30 August 2008; C. Bates, 'The Hidden Story of Partition and its Legacies', *BBC History*, 3 March 2011, http://www.bbc.co.uk/history/british/modern/partition1947_01.shtml; T. Basu, 'The Fading Memory of South Asia's Partition', *The Atlantic*, 15 August 2014, http://www.theatlantic.com/international/archive/2014/08/the-fading-memory-of-partition-india-pakistan-bangladesh/376120/.

p.49 By 1951, Pakistan was home to seven million refugees: American Consul Lahore to Department of State, 25 May 1960, 790D.00(W)6-162-790D 1/2-1060, National Archives at College Park, cited in I. Talbot, *Pakistan: A Modern History* (New York: Palgrave Macmillan, 2005), p.101.

p.49 they slaughtered one another in hundreds of thousands: Jalal, *The Struggle for Pakistan*, op. cit., p.39; Talbot, *Pakistan: A Modern History*, p.101.

p.49 Kashmir – a territory that would be fought over by Pakistan and India from Partition until today: for a discussion of the ongoing conflict in Kashmir, see, amongst others: Jalal, *The Struggle for Pakistan*, pp.67–72 and 117–27; A. Lieven, *Pakistan: A Hard Country* (London: Allen Lane, 2011), pp.186–92; A. Jalal, *The State of Martial Rule: The Origins of Pakistan's Political Economy of Defence* (Cambridge; New York; Port Chester: Cambridge University Press, 1990), pp.56-60; P. Mishra, 'Kashmir: The Unending War', *New York Review of Books*, 19 October 2000.

p.50 Hindu and Muslim lower castes: L. Wallbridge, *The Christians of Pakistan: The Passion of Bishop John Joseph* (London: Routledge Curzon, 2003), pp.15-17; T. Gabriel, *Christian Citizens in an Islamic State: The Pakistan Experience* (Aldershot: Ashgate, *c.*2007), p.20.

p.50 determined everything from career and marriage prospects to the area of town they could live in: Wallbridge, *The Christians of Pakistan*, p.16; D. Ibbotson, *Panjab Castes: Races, Castes and Tribes of the People of the Panjab* (New Delhi: Cosmo Publications, 1916 and 1981).

p.50 Christians in Pakistan: although many of Pakistan's Christians are descendants of these nineteenth-century converts, South Asia's history has seen other sources of Christianity. Many of Pakistan's Christians, for example, see themselves as descended from the men and women converted by St Thomas, when he visited Taxila (a site between Lahore and Islamabad) in the first century AD. Others, usually Catholics, are descended from the converts of Portuguese missionaries, who came to Goa and the south of India in the sixteenth century. See Gabriel, *Christian Citizens in an Islamic state*, p.17.

p.50 who make up roughly 1.6 per cent of the country's population: P. R. Blood, *Pakistan: A Country Study* (Washington, DC: Federal Research Division, Library of

Congress, 1995); Population Distribution by Religion, based on 1998 census, published by Pakistan Bureau of Statistics, http://www.pbs.gov.pk/sites/default/files/other/yearbook2011/Population/16-16.pdf.

p.50 21 per cent of blasphemy cases registered are against Christians: M. Nafees, *Blasphemy Laws in Pakistan: a Historical Overview* (Islamabad: Center for Research and Security Studies), p.52, http://www.csi-int.org/file-admin/Files/pdf/2014/blasphemylawsinpakistan.pdf; 'Blasphemy laws: a fact sheet', *Dawn*, 15 April 2010, http://www.dawn.com/news/845129/blasphemy-laws-a-fact-sheet.

p.51 Christian residential areas are vulnerable to sporadic attacks by lynch mobs: a few recent examples include 'Police save Christian couple from "blasphemy" mob near Lahore', *Dawn*, 2 July 2015, http://www.dawn.com/news/1191891; 'Pakistan mob burns man for "blasphemy"', Al-Jazeera, 22 December 2012, http://www.aljazeera.com/news/asia/2012/12/20121222114547753697.html; S. Jillani, 'Pakistan Christian community living in fear after mob killings', BBC News, Kasur District, Pakistan, 8 November 2014, http://www.bbc.co.uk/news/world-asia-29956115; M. Haider, 'The lynch mob nation', *Dawn*, 13 March 2013, http://www.dawn.com/news/792335/the-lynch-mob-nation.

p.51 on several occasions whole church congregations have been the target of suicide bombs: in September 2013, All Saints Church in Peshawar was bombed by the Taliban (see J. Boone, 'Pakistan church bomb: Christians mourn 85 killed in Peshawar suicide attack', the *Guardian*, 25 September 2015, http://www.theguardian.com/world/2013/sep/23/pakistan-church-bombings-christian-minority). In March 2015, two churches in Lahore were bombed by the Taliban (see 'Worshippers killed in Pakistan church bombings', Al-Jazeera, 15 March 2015, http://www.aljazeera.com/news/2015/03/lahore-churches-hit-deadly-bomb-attacks-150315074103093.html).

p.52 prefaced with confirmation of Islam's position at the heart of the country: every constitution of Pakistan since 1956 had been prefaced with the Objectives Resolution, until it was made part of the constitution itself in 1985, by General Zia. See Jalal, *The Struggle for Pakistan*, pp.56–9: and C. Kennedy, 'Repugnancy to Islam: Who Decides? Islam and Legal Reform in Pakistan', *The International and Comparative Law Quarterly*, Vol. 41, No. 4 (October 1992), pp.769–87.

p.52 In keeping with a wave of similar projects across the Islamic world: the 1960s and 1970s saw a number of programmes of Islamic legal reform across the globe. In Libya, Gaddafi seized power through a military *coup d'état* in 1969 and began to introduce Islamic legislation from 1971. This included setting up a committee (not dissimilar to Pakistan's Council of Islamic Ideology) to prepare for the Islamisation of the Libyan legal system. Early in 1979, revolutionary Islamic courts were set up in Iran. Four laws to codify Islamic criminal law were enacted in 1982 and 1983. In Sudan, al-Nimeiri seized power in 1969 and set up a Committee for Law Revision in 1977, in order to prepare for the Islamisation of Sudanese law. He introduced Islamic legislation in 1983. See R. Peters, *Crime and Punishment in Islamic Law* (Cambridge, UK; New York: Cambridge University Press, 2005) Chapter 5.

p.53 Zia intended to Islamise his country's legal system: as his source of Islamic law, General Zia relied on the recommendations of the Council of Islamic Ideology (founded by President Ayub Khan in 1962 as the Advisory Council of Islamic Ideology before becoming the Council of Islamic Ideology in 1973). He strengthened the council by increasing its membership to twenty (Section 228, Constitution of Pakistan 1973) and, in 1980, appointing Justice Tanzil-ur-Rehman – renowned Pakistani jurist and Islamic scholar – as chairman. For further detail, see P. Shaukat Ali, *Politics of conviction: the life and times of Muhammad Zia-ul-Haq* (London: London Centre for Pakistan Studies, 1997), p.58. For more details of General Zia's thoughts on Islamisation, see Z. ul-Haq, *Introduction of Islamic Laws: Address to the Nation* (Islamabad: Ministry of Information & Broadcasting, Directorate of Films & Publications, Government of Pakistan, 1979), and Z. ul-Haq, *Interviews to Foreign Media* (Islamabad: Ministry of Information & Broadcasting, Directorate of Films & Publications, Government of Pakistan, Vol. VI, Jan.–Dec. 1983), p.148. For the views of those close to General Zia at the time, see the memoirs of Abdul Qayyum, self-titled 'one-man think tank' for both the Chief Martial Law Administrator and Chief of Army Staff during General Zia's period in office: A. Qayyum, *Zia-ul-Haq and I* (Islamabad: Consortium of Consultants and Technical Services, 1997). For an overview of Pakistan's return to Islamic criminal law, see Peters, *Crime and Punishment in Islamic Law*, pp.155–60.

p.53 'Religion', Jinnah famously said, 'has nothing to do with the business of the state.': Jinnah said this in one of his first speeches following the creation of Pakistan, given on 11 August 1947, when the Constituent Assembly elected him as their first president. See M. A. Jinnah, *Speeches of Quaid-i-Azam Mohammad Ali Jinnah as Governor General of Pakistan* (Karachi: Sindh Observer Press, 1948), pp.9–10. Broadcast on American radio in February 1948, Jinnah also said: 'In any case, Pakistan is not going to be a theocratic state to be ruled by priests with a divine mission. We have many non-Muslims – Hindus, Christians and Parsees – but they are all Pakistanis. They will enjoy the same rights and privileges as any other citizens and will play their rightful part in the affairs of Pakistan.' Cited in L. H. Merchant, *Jinnah: A Judicial Verdict* (Karachi: East West Publishing Company, 1990), p.12. For a detailed analysis of Jinnah's vision for Pakistan, see A. Jalal, *The Sole Spokesman: Jinnah, the Muslim League and the Demand for Pakistan* (Cambridge: Cambridge University Press, 1994) and A. Ahmed, 'Why Jinnah Matters', in M. Lodhi (ed.), *Pakistan: Beyond the Crisis State* (London: C. Hurst & Co., 2011), pp.21–34.

p.53 since Jinnah's death, Pakistan's rulers have used Islam to their advantage, relying on Islamic idiom to co-opt conservative religious groups and contain a disparate electorate: see Jalal, *The Struggle for Pakistan*, pp.111–12.

p.54 unsuccessful attempts to impose dress codes on women, make the growing of beards compulsory and ban pigeon flying: see Talbot, *Pakistan: A Modern History*, pp.251 and 272, and Jalal, *The Struggle for Pakistan*, pp.249–50.

p.54 In 1980 ... he established a Federal Shariat Court: see Constitution of the Islamic Republic of Pakistan, Article 203C(1).

p.54 According to Zia's blueprint, the court would be supported by *ulema*: see M. Lau, *The role of Islam in the legal system of Pakistan* (Leiden; Boston: M. Nijhoff, c.2006), p.13.

p.54 During Zia's rule, the court declared repugnant a law that prescribed death by stoning as punishment for adultery: Jalal, *The Struggle for Pakistan*, p.249.

p.54 'ensure and guarantee all fundamental human rights and [to emphasise] social, economic, and political justice for all': see 'Quetta Declaration' at PLD 1991 J 142, p.142, cited in M. Lau, *The Role of Islam in the legal system of Pakistan* (London: University of London, 2002), pp.161–2.

p.54 And in fulfilment of this mandate, the court would rule handcuffs and extended prison sentences un-Islamic, and repeatedly emphasise the Islamic values of liberty, equality and freedom of expression: see *Dr Muhammad Aslam Khaki and others v. The State and others* PLD 2010 Federal Shariat Court 1. Likewise, the Supreme Court and Lahore High Court relied on Islamic principles to protect the rights of bonded labourers, challenge political corruption, and overturn wrongful death sentences. With regard to bonded labourers, see Justice Zullah's judgment in *Darshan Masih v. The State* PLD 1990 SC 513, where the court recommended that under the Objectives Resolution, a bill of fundamental rights should be read into Pakistan's constitution. With regard to political corruption, see *Al-Jehad Trust v. Manzoor Ahmad Watoo* PLD 1992 Lah 855, a case that ultimately brought Benazir Bhutto and Nawaz Sharif before the Lahore High Court, though note that this decision was ultimately overturned (also by the Lahore High Court) two years later (see *Manzoor Ahmad Watoo v. Abdul Wahabul Khairi* PLD 1994 Lah 466). With regard to overturning death sentences, see *Khalil-uz-Zaman v. Supreme Appellate Court* PLD 1994 SC 885, which concerned the operation of speedy trials courts and found that the lower court had wrongly sentenced a man to death. All these cases are discussed in greater details in Lau, *The Role of Islam in the legal system of Pakistan*, pp.159–69.

p.54 In an attempt to secularise the subcontinent's laws, the British had granted Indian courts a power to find local religious laws (such as Muslim and Hindu personal law) invalid where '*repugnant*' to (British concepts of) '*natural justice*': the East India Company, in administering Indian law, increasingly advised judges to appeal to 'natural law' in interpreting indigenous law codes; they were to be applied in accordance with 'justice, equity and good conscience'. This practice continued under the Raj. See S. Kugle, 'Framed, Blamed and Renamed: the Recasting of Islamic Jurisprudence in Colonial South Asia', *Modern Asian Studies*, Vol. 35, issue 2, April 2001, pp.257-313 (particularly pp.265–6). See also Lau, *The Role of Islam in the legal system of Pakistan*, p.78.

p.54 Pakistan's own repugnancy clause was first drafted in 1956: see Article 198(1) of 1956 Constitution of Pakistan, which states: 'no law shall be enacted which is repugnant to the injunctions of Islam as laid down in the Holy Quran and Sunnah, hereinafter referred to as the injunctions of Islam, and existing law shall be brought into conformity with such injunctions'. For a detailed discussion of this clause, see Lau, *The Role of Islam in the legal system of Pakistan*, p.30.

p.54 seventeen years before Islam was even declared Pakistan's state religion: see Jalal, *The Struggle for Pakistan*, pp.95 and 203; and Talbot, *Pakistan: A Modern History*, p.229.

p.54 twenty-four years before Zia established the Federal Shariat Court in 1980: see Lau, *The Role of Islam in the legal*

system of Pakistan, p.204; the Federal Shariat Court was established by *The Constitution (Amendment) Order 1980*, under
Article 203C. The court's principal seat was to be in Islamabad.

**p.55 But General Zia's legislative amendments were
far more thoroughgoing ... creation of a specialist
Islamic court:** see Lau, *The Role of Islam in the legal system
of Pakistan*, p.32.

p.60 ultimately became law in 1990: the provisions were
binding as a matter of judicial precedent from 1980; they
were then binding as a result of the ordinance from 1990,
and this ordinance was repeatedly promulgated until finally
passed into law by Parliament in 1997. See 'Slow march
to the gallows', p.34; and Lau, *The Role of Islam in the legal
system of Pakistan*, pp.212, 219 and 229. See also *Gul Hassan
Khan v. Govt. Of Pakistan and another PLD* 1980 Pesh 1,
Mumtaz Khan v. Government of Pakistan PLD 1980 Pesh 154,
Federation of Pakistan v. Gull Hassan Khan PLD 1989 SC 633
and *Muhammad Riaz v. Federal Government PLD* 1980 FSC
1. That the Qisas and Diyat provisions were not given the
force of law in 1977 has been cautiously attributed to a
reluctance on the part of the then government of Pakistan
to allow Zulfikar Ali Bhutto (the prime minister over-
thrown by General Zia and in 1977 jailed and awaiting
execution) to avoid the death penalty. For a discussion of
the effect of the Qisas and Diyat Ordinances on the death
penalty, see Amnesty International, *Pakistan: Legal changes
affecting application of the death penalty*, ASA 33/03/91.

**p.60 have sometimes led to last-minute reprieves at
the foot of the gallows:** prison superintendents have
witnessed compromises reached as a noose is put around
the prisoner's neck, or only a few hours before the scheduled execution. See 'Slow march to the gallows', p.35.

p.60 Broadly speaking, it is only in civil law that the parties can settle cases financially. Other than giving evidence, the victim and their family generally have no role in the criminal proceedings: in practice, in the UK, the victim can sometimes play a role in the police decision to charge an individual with an offence. Where a crime is relatively low-level – theft of a small sum, for example, or damage to a bicycle – the police will often ask the victim whether they would like the crime prosecuted. The victim's wishes will therefore have some bearing on whether the police consider charging a suspect to be in the public interest. Domestic violence cases, to give another example, are often only prosecuted if the victim wishes the police to do so (but in these cases, the intimacy of the relationship between suspect and victim goes a long way toward explaining this anomaly). With thanks to Fred Wilmot-Smith for discussion on this point.

p.60 *wali* (legal heirs): an Arabic word (from the triliteral verb root ولي) meaning 'helper', 'sponsor' or 'representative', but used in Pakistan's law to mean 'legal heirs', or 'person entitled to claim *qisas*' (see Pakistan Penal Code, Section 299). Definition given by J. M. Cowan (ed.), *The Hans Wehr Dictionary of Modern Written Arabic*, 4th edn (Urbana, IL: Spoken Language Services Inc., 1979), p.1289. With thanks to Bruce Wannell for spotting this particular Urdu/Pakistani usage.

Chapter 4

Except as set out below, this chapter and the following one are based on the court documents in Aftab Masih's case (all public records), my interviews with Nasar Hussain and my experience of having worked with Nasar since 2011.

p.71 Magistrates' Court to Sessions Court: although matters of police remand will be dealt with by a magistrate, generally all capital cases in Pakistan are tried in the Sessions Court, not the Magistrates' Court. In the Sessions Court, the case will be tried by an additional sessions judge. Death sentences must be confirmed by the High Court, so if the accused is found guilty and sentenced to death, the case will automatically be sent to the High Court.

p.72 old British carriage house: R. Sohrabji Sidhwa, *The Lahore High Court and its Principal Bar* (Lahore: Printed at the Pakistan Times Press, 1989).

p.78 when interviewed by a human rights organisation: see 'Slow march to the gallows'.

p.79 Under both domestic and international law, it is illegal in Pakistan to sentence a juvenile to death: for details of the development of Pakistan's domestic law on the execution of juveniles, see 'Slow march to the gallows', p.38.

Chapter 5

p.82 taking tea with a Lahore High Court judge one afternoon: this conversation, with a High Court justice who is currently overseeing a reform of the Lahore High Court's case management system, took place in May 2012.

p.82 Over the years, a host of wings have been added to what was once a simple quadrangle: R. Sohrabji Sidhwa, *The Lahore High Court and its Principal Bar* (Lahore: Printed at the Pakistan Times Press, 1989), pp.139–44.

p.82 Persian records offices: Sohrabji Sidhwa, *The Lahore High Court and its Principal Bar*, p.140. That there were allocated Persian records offices within the Lahore High Court is interesting, as the language of the British administration in India at the time was English or Urdu. These rooms must, therefore, have been archives of older Persian records.

p.84 the Lahore High Court was said to have been built in imitation of a fourteenth-century South Asian palace: Morris, *Stones of Empire*, pp.112–14.

p.90 *qahwah* (green tea): this tea – often made with saffron, cinnamon and cardamom – is drunk throughout Central Asia and northern India, particularly in Kashmir. Somewhat confusingly, it shares its name with the Arabic word for coffee, a result of the history of coffee drinking. Qahwah was initially, in the early Middle Ages, used to describe a drink of alcohol. It later described a coffee drink, as coffee beans spread from Ethiopia to Yemen in the early to mid-fourteenth century. In the mid-fifteenth century, Yemen began to export coffee beans, and by the mid-sixteenth century, the practice of drinking coffee had reached Egypt and the Indian Ocean. Coffee remained popular in India until the late nineteenth century, when tea replaced it as a widespread social drink (tea having been first introduced by the British in order to compete with the Chinese tea markets). In India, although tea drunk with milk was called *chai*, tea drunk without milk (as coffee was then drunk) was referred to as *qahwah*. Green tea was particularly popular in the northern Anglo-Indian sphere, in what is now Pakistan. (With thanks to Bruce Wannell for unpicking this somewhat complex etymology!)

p.92 If, as one nineteenth-century jurist put it, the life of the law has not been logic but experience: O. Wendell Holmes, *The Common Law* (Cambridge, MA; London: The Belknap Press of Harvard University Press, 2009), 'Lecture 1: Early Forms of Liability', pp.3–36; and O. Wendell Holmes, 'Common Carriers and the Common Law', *American Law Review* 609 (1879).

Chapter 6

Other than as stated below, this chapter is based on interviews with Sohail and conversations with other former prisoners and lawyers who have worked in Sahiwal jail.

p.96 *kafala* system: See A. Khan, 'Why it's time to end Kafala', *The Guardian*, 26 February 2014, http://www .theguardian.com/global-development/2014/feb/26/time-to-end-kafala; Migrant Rights 'End the Kafala System' campaign, http://www.migrant-rights.org/campaign/end-the-kafala-system/; P. Motaparthy, 'Understanding Kafala: An Archaic Law at Cross Purposes with Modern Development', Migrant-Rights.org, 11 March 2015, http:// www.migrant-rights.org/2015/03/understanding-kafala-an-archaic-law-at-cross-purposes-with-modern-development/; N. Vora, *Impossible Citizens: Dubai's Indian Diaspora* (Durham; London: Duke University Press, 2013).

p.97 accounting for almost half of Pakistan's exports, textiles form the backbone of the country's economy: of Pakistan's £17 billion export revenue (2013 estimate, see http://www.indexmundi.com/pakistan/economy_profile.html), £8.5 billion results from the export of textiles: K. Baig, 'Why the Pakistan textile industry cannot die', *The Express Tribune*, 18 March 2013, http://tribune.com.pk/story/522293/anatomy-of-an-indispensable-sector-why-the-pakistan-textile-industry-cannot-die/; M. Ahmad, 'Pakistan accounts for only 5.7pc of textile imports by 20 nations', *The News International*, 23 February 2013, http://tribune.com.pk/story/522293/anatomy-of-an-indispensable-sector-why-the-pakistan-textile-industry-cannot-die/.

p.99 Model Town: this area of Lahore was built in the 1920s under the chairmanship of Sir Ganga Ram. Hindu philanthropist, Executive Engineer of Lahore, chief architect of the Imperial Assemblage at Delhi and son of a court copywriter, Ganga Ram was responsible for most of British Imperial Lahore, including the Lahore High Court, General Post Office and museum. For more detail on him, see F. M. Bhatti, *Sir Ganga Ram: A Man of All Seasons* (Delhi: Deepak Prakashan, 2006).

p.100 Sahiwal, one of the largest prisons in Pakistan: according to the government of the Punjab, Sahiwal Central Jail has the region's third largest prison population (at 3,652), behind Rawalpindi Central Jail (4,746) and Lahore Central Jail (3,896): see http://prisons.pitb.gov.pk/prisoners_statistics_jail_wise.

p.102 1,500 of the approximately 4,500-man (most of Pakistan's inmates are men) prison population had been condemned to death: it is difficult to get any historical statistics from Pakistan's jail authorities as to the exact number of people on death row in each prison; I rely here on Sohail's estimate, and the opinion of several criminal lawyers in Lahore who have worked with condemned prisoners in Sahiwal. Today, according to the government of the Punjab, there are 3,652 prisoners in Sahiwal (over double the official jail capacity of 1,565), 400 of whom have been sentenced to death: http://prisons.pitb.gov.pk/prisoners_statistics_jail_wise. With regard to the proportion of women to men on Pakistan's death row, see 'Slow march to the gallows', pp.26–30.

p.103 the 1850s British jail manual provided for the following meals: see Chapter XXXVI, Section 915(1), *Manual for the superintendence and management of jails in the Punjab – corrected up to August 1975* (Patiala: Government Press, 1975).

p.103 In the nineteenth and twentieth centuries: see Chapter XXXVII, Section 945, *Manual for the superintendence and management of jails in the Punjab.*

p.103 'agreeable shade if planted within the jail enclosure but must not be planted so thickly as to interfere with free ventilation': see Chapter XXXVII, Section 956(1), *Manual for the superintendence and management of jails in the Punjab.*

p.104 This labour economy followed the nineteenth-century British model of the prison, which made of the Punjab's petty criminals a formidable labour force: the division of labour in the Punjab's jails is detailed at Chapter XXII, Section 677 of *Manual for the superintendence and management of jails in the Punjab.*

p.104 In the early nineteenth century, some theorists saw labour as inherently beneficial to both prisoner and society: for example, M. Foucault, *Discipline and Punish: The Birth of the Prison* (London: Penguin Books,

1991), p.240, cites Jean-Baptiste Treilhard's *Motifs du code d'instruction criminelle* (1808): 'Although the penalty inflicted by the law has as its aim the reparation of a crime, it is also intended to reform the convict, and this double aim will be fulfilled if the malefactor is snatched from that fatal idleness which, having brought him to prison, meets him again within its walls and, seizing hold of him, brings him to the ultimate degree of depravity.' And at p.319, instructions from the French Ministry of the Interior in 1816: 'It is of the greatest importance to keep prisoners occupied as much as possible. One must instil in them a desire to work, distinguishing between the fate of those who are occupied and that of prisoners who wish to remain idle. The first will be better fed and have more comfortable beds than the second.'

p.104 Others saw penal labour as further means whereby the prison asserted power over the prisoners, forcing them to labour in submission: for example, Foucault, *Discipline and Punish*, pp.242–4.

p.105 As had been the case for over a century: see Chapter XVIII, Sections 581 and 587, *Manual for the superintendence and management of jails in the Punjab*.

p.107 'reformatory principles ... contaminating effect': address delivered before the reformatory section of the Social Science Association on the 'Treatment of Criminals in the Punjab' by Major G. Hutchinson, Inspector General of Police, cited in M. Lewin, *Torture in Madras* (report) (London: Thomas Brettell, 1855).

p.107 Criminologists from Ireland to France to Calcutta: Hutchinson, 'Treatment of Criminals in the Punjab'.

Chapter 7

This chapter, other than as set out in the notes below, is based on the court documents in Sohail's case (all public records) and interviews with Sohail.

p.114 As all oral evidence taken in police custody (including confessions) is inadmissible unless it leads the police to material evidence, the judgment was unlawful in relying on these 'disclosures': see Articles 38 and 39, Qanoon-e-Shahadat Order 1984: 'Confession to police officer not to be proved' and 'Confession by accused while in custody of police not to be proved against him'.

p.115 Muslim Students Federation of Government College, Lahore: Pakistan's politicians had historically been wary of student politics: a student uprising ended Ayub Khan's regime in the late 1960s, and in 1984, General Zia banned student unions across Pakistan. See L. Gayer, *Karachi: Ordered Disorder and the Struggle for the City* (London: C. Hurst & Co., 2014), p.71.

p.117 applied to the court to have his sentence suspended: under Section 401 of the Criminal Procedure Code 1898, the provincial government may suspend or remit a person's sentence at any time; suspension may be conditional or unconditional, with breach of a condition possibly resulting in arrest and re-imprisonment.

p.118 making a total of between 400 and 600 condemned prisoners in Sahiwal, roughly five hundred times the prison's nineteenth-century death row population: in 1881, there were 510 prisoners imprisoned in Montgomery Jail (now Sahiwal Central Jail), and only one of them had been sentenced to death: see *Report on the jails of the Punjab* (Lahore: Government Press, 1870–94); in 2013, according to the government of the Punjab, there are 400 condemned prisoners in Sahiwal: http://prisons.pitb.gov.pk/prisoners_statistics_jail_wise.

p.119 'manilla, one-inch diameter, 19 foot long': see Chapter XXXI, Section 866, *Manual for the superintendence and management of jails in the Punjab.*

p.123 no word from... the Multan High Court: it wasn't until late 2014, over thirteen years after he was first arrested, that Sohail was finally acquitted of all charges.

Chapter 8

Other than the notes set out below, where not experienced first hand, this chapter is based on my interviews with Sohail.

p.129 which, in a capital case, is punishable with a life sentence: see Section 194, Pakistan Penal Code 1860.

p.131 Even if it couldn't be used in court, this information would be helpful in drafting a mercy petition to the provincial government and the President: proof that Aftab Masih was convicted on the basis of a false eyewitness account could have led to a retrial. Where a conviction is based on evidence that one party objects to (false evidence, for example), and there is no other independent evidence to warrant the conviction, that conviction can be set aside or reversed and a retrial ordered (*Government of Sindh v. Sabur-ur-Rehman* 1989 PLD 572, and Article 162, Qanoon-e-Shahadat Order 1984).

Chapter 9

Except as set out below, this chapter and the next one are based on the court records of Altaf Rehman's case (all public records) and my own meetings with Altaf Rehman. Altaf Rehman is not his real name.

p.135 Cyber crime: see Prevention of Electronic Crimes Ordinance 2007, Section 20/22.

p.135 The National Response Centre for Cyber Crime: see their website: http://www.nr3c.gov.pk/index.html.

p.136 'risked the dissolution of society': Indian Penal Code, Act XLV of 1860 (Krishen Lal & Co. Law Publishers, 1929), 1322, cited in O. Siddique and Z. Hayat, 'Unholy Laws & Holy Speech: Blasphemy Laws in Pakistan – Controversial Origins, Design Defects and Free Speech Implications', *Minnesota Journal of International Law*, Volume 17, Spring 2008, p.337.

p.137 'ascertain whether the intention of the person was deliberately to wound religious feelings': see T. S. Macpherson's notes on the Indian Penal Code, which can be found in the British Library at IOR:MSS Eur F523/41.

p.137 'distinctly [prove] that there was an intention on the part of the accused to insult the religion of a class of persons': commentary on the Indian Penal Code, cited in Siddique and Hayat, 'Unholy Laws & Holy Speech', p.340.

p.137 risked 'unsafe' judgments: T. S. Macpherson in his notes on the Indian Penal Code stated, with regard to the blasphemy laws: 'One difficulty is to ascertain whether the intention of person was deliberately to wound religious feelings. Evidence of intention – he must assure judge of intention by consequence of acts because we hold a [illegible]. Under 298 it is not, however, reasonable to judge intention by consequence of act e.g. producing feeling of pain – unsafe to infer that this was intention.'

p.137 Section 295 remained relatively unproblematic for over a hundred years: the British government amended the law in 1927, but it still applied to all religious sentiment. The 1970 s.295-A was added to the Pakistan Penal Code by the Criminal Law Amendment Act XXV of 1927, and read: 'Whoever, with deliberate and malicious intention of outraging the religious feelings of any class of His Majesty's subjects, by words, either spoken or written, or by visible representations, insults or attempts to insult the religion or the religious beliefs of that class, shall be punished with imprisonment of either description for a term which may extend to two years, or with a fine, or with both.'

p.137 Legislative change was its undoing: for an extremely thorough discussion of the legislative development of Section 295, see Siddique and Hayat, 'Unholy Laws & Holy Speech'.

p.137 in April 1991, the Federal Shariat Court made execution the mandatory punishment for blasphemy: see *Muhammad Ismail Qureshi v. Pakistan* PLD 1991 FSC 10; and for a detailed analysis of this judgment, Lau, *The Role of Islam in the legal system of Pakistan*, pp.306–7.

p.137 The broad British code was narrowed from a provision that prevented all blasphemy against any religion to one that only prevented blasphemy against Islam: General Zia's amendments to the blasphemy laws also had the effect of targeting one religious minority.

Practising as an Ahmadi – a follower of Mirza Ghulam Ahmad, a Muslim preacher who in the 1880s had declared that he, not the Prophet Muhammad, was the saviour of humanity – is of itself an act of blasphemy in Pakistan. For further discussion, see S. Kadri, *Heaven on Earth: A journey through Shari'ah law* (London: Bodley Head, 2011), pp.235–8; Jalal, *The Struggle for Pakistan*, pp.58–60 and 203–8; R. Peters, *Crime and Punishment in Islamic Law* (Cambridge, UK; New York: Cambridge University Press, 2005), p.158.

p.137 insults to the Prophet and the Holy Qur'an were punishable: see s.298-A (amended in 1980), s.295-B (amended in 1982) and s.295-C (amended in 1986), Pakistan Penal Code.

p.137 The abbreviation **pbuh** stands for 'peace be upon him'.

p.138 With no requirement of criminal intent: see Siddique and Hayat, 'Unholy Laws & Holy Speech', pp.340–51, for a more detailed discussion of the element of intent in the offence of blasphemy. The case law provides a fascinating discussion of the required intent; for example: 'the intention contemplated by section 295-A of the Pakistan Penal Code is not just the ordinary intention that one finds mentioned with regard to almost all other offences made punishable by the Pakistan Penal Code but a deliberate and malicious intention to do the thing mentioned therein . . . [I]n section 295-A . . . the legislature hedged "mention" with "deliberately" and "maliciously" because it was proven punishment for insulting or attempting to insult the religion or religious beliefs of a person and it is well-known that when followers of a religion try to show that their religion is the best in the world, words which will not be palatable to the followers of other religions are difficult to avoid and if it were not made necessary that the intention to do the things mentioned in the section be deliberate and malicious the door would have been closed on all religious discussions.' (Lahore High Court judgment in *Punjab Religious Book Society, Lahore v. The State*, cited in Siddique and Hayat, 'Unholy Laws & Holy Speech', p.342.)

p.138 known for adopting a less Islamic stance when sitting in judgment: Lau, *The Role of Islam in the legal system of Pakistan*, p.311.

p.138 the Federal Shariat Court had fully upheld only 19 per cent of the cases that came before it: for a detailed study of the number of cases brought before the Federal Shariat Court and an analysis of their resolution, see C. Kennedy, 'Islamization in Pakistan: Implementation of the Hudood Ordinances', *Asian Survey*, Vol. 28, No. 3 (March 1998), pp.307–16.

p.138 announced itself loath to apply severe penalties: see *Ghulam Ali v. The State* PLD 1986 SC 741, and further discussion at Peters, *Crime and Punishment in Islamic Law*, pp.159–60.

p.138 blasphemy convictions and sentences of death continue to increase: see Siddique and Hayat, 'Unholy Laws & Holy Speech', pp. 380–1; and Kadri, *Heaven on Earth*, p.235.

p.140 almost a quarter of the population are Muslim, and there are over eighty mosques in the city: 24.7 per cent of Bradford's population are Muslim (http://www.

bradford.gov.uk/bmdc/community_and_living/popula-
tion); there are 86 mosques (http://mosques.muslimsin-
britain.org/maps.php#/town/Bradford).

p.140 largely composed of Pakistani émigrés: today
Bradford has the largest proportion of people of Pakistani
ethnic origin in England (http://www.bradford.gov.uk/
bmdc/community_and_living/population).

**p.141 the year after Altaf Rehman's return was the
most violent Karachi had ever seen:** Gayer, *Karachi:
Ordered Disorder*, p.31.

Chapter 10

**p.150 The lower courts rarely acquit on blasphemy
charges:** for details of the successful appeals of those
convicted of blasphemy in the lower courts and the
grounds of such appeals, see Siddique and Hayat, 'Unholy
Laws & Holy Speech', pp.325–7.

p.150 as contrition was a central tenet of Islamic law:
see the 'Case of *Ma'iz*', as discussed in I. Rabb, *Doubt in
Islamic Law: A History of Legal Maxims, Interpretation, and
Islamic Criminal Law* (New York: Cambridge University
Press, 2015), Part 1, Section 1, pp.25–48; see also
Muhammad Ismail Qureshi v. The State PLD 1991 FSC 10,
a Federal Shariat Court judgment that discussed the
requirement of intent for blasphemy offences and stated
that penitence would 'wipe out an intended contempt'.

p.151 She went to the Supreme Court: in getting permission to appeal this point to the Supreme Court, Sarah
worked with another advocate, based in Karachi.

p.152 Created by martial law in 1959, designed by a Greek modernist architect and urban planner in 1960: M. Hull, *Government of Paper: The Materiality of Bureaucracy in Urban Pakistan* (Berkeley; Los Angeles: University of California Press, 2012), p.2.

p.152 named 'Islamabad', the 'Abode of Islam', in February 1960 by an ambitious young Information Minister: see Gayer, *Karachi: Ordered Disorder*, p.28.

p.154 first empowered to enforce fundamental rights by the Constitution of 1956: see Jalal, *The Struggle for Pakistan*, p.95.

p.154 by Zulfikar Ali Bhutto in 1971: A. Cowasjee, 'Fundamental Rights', *Dawn*, 8 May 2011, http://www.dawn.com/news/627005/fundamental-rights.

p.154 General Zia in 1981: Jalal, *The Struggle for Pakistan*, p.238.

p.154 Nawaz Sharif in 2014: 'Pakistan: Revoke Suspension of Rights in Islamabad', *Human Rights Watch*, 8 August 2014, https://www.hrw.org/news/2014/08/08/pakistan-revoke-suspension-rights-islamabad.

p.154 championing its independence from the government: see, for example, *Government of Sindh v. Sharaf Faridi* PLD 1994 SC 105, in which the Supreme Court held it to be a principle of Islamic law that the 'independence of the judiciary should be fully secured' (cited in Lau, *The Role of Islam in the legal system of Pakistan*, p.169).

p.154 charged prime ministers with contempt: during a constitutional crisis in the late 1990s, the Supreme Court charged Prime Minister Nawaz Sharif with contempt of court (although during the hearing, government ministers stormed the court and attempted to arrest the Chief Justice). The Supreme Court also charged Prime Minister Gilani with contempt of court in 2012. For more details, see Jalal, *The Struggle for Pakistan*, pp.297 and 367.

p.154 vetoed laws and constitutional amendments: see Jalal, *The Struggle for Pakistan*, p.353.

p.154 and disqualified politicians from holding office: in 2009, the court barred Nawaz Sharif and his brother from holding elected office. See Jalal, *The Struggle for Pakistan*, p.352.

p.155 'because of a disease of mind, did not know the nature of his act or he did not know that it was wrong': see *M'Naughten's Case* 1843 10 C & F 200.

p.156 As Section 84 of the Pakistan Penal Code reads: under Section 84, unsoundness of mind at the time of committing the offence can be pleaded as a full defence to any offence in Pakistan's Penal Code. The defence bears the burden of proof to show on the balance of probabilities that the accused was of unsound mind at the time of committing the offence and that this unsoundness of mind rendered the accused incapable of knowing the nature of his actions, or that those actions were either wrong or contrary to law. If the defence can prove this, the accused should be acquitted.

p.156 The Criminal Procedure Code – section 465: under Section 465 if it appears to the court that the accused is of unsound mind at the time of trial and thereby incapable of making his defence, then the proceedings must be stayed. If the accused is then acquitted on this basis, the court cannot release him but must order detention in safe custody, awaiting a final order for release or detention from the provincial government.

p.158 in Pakistan, where a person charged with a capital offence has been detained for over two years without their trial being concluded, they may be released on bail: see Section 497, Criminal Procedure Code 1898.

p.160 There is no requirement of intent in Pakistan's blasphemy laws, an element central to Sharia jurisprudence: under the traditional Sharia offence, a person has to have acted willingly to be deemed an apostate/blasphemer, and they must have done so with an awareness of the penalty attaching to acts of blasphemy. See Hallaq, *Shari'a*, p.319, and A. Mansour, 'Hudud crimes', *The Islamic Criminal Justice System* (London; New York; Oceana Publications, *c*.1982), p.197.

p.160 (a point that Pakistan's Federal Shariat Court made when reviewing the laws): see Lau, *The Role of Islam in the legal system of Pakistan*, pp.306–7, and Justice Khan's judgment at p.30 in *Muhammad Ismail Qureshi v. Pakistan* PLD 1991 FSC 10. The requirement for intention (or *mens rea*) was particularly controversial in the cases of Ahmadis, who under Pakistan's law are effectively all considered blasphemers. (see *Riaz Ahmad v. State* PLD 1994 Lah 485).

p.160 Persons accused of blasphemy are not given the full evidentiary protections of Sharia – which, in many schools, bar circumstantial evidence and require the testimony of four adult male witnesses or a repeated,

voluntary confession: Peters, *Crime and Punishment in Islamic Law*, pp.12–19.

p.160 More than 1,200 people have been charged with blasphemy: see 'Timeline: accused under the blasphemy law', *Dawn*, 8 August 2013: http://www.dawn.com/news/750512/timeline-accused-under-the-blasphemy-law.

p.160 these executions are never carried out: Kadri, *Heaven on Earth*, p.238.

p.160 poisoned to death in jails, stabbed to death in hospitals, tortured to death in police custody, shot dead outside courtrooms, mauled to death by mobs: for an extraordinary overview of the fates suffered by those charged with blasphemy, see 'Timeline: accused under the blasphemy law', and 'Blasphemy in Pakistan: Anatomy of a Lynching', Al-Jazeera America, 20 June 2015, http://america.aljazeera.com/articles/2015/6/20/blasphemy-in-pakistan-anatomy-of-a-lynching.html.

Chapter 11

Other than as set out below, this chapter is based on Yasir Ansari's court records, my own experience and interviews with Nasar Hussain and Arthur Wilson. Yasir Ansari is not a real name.

p.164 in a country where angry mobs have often bludgeoned alleged blasphemers to death: see, for example, 'Pakistan mob kills Christian couple over "blasphemy"', BBC News, 4 November 2014, http://www.bbc.co.uk/news/world-asia-29893809; Z. Baber, 'Pakistani mob torches Christian homes in Lahore over prophet Mohamed "blasphemy"', *The Independent*, 9 March 2013, http://

www.independent.co.uk/news/world/asia/pakistani-mob-torches-christian-homes-in-lahore-over-prophet-mohamed-blasphemy-8527641.html.

p.169 Islamic compensation payments – *Qisas* and *Diyat* – are not applicable to such charges: the *Qisas* and *Diyat* provisions only relate to offences affecting the human body – murder, manslaughter and bodily harm (see Sections 299-338, Pakistan Penal Code 1860), and the Federal Shariat Court has held that even the President of Pakistan cannot pardon a person accused of blasphemy: 'no one after the Holy Prophet (pubh) exercised or was authorised [to exercise] the right of reprieve or pardon': see *Muhammad Ismail Qureshi v. Pakistan* PLD 1991 FSC 10, and *Habib-ul-wahab Alkhairi v. Federation of Pakistan* PLD 1991 FSC 236, cited in Amnesty International, 'Pakistan: the death penalty', ASA 33/10/96, pp.15-16, available at https://www.amnesty.org/download/Documents/.../asa330101996en.pdf.

p.169 I had read Jean-Jacques Rousseau's warning that 'laws are always useful to those with possessions and harmful to those who have nothing': J. J. Rousseau, *On the Social Contract, with Geneva Manuscript and Political Economy*, ed. R. D. Masters, trans. J. R. Masters (New York: St Martin's Press, 1978), p.58.

Chapter 12

All information about Bagram's detention conditions and interior layout is from my interviews with an ICRC employee who worked with Pakistani third-country nationals in DFIP. Details of Karim Muhammad's case come from his case notes or interviews with him. Except as set out below, all other information is from my own experience. Karim Muhammad is not his real name.

p.174 'detainee review boards', both as a basic guarantor of detainee rights: see 'The Bagram Detainee Review Boards: Better, But Still Falling Short', *Human Rights Watch*, 1 June 2010, http://www.hrw.org/news/2010/06/02/bagram-detainee-review-boards-better-still-falling-short; and, 'Detained and Denied in Afghanistan: How to Make US Detention Comply with the Law', *Human Rights First*, May 2011, available at https://www.humanrightsfirst.org/wp-content/uploads/pdf/Detained-Denied-in-Afghanistan.pdf.

p.175 In 2010, the year of Karim Muhammad's capture . . . beyond the scope of a US courtroom: see *Maqaleh, et al. v. Gates* (circuit docket 09-5265). Broadly the same decision was reached by the DC Circuit Court in December 2013: see *Fadi Al Maqaleh, et al. v. Hagel* (circuit docket 12-5404); *Amanatullah et al. v. Obama* (circuit docket 12-5407); *Hamidullah et al. v. Obama* (circuit docket 12-5410). See also *Boumediene v. Bush* 553 US 723 (2008), which established the legal framework governing the scope of habeas corpus rights with regard to enemy combatants detained abroad, i.e. outside of the US, and which is cited in these cases as the basis for the detainees' rights.

p.175 The trial: for a history of the trial, see S. Kadri, *The Trial: A History from Socrates to O. J. Simpson* (London: Harper Collins, 2005).

p.175 'open justice': in 1924, an English High Court judge held it imperative that during a trial, justice should not only be done, but should also be seen to be done, and this principle came to be known as 'open justice'. See *R v. Sussex Justices, ex parte McCarthy* [1924] 1 KB 256.

p.176 at times there was only one for every hundred detainees: see 'The Bagram Detainee Review Boards'.

p.176 'There is no reporting on this guy . . .': Bagram/Centcom/001608-001609 ACLU FOIA request files (personal representative speaking).

p.177 on the basis of 'mistaken identity': see, for example, Bagram/Centcom/001544 ACLU FOIA request files.

p.177 Rather, local power-brokers in Afghanistan learnt that describing a rival or enemy as 'Taliban' was an easy way to get rid of them ... But this did not stop many innocent Afghans ending up in Bagram or Guantanamo, the surreal product of an international superpower's unwitting entanglement in local feuds: for detailed narratives of these dynamics, see A. Gopal, *No Good Men Among the Living: America, the Taliban, and the War Through Afghan Eyes* (New York: Metropolitan Books, 2014); M. Martin, *An Intimate War: An Oral History of the Helmand Conflict 1978–2012* (London: C. Hurst & Co., 2014); G. Smith, *The Dogs Are Eating Them Now: Our War in Afghanistan* (Toronto: Knopf, Canada, 2013).

p.177 'Maybe my enemy gave wrong information': Bagram/Centcom/001625 ACLU FOIA request files.

p.178 a cell phone or SIM card with perhaps some money, pocket litter: the ACLU FOIA Bagram files can be accessed at https://www.aclu.org/bagram-documents-released-under-foia, which details the arrest of many of the detainees in Bagram.

p.178 Many gave very similar explanations: see the ACLU FOIA Bagram files.

p.178 'either English, Pashtu or in Dari ...': Bagram/ Centcom-DRB-715 ACLU FOIA request files.

p.180 'habeas writ' in both American and English courts: see *Secretary of State for Foreign and Commonwealth Affairs and another v. Yunus Rahmatullah* [2012] UKSC 48, and *Maqaleh, et al. v. Gates* (circuit docket 09–5265).

p.181 in England, in 1772, a habeas writ ended slavery: see *Somerset v. Stewart* (1772) 98 ER 499.

p.181 But President George W. Bush had, in 2004, construed anyone suspected of association with the Taliban or al-Qaeda as ineligible for these protections: see 'Press briefing by White House Counsel Judge Alberto Gonzales, DoD General Counsel William Haynes, DoD Deputy General Counsel Daniel Dell'Orto and Army Deputy Chief of Staff for Intelligence General Keith Alexander', 22 June 2004, available at http://www.presidency.ucsb.edu/ws/?pid=66011.

p.182 'an enemy that lies in the shadows . . .': see opening statement of Judge Gonzales in 'Press briefing by White House Counsel Judge Alberto Gonzales'.

p.183 a fifth of Pakistan's land was under water: see Jalal, *The Struggle for Pakistan*, p.361.

p.183 The floods caused more destruction than the Indian Ocean tsunami of 2004: see Jalal, *The Struggle for Pakistan*, p.361.

p.183 *Vakil,* **the Urdu word for lawyer, literally translates as 'representative':** The word is originally Arabic; the definition of وكيل given in J. M. Cowan (ed.), *The Hans Wehr Dictionary of Modern Written Arabic,* 4th edn (Urbana, IL: Spoken Language Services Inc., 1979), p.1284, is 'authorised representative; attorney in fact; authorised signatory, proxy; lawyer, attorney; manager; deputy, vice-; agent; commercial representative . . .'

p.185 and are accused by many of responsibility for Pakistan's several hundred 'disappeared' persons: see ' "We can torture, kill or keep you for years" – Enforced disappearances by Pakistan Security Forces in Baluchistan', *Human Rights Watch,* July 2011.

p.186 first articulated by Aristotle: see *On Rhetoric,* trans. G. Kennedy (Oxford: Oxford University Press, 1991), p.31 (Bk 1, Ch. li, 1354a): 'It is highly appropriate for well enacted laws to define everything as exactly as possible and for as little as possible to be left to the judges'; *The Politics,* ed. S. Everson (Cambridge: Cambridge University Press, 1988), p.78 (Bk III, Ch. xvi, 1287a): '. . . it is thought to be just that among equals everyone be ruled as well as rule, and therefore that all should have their turn. We thus arrive at law; for an order of succession implies law . . . [T]here may indeed be cases which the law seems unable to determine, but . . . the law trains officers for this express purpose, and appoints them to determine matters which are left undecided by it, to the best of their judgement'; *Nichomachean Ethics,* trans. D. Ross (London: Oxford University Press, 1954), p.133 (Bk V, Ch. 10, 1137b): 'For when the thing is indefinite the rule also is indefinite, like the leaden rule in making the Lesbian moulding; the rule adapts itself to the shape of the stone and is not rigid.' For a discussion of the history of the phrase, see

J. Waldron, 'Is the Rule of Law an Essentially Contested Concept (in Florida)?', *Law and Philosophy*, Vol. 21, No. 2 (March 2002), pp.137–64.

p.186 Much debated since the fourth century BC: as the main British discussant of the rule of law, see A. V. Dicey, *Introduction to the Study of Law and the Constitution* (London: Macmillan, 1889). One of the best-known legal debates of the twentieth century was the exchange between H. L. A. Hart and Lon Fuller following Hart's delivery in 1957 (he was at the time Professor of Jurisprudence at Oxford) of the annual Oliver Wendell Holmes Lecture at Harvard Law School (where Fuller was then Carter Professor of General Jurisprudence). Hart's topic was 'Positivism and the Separation of Law and Morals'. Hart essentially denied any connection between law and morality; these thoughts were then developed into a book, *The Concept of Law*. Contrary to Hart, Fuller's legal thought was preoccupied with the immanence of moral values within the law, which was also later developed into a book, *The Morality of Law*. Their initial exchange was published as H. L. A. Hart, 'Positivism and the Separation of Law and Morals', *Harvard Law Review*, Vol. 71, No. 4 (February 1958), pp.593-624, and L. Fuller, 'Positivism and Fidelity to Law – a Reply to Professor Hart', *Harvard Law Review*, Vol. 71, No. 4 (February 1958), pp.630–72. Although Hart and Fuller were concerned with the concept of law itself, rather than the concept of the rule of law, the question of moral immanence within the law has influenced much thinking on the subject.

p.186 So where a legal system's aspiration may be 'justice', its operation depends instead on procedural

guarantees, upon genealogies – be they from statute or case law – of authority, or justification. I should make clear that the thoughts in this paragraph are relevant only to common law systems rather than civilian legal systems. They are relevant, therefore, to Pakistan, India, Britain and America, but could not be extrapolated to apply to many continental European legal systems in the same way.

p.187 rules *'easily learned and easily retained'*, wrote the English judge Lord Mansfield: see *Hamilton v. Mendes* (1761) 2 Burr 1198 at 1214.

p.189 helped overturn ingrained injustices from apartheid rule in South Africa to racial sentencing in America's southern states: for details of these trials, see P. Harris, *In a Different Time: The Inside Story of the Delmas Four* (Roggebaai: Umuzi, 2008); B. Stevenson, *Just Mercy* (New York: Spiegel and Grau, 2015); and, C. Stafford Smith, *Injustice: Life and Death in the Courtrooms of America* (London: Harvill Secker, 2012).

p.192 the country's senior judges had been more assertive in openly opposing government policy: See Jalal, *The Struggle for Pakistan*, p.353.

p.193 Pakistan first asked the US for money ($2 billion) mere months after it was founded, in October 1947: See Talbot, *Pakistan: A Modern History*, p.119. The request was unsuccessful. See also Jalal, *The State of Martial Rule*.

p.194 If the government failed to comply with these orders . . . punitive action as he saw fit. Sarah had brought the petition under Article 199 of the Constitution of Pakistan 1973, which allows any aggrieved party to apply to the High Court for a mandatory or prohibitory injunction against public officials; any aggrieved party to apply to the High Court asking that they order the government to comply with the fundamental rights set out in the Constitution; and any person to file a habeas writ at the High Court. Under Section 82 of the Civil Procedure Code 1908, if the government failed to comply with any decree of the court within a certain time, the court could order that an official be detained in prison, or pay a fine, or be subject to other punitive action. Under Section 4 of the Contempt of Court Act 1976, it is a criminal offence, punishable with up to six months' imprisonment, to disobey an order of the court.

p.196 'the only conceivable meaning . . . the atrocities and their perpetrators': I. Kant, *Perpetual Peace: a Philosophical Sketch* (1975), cited in M. Mazower, *Governing the World: The History of an Idea* (New York: The Penguin Press, 2012), pp.16–17.

p.196 'laws should be adapted in such a manner to the people for whom they are framed that it would be merely lucky if those of one nation suit another': Montesquieu, *The Spirit of the Laws*, trans. and ed. A. Cohler, B. Miller, H. Stone (Cambridge: Cambridge University Press, 1989), Book 1, pp.8–9.

p.197 Whilst Karim Muhammad was in Bagram, the Taliban had stormed two large prisons in north-west Pakistan, freeing well over 500 prisoners: see 'Pakistan jailbreak: Taliban free 248 in Dera Ismail Khan', BBC News, 30 July 2013 http://www.bbc.co.uk/news/world-asia-23493323; I. Khan and D. Walsh, 'Taliban free 384 inmates in Pakistan', *New York Times*, 15 April 2012, http://www.nytimes.com/2012/04/16/world/asia/pakistani-taliban-assault-prison-freeing-almost-400.html?_r=0.

p.197 Sahiwal was one of the first: see F. A. Ghumman, 'High Security Prison in Sahiwal Shortly', *Dawn*, 3 July 2014, http://www.dawn.com/news/1116694; M. Bilal, 'Foolproof detention: Govt turns 5 Punjab jails into high security prisons', *The Express Tribune*, 17 March 2014, http://tribune.com.pk/story/683727/foolproof-detention-govt-turns-5-punjab-jails-into-high-security-prisons/.

p.197 and the other Bagram detainees: for further details of the experiences of other Pakistani Bagram detainees, see O. Belhadi, I. Buchanan, S. Belal, *Closing Bagram, The Other Guantanamo: Repatriating Pakistani detainees from US detention in Pakistan* (2013), available at: http://www.jpp.org.pk/bagram/.

Epilogue

Except as set out in the notes below, this epilogue is based on my experience and conversations with Arthur, Sohail and Sarah during late 2014 and 2015.

p.199 killing 132 children, along with nine of the school's staff: for further accounts of the attack, see 'Peshawar school attack: Death toll stands at 141, PM Modi calls up Nawaz Sharif to express condolence', *DNA India*, 16 December 2014, http://www.dnaindia.com/world/report-peshawar-school-attack-death-toll-stands-at-141-pm-modi-calls-up-nawaz-sharif-to-express-condolence-2044341; 'TTP militants storm Peshawar school: 131 killed, more than 100 injured', *Pakistan Today*, 16 December 2014; 'Pakistan Taliban: Peshawar school attack leaves 141 dead', BBC News, 16 December 2014, http://www.bbc.co.uk/news/world-asia-30491435.

p.200 At the time, there were roughly 800 people on death row for terrorism-related offences, and a further 17,000 being prosecuted: see 'Pakistan: Reinstate Death Penalty Moratorium', *Human Rights Watch*, 17 December 2014, https://www.hrw.org/news/2014/12/17/pakistan-reinstate-death-penalty-moratorium.

p.200 at a rate of one a day: see C. Lamb, 'Day 150: Pakistan's gallows await next victim', *Sunday Times*, 7 June 2015, http://www.thesundaytimes.co.uk/sto/news/world_news/Asia/article1565539.ece.

p.201 In 2013, shortly after coming into power ... and international rights groups: see J. Boone, 'Taliban warns Pakistan government against execution of militants in jail', *The Guardian*, 13 August 2013, http://www.theguardian.com/world/2013/aug/13/taliban-pakistan-execution-militants; O. Waraich, 'Return of death penalty in Pakistan condemned', *The Independent*, 5 July 2013, http://www.independent.co.uk/news/world/asia/return-of-death-penalty-in-pakistan-condemned-8691187.html; Reuters, 'Pakistan to continue moratorium on capital punishment', *Dawn*, 3 October 2013, http://www.dawn.com/news/1047193.

p.201 It was not hard to pick holes in the government's reasoning: for international criticism of the move, see 'Thousands at risk of execution after Pakistan's "shameful retreat to the gallows"', *Amnesty International*, 10 March 2015, https://www.amnesty.org/en/latest/news/2015/03/pakistan-lifts-death-penalty-moratorium/; and 'Pakistan: Reinstate death penalty moratorium'.

p.202 plaything of foreigners: see A. Abbasi, 'Foreign funding behind "Save Shafqat" campaign', *The News International*, 1 April 2015, http://www.thenews.com.pk/ Todays-News-2-310110-Foreign-funding-behind-Save-Shafqat-campaign.

p.202 she be imprisoned for contempt of court: see S. Anjum, 'Action recommended against those who distorted facts', *The News International*, 20 April 2015, http://www.thenews.com.pk/Todays-News-2-313781-Action-recommended-against-those-who-distorted-facts; A. Abbasi, 'After FIA, IHC tears apart bogus "Save Shafqat" campaign', *The News International*, 12 May 2015, http:// www.thenews.com.pk/Todays-News-2-317696-After-FIA-IHC-tears-apart-bogus-'Save-Shafqat'-campaign.

p.202 'self-aggrandising', 'social media hungry', 'reckless', 'Bolshevik': see A. S. Zia, 'Some principles in the Shafqat case', *The News on Sunday*, 12 April 2015, http://tns.thenews. com.pk/some-principles-in-shafqat-case/#.VaDfIFse5UR.

Appendix: Criminal Procedure

This book is not, nor does it purport to be, a comprehensive study of Pakistan's criminal law. The lawyers amongst its readers may, however, find the following broad overview of some elements of criminal procedure helpful in understanding the context of the cases discussed.

Investigation of an offence

Murder and blasphemy are both categorised as 'cognisable' offences, which means that they are offences for which a police officer can make an arrest without a warrant and may begin investigation without the permission of a magistrate. For murder and blasphemy charges, therefore, the police officer in charge of the police station (the 'incharge') directs the investigation of the offence.

Witnesses

The police may require that witnesses attend the police station for questioning. They must answer all questions put by the police officer (unless those questions would expose the witness to criminal charges). A note may be taken of the interview by the police officer conducting it, but this cannot be used as evidence at trial (nor can any statement, or confession, made to the police by the accused, unless that confession refers to material evidence relevant to the offence). However, the defence may ask the court to consider a statement made by a witness to the police where it is inconsistent with the evidence given at trial by that witness.

If the police wish to rely on the statement or confession of a person at trial, then they must bring that person before a magistrate, who can record the statement or confession. This record will be admissible at trial.

Detention of a suspect

Having arrested a suspect, if the investigation cannot be completed within twenty-four hours, the incharge must present the accused and the police diary entries to a magistrate, who can approve further detention up to a maximum of fifteen days.

Completion of investigation

The investigation is to be completed without unnecessary delay. Once completed, the incharge must send a report to the magistrate. If it appears to the incharge that the investigation will not be completed within fifteen days, then by day 11 of the investigation he must send an interim report to the magistrate, who, upon receipt, can either commence trial or postpone trial until the completion of the investigation.

Sessions Court

All capital offences are tried in the Sessions Court.

Trial procedure

1. Prosecution documents are provided to the defence and the court.
2. The court reviews the documents and evidence and decides whether there are grounds for proceeding

to trial. If so, the court will frame the charge in writing.

3. The charge is read to the accused in court.

4. The accused enters a plea of guilty or not guilty.

5. The prosecution will inform the court of the witnesses they wish to call. The court will rule on the admissibility of this evidence.

6. The prosecution witnesses are examined-in-chief; they are then cross-examined (if the defence elects to do so); then re-examined (if the prosecution elects to do so).

7. The accused may be asked questions by the court, in response to the prosecution evidence. Answers to these questions are not given on oath. The court may draw adverse inferences if the accused refuses to answer any of these questions.

8. The defence will be asked if they intend to call any witnesses, and if so, those witnesses may be examined-in-chief, cross-examined and re-examined.

9. If the defence does not call witnesses, then the prosecution will make a closing speech. The defence can make a closing speech in response to the prosecution.

10. If the defence does call witnesses, then upon the close of their case, the defence will make a closing speech. The prosecution will then make a closing speech.

11. If the court finds the accused not guilty, they will record an order of acquittal.

12. If the court finds the accused guilty, they will proceed to sentence.

Sentencing procedure

1. The court will consider the accused's previous convictions and whether they mean for an enhanced sentence.

2.   If there are no relevant previous convictions, then the court will sentence according to the offence(s) of which the accused has been convicted.

3.   If the accused is sentenced to death, the court will inform the accused of the period within which to file an appeal.

4.   Sentences of death passed by a Sessions Court must be confirmed by a High Court bench of at least two judges before they can be carried out. When considering the sentence, the High Court has the power to: confirm the death sentence; pass any other lawful sentence; annul the conviction and convict the accused of any offence that the Sessions Court might have convicted him of; order a retrial on the same or an amended charge; acquit.

Constitution of the bench

Sessions Court judges sit alone when trying capital cases.

High Court

Appeals from judgments of the Sessions Court lie to the High Court.

Appeal against conviction

A party can appeal the conviction on a point of law. No permission to appeal is required.

A party can appeal the conviction on a point of fact or a point of mixed fact and law, or any matter that appears to the appellate court to be a sufficient ground of appeal. In order to appeal in these circumstances, the party must apply to the appellate court for permission to appeal or have the trial court certify that the case is fit for appeal.

Appeal against sentence

A party can appeal the sentence awarded (unless that sentence is mandatory). In order to appeal in these circumstances the party must apply to the appellate court for permission to appeal.

In all cases, the appeal (against either sentence or conviction) must be made in writing to the appellate court. If the appeal is not dismissed, the appellate court will send for the case record and study it before hearing from the appellant and the public prosecutor (in that order). The appellate court may hear fresh evidence, if it so directs, and generally the accused must be present when this evidence is being given.

Constitution of the bench

Appeals will be heard by a bench of at least two judges, who must be different to the judge(s) who heard the case at first instance.

Federal Shariat Court

Repugnancy jurisdiction

The Federal Shariat Court has the power to determine whether any of Pakistan's laws are repugnant to the injunctions of Islam. If the court holds a law to be repugnant, then that law will cease to have effect from the date stated in the court's judgment (this is the case even if the legislature does not amend the statute or wording of the law). The court can exercise this power either on the petition of a citizen or of its own motion.

Appeal against hudood

The Federal Shariat Court also has the power to examine the record of any case decided by any criminal court in relation to *hudood* offences, with the purpose of ascertaining whether the criminal court's sentence was lawful under Islamic law.

The court's judgments are binding on the High Court and all lower courts.

Constitution of the bench

The court is composed of a maximum of eight Muslim judges, up to three of whom must be *ulema* with at least fifteen years' experience in Islamic law, research or instruction. Generally, any appeal against a *hadd* sentence or death sentence will be heard by at least three judges, at least one of whom must be an *alim* (an Islamic legal scholar). An appeal against a sentence of over ten years will be heard by at least two judges. A single judge will hear revisions and applications that do not fall into either of the preceding categories.

Supreme Court

Appeals from decisions of the High Court when exercising its appellate jurisdiction lie to the Supreme Court. Appeals from decisions of the Federal Shariat Court lie to the Supreme Court Shariat Appellate Bench.

Appeals from the High Court

In all but some exceptional cases, where there is an automatic right of appeal, a decision of the High Court can only be appealed to the Supreme Court where the latter has granted permission to appeal.

Generally, a bench of at least three judges hears every matter before the court. Petitions for leave to appeal, appeals from decisions made by a single judge in the High

Court, appeals from decisions of certain tribunals and appeals regarding the grant of bail may be heard by only two judges.

Supreme Court Shariat Appellate Bench

This bench is a division of the Supreme Court and is composed of three Muslim Supreme Court judges and up to two *ulema* selected by the president from the judges of the Federal Shariat Court. In all but some exceptional cases, where there is an automatic right of appeal, a decision of the Federal Shariat Court may only be appealed to this bench where the bench has granted permission to appeal.

Generally, appeals against acquittal will be heard by at least three judges, one of whom is an ad hoc member of the bench. Other appeals will be heard by at least two judges.

Structure and regulation of the legal profession

Public prosecution

In every Sessions Court trial, the prosecution is conducted by a public prosecutor or senior police officer (so long as that police officer has not taken part in the investigation of the offence). Private prosecutors may be employed, however, where no departmental prosecutor is able to take the case. In specialised courts, such as the anti-terrorism courts, specialised prosecutors are contractually appointed to act as prosecutor in individual cases.

Legal representation and government funding

If an accused or appellant cannot afford legal representation, the court will appoint counsel at government expense. However, rates for this work are low.

Professional ethics

A code of professional ethics does regulate the practice of Pakistan's advocates, although to the best of my knowledge it is rarely enforced.